‖‖‖‖‖‖‖‖‖‖‖‖‖‖‖‖‖‖‖‖ VAL

⊲ **W9-BWX-724**

Fithian, Lisa, author
Shut it down
33410015681614 01-05-2021

DISCARD

PRAISE FOR S

"As the left gets serious about electoral organizing, it's more important than ever that our movements also stay mobilized, disobedient, and in the streets. Lisa Fithian has helped drive some of the most creative, game-changing organizing of our time—and her wise and warm book will help us build real power."

—NAOMI KLEIN, author of *No Is Not Enough* and
This Changes Everything

"Direct action must be strategic, precise, calculated, and intentional—words that also describe Lisa Fithian. She is a movement veteran, and we stand on shoulders of women like her. Lisa has taken a new generation of leaders under her wing at a critical time, and I am honored to be among them."

—LINDA SARSOUR, Palestinian-Muslim-American activist;
cochair, Women's March on Washington

"Lisa Fithian is a treasure to social justice movements in the United States and an inspiration to all who have been touched by her energy and commitment. From workers' struggles to Occupy Wall Street, from the Battle of Seattle to the Katrina disaster, Lisa has been there—teaching, leading, following, and building a toolbox for direct action. In *Shut It Down*, Lisa brings the past four decades of activism alive with dynamic storytelling skills that allow the reader to relive those moments and know that they, too, can pick up the banner and run with it."

—ROXANNE DUNBAR-ORTIZ, author of
An Indigenous Peoples' History of the United States and *Loaded*

"Lisa Fithian's book shows both the craft and the heart essential for these times. Her wide organizing experience enables her to describe both the toolbox police use against activists and how grassroots movements rise again despite everything. Get this book if you like stories and you want to win."

—GEORGE LAKEY, author of *How We Win*;
columnist, W

Valparaiso Public Library
103 Jefferson Street
Valparaiso, IN 46383

"Ready to rise up and shut down injustice? You can find no better guide than this dynamic collection of stories and lessons from powerhouse organizer Lisa Fithian. This brilliant book, a vital addition to every resister's library, will take you right to the frontlines of some of the boldest and most consequential protest campaigns of the last four decades, leaving you with everything from nuts-and-bolts tactical tips to frameworks for deep strategic thinking."

—L.A. KAUFFMAN, author of *Direct Action* and *How to Read a Protest*

"Lisa Fithian is a legend. I hope this book becomes one, too."

—DAVID GRAEBER, author of *Debt* and *Bullshit Jobs*

"In my own long life of activism, Lisa Fithian is the person who has taught me the most about strategy, organizing, and sheer, stubborn courage. She's also gotten me into more trouble than any other single person! So—full disclosure—she's a dear friend. I'm in the book, and she says nice things about me. But even if she didn't, I would still have to honestly say that she's done a brilliant job of weaving activist stories together with practical, how-to advice. The book reads like an adventure story, but at the end you will come away with solid information on how to organize and make transformative social change. In these challenging times, this book is a much-needed gift!"

—STARHAWK, activist; director, Earth Activist Training; author of
The Fifth Sacred Thing and *The Empowerment Manual*

"*Shut It Down* is an annotated travelogue of a lifetime of resistance, full of the nitty-gritty of real movements: deep strategy and think-on-your-feet decisions, friendships and alliances, best practices, worst mistakes and key lessons, real life exhaustion, and the exhilarating, world-changing power of fighting back. It's jam-packed with tips for a journey we all need to take, shared through detailed and richly personal stories that transform the ideas of struggle into usable muscle memory."

—AURORA LEVINS MORALES, author of *Medicine Stories*

"Based on lessons of struggle over the past few decades, *Shut It Down* is one of the best guides to, and reflections on, social transformation that I have ever read. It is both deeply profound and educative, direct and unpretentious. Everyone, whether experienced or new to wanting to change the world, needs to read and share it."

—**MARINA SITRIN**, author of *Horizontalism* and *They Can't Represent Us!*

"*Shut It Down* traces the course of radical resistance in the United States through Lisa Fithian's astounding experiences sowing the seeds of struggle. Rather than analyzing protest movements from afar, Fithian brings her readers into the streets in this essential chronicle of direct action from below."

—**MARK BRAY**, historian, Dartmouth College; author of *Antifa*

"Lisa Fithian's *Shut It Down* is an invaluable tool and a must-read for organizers and activists. She explains both *why* we need to shut it down and the nitty-gritty of *how* to shut it down. She has been a key strategist in organizing hundreds of thousands of workers in the Justice for Janitors campaign—from blocking bridges in order to shut down DC to enduring mass arrests in the face of police violence during the Houston janitors' strike. Lisa's book inspires us to confront the powerful and teaches us how to beat them."

—**STEPHEN LERNER**, fellow, Georgetown University Kalmanovitz Initiative for Labor and the Working Poor; architect, Justice for Janitors campaign

"A firsthand account from the front lines of direct action over the past four decades. A story not simply of resistance, but of building something better. The young movements of our time will only benefit from Fithian's experiences and insights."

—**SHAUN CHAMBERLIN**, editor of *Surviving the Future* and *Lean Logic*; Extinction Rebellion arrestee

SHUT IT DOWN

Stories from a Fierce, Loving Resistance

LISA FITHIAN

Foreword by Frances Fox Piven

Chelsea Green Publishing
White River Junction, Vermont
London, UK

Copyright © 2019 by Lisa Fithian
All rights reserved.

Unless otherwise noted, all photographs copyright © 2019 by Lisa Fithian.

Lyrics to the song "Like a Mountain" on page 89 were written by Naomi Littlebear Morena. Reprinted with permission.

No part of this book may be transmitted or reproduced in any form by any means without permission in writing from the publisher.

Editor: Katherine Don
Project Editor: Michael Metivier
Project Manager: Sarah Kovach
Copy Editor: Laura Jorstad
Proofreader: Eliani Torres
Indexer: Linda Hallinger
Designer: Melissa Jacobson

Printed in Canada.
First printing August 2019.
10 9 8 7 6 5 4 3 2 1   19 20 21 22 23

Our Commitment to Green Publishing
Chelsea Green sees publishing as a tool for cultural change and ecological stewardship. We strive to align our book manufacturing practices with our editorial mission and to reduce the impact of our business enterprise in the environment. We print our books and catalogs on chlorine-free recycled paper, using vegetable-based inks whenever possible. This book may cost slightly more because it was printed on paper that contains recycled fiber, and we hope you'll agree that it's worth it. *Shut It Down* was printed on paper supplied by Marquis that is made of recycled materials and other controlled sources.

Library of Congress Cataloging-in-Publication Data
Names: Fithian, Lisa, author.
Title: Shut it down : stories from a fierce, loving resistance / Lisa Fithian.
Description: White River Junction, Vermont : Chelsea Green Publishing, [2019]
Identifiers: LCCN 2019018116| ISBN 9781603588843 (paperback) | ISBN 9781603588850 (ebook)
Subjects: LCSH: Civil disobedience—United States. | Protest movements—United States.
Classification: LCC JC328.3 .F57 2019 | DDC 303.6/1—dc23
LC record available at https://lccn.loc.gov/2019018116

Chelsea Green Publishing
85 North Main Street, Suite 120
White River Junction, VT 05001
(802) 295-6300
www.chelseagreen.com

This book is dedicated to my father, Douglas Brooks Fithian,
who opened me up to the world and the woods, showing me
that another world is possible. He told me, "Once upon a time,
poetry and science were one, and they called it magic."
I have carried that within me ever since.

To all my teachers, seen and unseen,
who have offered me guidance and love.

To all those who struggle for justice,
embracing creative direct action to
heal themselves and the world.

CONTENTS

FOREWORD

You are about to enter the life, joys, and passions of Lisa Fithian, and the experience may well change your life for the better.

Lisa is a firebrand who has been at the center of some of the most important campaigns of the American resistance movement in the past four decades. Some of you will already know her, because Lisa's energy and commitment take her everywhere that important movement actions are welling up. She was a young woman when she worked with Abbie Hoffman at Save the River and then participated in the Pledge of Resistance campaign. If you weren't there, you'll read in the pages that follow about their March for Peace and Justice in Central America and Southern Africa and their bold but also hilarious action to shut down the CIA. As always with Lisa, the account is detailed and vivid, and you'll also learn specifically and concretely how to mount actions that matter.

When Lisa tells a story, you are *there*, and what's more, you learn how to create actions of resistance that together may yet save us.

The Pledge was just the beginning of Lisa's career as agitator and organizer. Her lifework became *the resistance* in all its forms. She went from the Pledge of Resistance to play a key role in the Washington, DC, arm of the Justice for Janitors labor organizing campaign. Steve Lerner, another legendary organizer who is credited for the success of that campaign, describes Lisa as a critically important strategist and tactician, saying that she "pushed, cajoled, and inspired us to go beyond traditional and ineffective tactics. And she helped develop the broader strategy that forced billionaire building owners to deal with their formerly invisible janitors."

Lisa was of course also there in 1999 when the huge protests known as the Battle of Seattle erupted, where the Turtles and the Teamsters, the labor unions and the environmental activists joined together in the first of a series of challenges to the emerging neoliberal world order. Seattle was followed by the protests against the World Bank meeting in Washington, DC, and then the protests that challenged the Los Angeles Democratic convention as election 2000 approached. Lisa was also part of the campaign to target the World Bank meeting in Prague in 2000, followed by similar mobilizations against the architects of neoliberal globalization in Quebec in 2000 and in Genoa in 2001.

In 2005, in the wake of Hurricane Katrina, Lisa joined with other resistance organizers to birth Common Ground Relief in a kind of collective action, an effort to bring aid, comfort, and recovery to the New Orleans neighborhoods that the federal government was ignoring. In 2009 Lisa joined with others in the Gaza Freedom March. In 2010 she helped launch the US Boat to Gaza as part of the International Freedom Flotilla. And in 2013 she played a central role in the failed but inspiring Rise Up Texas struggle to save abortion rights. She has continued to agitate and organize in many more recent movements for justice.

So how should we make sense of this whirlwind of activism? Lisa tells us her view, and I think she is basically right. She offers a kind of chaos theory of social change. For Lisa the objective of protest is to disturb complex social systems, to interfere with ongoing institutional processes in a way that demands action by the authorities. Protest can thus create the space for change, for negotiation, and perhaps for reform.

A glance backward at the history of democratizing change in the United States shows us the truth of this view, from the risings of farmers in the revolutionary era, to the white and Black abolitionists of the nineteenth century, to the recurrent strikes and sit-ins of workers, to the struggles for recognition and rights by marginalized groups of our own time. People win when they win because they find the courage and imagination to refuse the cooperation that dominant institutions require.

Lisa's special talent is as the mastermind of the collective actions that sometimes take us to the brink of significant social change. In other words, she is an organizer. Organizers come, of course, in all varieties. There are labor organizers who try to build unions and community organizers who work to create neighborhood-based organizations. But Lisa's kind of organizing is distinctive to our time, and it is what many of the activists in the resistance aspire to do.

Lisa and her cohort eschew the typical hierarchical models of organization in favor of horizontal networks, with the emphasis on both *horizontal* and *networks*. People group together and have relationships, but the glue is not formal membership and a formal organizational role. Instead they come together in what are called affinity groups, and these groups coordinate their activities through a kind of representative assembly called a spokes council.

Something else that is distinctive about Lisa's approach is the emphasis on "direct action." At first glance this may seem to mean taking a sledgehammer to the target that is responsible for our grievances. And sometimes that *is* what it means, as when angry protestors smash the noses of missiles, for example.

But the advocates of direct action are also strategic thinkers, and Lisa exemplifies strategic thinking. For Lisa the escalating forms of non-cooperation, the shutdowns, sit-ins, and blockades that characterize direct action, are the tactics that are needed to win the struggle. She also embraces complementary electoral organizing, corporate campaigns, coalition building, and media outreach, and the more the better because more contentious action increases the chances of success.

The accounts of resistance actions in the pages that follow are much more than good stories, and they're even more than good stories illuminated by a political philosophy. They also serve as examples in a handbook, with multiple sets of instructions for resistance campaigns. So in the pages that follow, you'll learn how to do banner drops in ten easy steps, tips for slapping wheat-paste posters all over town, action grids and calendaring to frame the action, tactics that take space, and, not least, step-by-step instructions for getting arrested.

This book is not only an account of the resistance and an explanation of the principles that inform it but also a handbook to help you become part of the struggle. Read it, and then hold on to it. Hopefully, you'll need it.

—FRANCES FOX PIVEN
New York, New York

PREFACE

This book has been one of the greatest challenges of my life. Ever since I was young, my dyslexia, along with school papers filled with correction marks on grammar, spelling, and punctuation, deterred me from thinking that writing was possible for me. My work as an organizer taught me that I'm a good communicator, but that early lack of confidence left its mark. Over the years I tried to write accounts of some of my experiences, but I questioned myself, thinking, *What could I possibly have to say? Who cares what I think!* So my folder of half-written pieces continued to grow.

As the years passed, more people were saying, "You need to write a book." Yeah, right! But the requests kept coming. I started to see that people were writing about historical moments that I myself had lived through. They were the experts, but they had not been there to see it all firsthand.

I'm not concerned about being an expert, but I realized I had a unique perspective, and it wasn't fair to keep it to myself. Still, I resisted. I told myself that I didn't need to write a book because I taught people through my trainings—and that was a lot of people! One day I was talking to my friend Laurie Arbeiter, and she said, "Lisa, only so many people can attend your trainings. Many more could access your book. People learn in different ways, and a book is just another vehicle to share what you have learned." Laurie is a wise friend, and I listened to her advice.

In the summer of 2011, I wrote a fifty-six-page manual called *Kicking Corporate Booty* for the staff of the New Bottom Line campaign. I thought about turning these lessons into a book, so in 2012 I took a year's sabbatical to expand *Kicking Corporate Booty* and to heal my body, mind, and spirit from years of injury and trauma. As I wrote, I saw that the manual needed to have stories and some theory to support my lessons. But it was hard for me to be away from movement life, and in 2013 I became involved with initiatives to fight for reproductive rights and against racism in Austin, Texas, where I have lived since 2002. I also participated in efforts to help the people of Austin after some catastrophic flooding in the area. Need-less to say, my attention to the book was challenged. Flood Wall Street happened. Ferguson happened. Standing Rock happened. The year of my father happened, which ended with his passing in September 2015.

The year I thought it would take to write a book became years. The manuscript I finally completed was not great, but with the help of a skilled editor, Katherine Don, I set about significantly rewriting and restructur-ing the material. Katherine said, "Lisa, you have written yourself out of the book. *You* are the protagonist. People will want to know your story!" Right—but years of PTSD had stripped a lot of sensory perceptions from my memory, and there was an overwhelming amount of life experiences to choose from. My first manuscript came in at 180,000 words! Yikes. Much was cut out, and important tidbits ended up in the endnotes. The process of writing, rewriting, and deletions reminded me of something Abbie Hoffman once told me, "Not all great ideas need to be implemented." Not all stories need to be told. But some do, and I hope this book contains the stories that will be of use and that needed to be told.

I have also been keenly aware that I'm a white woman who has had the privilege of supporting many POC struggles, some of which are written about in this book. I have worked hard to show up in a good way in those struggles and in how I write about them. My efforts are to honor the work and bring to life the wisdom and lessons that were offered. For those of you who lived these struggles, things may be left out, or not as you remember. If I got something wrong, please forgive me. I am so grateful to my dear friends Remy, Vega, and Laurie for their words of wisdom about all of this, accepting that this book will not be perfect.

I have been humbled by this work and excited that it has come to fruition. May it ignite your imagination. May it inspire you to organize and act against oppression and injustice. May it convince you to love and care for yourself and others. Most of all, may it offer you hope that the power of the people to create and to resist with love in our hearts really can change the world. To paraphrase Margaret Mead, it is the only thing that ever has.

ACKNOWLEDGMENTS

I have deep gratitude and praise for Katherine Don from Yellow Bird Editors—my cowriter, editor, and guide. Without her help, this book may never have come into being. And to Michael Metivier and my new family at Chelsea Green, who contacted me an hour after receiving my book proposal to say, "We want to read more!" I felt so honored, and I am so grateful for the care and support I have received. Thank you!

I could not have done this, or many things for that matter, without the loving support, encouragement, and contributions of time and skill from my friend Samantha Miller and her family Jonathan Williams and Riley.

To Laurie Arbeiter and Jennifer Hobbs, whose love, kindness, and support have made all the difference in my life.

To my friends who have supported me, given feedback, and cheered me on: Delight Stone, Cliff Curry and the Curry Stone Foundation, Starhawk, Donna Reed, Johanna Lawrenson, Jennifer Beach, Ted Nace, Marisa Holmes, L. A. Kauffman, Colin Clark, Ted German, Jill Kneerim, Lucy Cleland, Banafsheh Madaninejad (who turned me on to Yellow Bird Editors), Athena Lee Bradley, Leslie Cagan, Stephen Lerner, Bill Ragen, Mary Ann Hohenstein, Hilary McQuie, Emily Posner, Carolina Reyes, Elizabeth West, Ann Wright, Michael McPhearson, Molly Gott, Julia Ho, Remy from Black Mesa, Berkley Carnine, Kam Magor, Mark Bray, Marina Sitrin, David Graeber, Dawnielle Castledine, Robert King, Kenyatta Williams, scott crow, Ann Harkness, Ingrid Burrington, Undoing White Supremacy Austin, Rachel Manning, Andrea Black, Juniper Lauren Ross, and everyone who contributed to my *Kicking Corporate Booty* funding appeal. I also want to express my gratitude to Aurora Levins Morales for her love, wisdom, and insight.

I would not be who I am today without the anti-racist teachings about organizing and how to reclaim our humanity from my mentors at the People's Institute for Survival and Beyond, with special thanks to Ron Chisom and Dr. Kimberley Richards.

To Negar Kidman and her two beautiful daughters, Aaliyah and Raven, for reminding me to play and embrace joy in my life.

Thank you to all the photographers and artists who were willing to contribute their work: Kisha Bari, Diane Lent Green, Ann Harkness, Desiree Kane, Erik McGregor, Angus McGuire, Rick Reinhart, Angela Sevin, Emily Simmons, and Seth Tobocman.

Thanks to my family: my mom, Trudie Caruso, and stepdad, Joe, my sister, Dianne, my brother, David, and my stepsister, Diane, who have all encouraged me along the way. And my father, Douglas Brooks Fithian, who loved books and the art of writing. Hey, Dad—look, I did it! I am also grateful to all of my ancestors whose choices in life created mine.

I wanted to mention all the people, organizers, healers, friends, and coconspirators who have worked with me, but I have learned so much from so many people along the way that it would become a very long list! Please know that I love and value you.

INTRODUCTION

I have always been a rocker. Yes, I'm talking about rock 'n' roll, and yes, I'm talking about rocking the boat, but really it goes back further than that. When I was a toddler, I was literally rocking on the sofa, in the car, on the rocking horse, or back and forth in a high chair. There are stories of me rocking my crib clear across the room. Born in 1961, I was raised by a generation of women who were introduced to baby formulas and Swanson TV dinners, and who were counseled not to coddle their children, but in fact to ignore them, no matter how loud they cried or ran around raising a ruckus.

Even at that young age, I must have understood the anonymous quote loved by activists: *The most common way people give up their power is thinking they don't have it.* I continued to raise my voice. By the second grade a teacher noted on my report card that "Lisa is an instigator." Troublemaking was something I was good at. In high school I saw that all the tables in the cafeteria were littered with trash, and I felt so pissed off at the lack of respect that I started a student newspaper, *The Free Thinker*, to spread information about school issues, community accountability, and respect. My mom brought home a mimeograph machine from work so we could run the paper from our garage. Inspired by the impact of the paper, I ran for and won student council president. By the end of high school, I was voted "Most likely to do things for the school." I was also voted "Most likely to do things *to* the school."

I am grateful that I found my life's purpose at a young age, and over the years I have seen, time and again, that organizing and nonviolent direct action *work*. I've had the opportunity to be a part of many different movements, struggles, victories, and defeats over the past forty-plus years. I have raised up many powerful young organizers and have trained tens of thousands of people in the dynamics of power, fear, and oppression; the art and science of strategic nonviolent direct action; and the processes and structures that support liberation by running counter to forces of oppression. I have witnessed, firsthand, the growth of networks of resistance that are still in place today, and I have learned why some networks are strong while others collapse.

In my years as an anti-racist organizer, I have shut down the CIA, disrupted the World Trade Organization's first major meeting during the Battle of Seattle, and helped launch Common Ground Relief, a grassroots organization that supported communities in New Orleans after Hurricane Katrina. I have camped in a ditch with Cindy Sheehan, the Gold Star mom who protested the Iraq War. I have stood my ground in Tahrir Square and set sail on the US and Women's Boats to Gaza. I have occupied Wall Street, taken action for climate justice, marched on the streets of Ferguson, and walked in solidarity with tribal leaders at Standing Rock. During the anxious months after the 2016 election, I protested Trump's inauguration, marched in Washington, and organized anti-racist trainings in my adopted hometown of Austin, Texas, in response to the white supremacists who have violently exposed themselves in our community.

Today more than ever, we are reminded of the enduring relevance of the words of Spanish American philosopher George Santayana: "Those who cannot remember the past are condemned to repeat it." I have not forgotten my own past experiences in the ongoing struggle for human freedom and dignity. Indeed, after being arrested well over one hundred times for my acts of civil disobedience, my experiences are seared rather indelibly in my mind in the form of painful sensory memories.

This book is my attempt at sharing concrete, hands-on, replicable lessons from historic movements in the struggles against empire. I want to show how individuals like myself link together to form networks that create change and make a new history. In the history of the US Empire, settler colonialism, racism, sexism, capitalism, homophobia, ageism, ableism, and other forms of oppression are woven into every system. These deeply woven roots bind us to a dominant culture of oppression, violence, and death.

Throughout this book, I will advocate for the use of civil disobedience and other forms of nonviolent direct action as the primary means of dismantling and battling today's oppressive power structures while simultaneously creating structures that embody love and liberation. This work isn't only for those who can risk arrest. Everyone can contribute no matter your age, gender, race, or ability. We need grandmothers and grandfathers, artists, cooks, musicians, storytellers, researchers, lawyers, and more! I have always believed there are two necessary strategies for change: dismantling structures and processes of oppression, and creating structures and processes of liberation. Every story in this book is an example of both.

Sometimes there are aha! moments when the whole world shifts, and sometimes change is long and slow. In either case organizing is about personal relationships—beginning with one-on-one friendships and building to groups, networks, councils, and assemblies, all aligning for a common cause with common values, engaging collectively in alternative infrastructures and strategic actions as we dismantle what no longer serves us. Social justice organizing means amassing the energy we need to tip, crack, topple, or flatten the dominant paradigm, creating the space for a healthier, more humane society to emerge.

Each chapter in the book tells the story of a major action I have helped organize, along with instructional information and lessons learned. In chapter 1, I focus on the challenges of the Trump era and argue that networked groups capable of creating direct-action campaigns or uprisings are the best way to ensure a sustained resistance, both during and after his presidency. In chapter 2, I tell the story of the first major national action that I organized, shutting down the CIA in 1987 to protest the Reagan administration's dirty wars in Central America and southern Africa. I introduce organizational concepts such as formal consensus decision making, spokes councils, affinity groups, facilitation, accountability, and organized meetings and assemblies, all of which are fundamental to horizontal organizing.

In chapter 3, I take my readers to Washington, DC, in 1995, where I helped organize a historic campaign as part of the national Justice for Janitors movement. Chapter 4 is about the Battle of Seattle in 1999, when we came sixty thousand strong to stop the World Trade Organization (WTO) from consolidating its power as an undemocratic arbitrator of global trade conflicts. Chapter 5 will recount my wild experiences during the rise of the Global Justice movement, including the collapse of the WTO Ministerial Conference in Cancun in 2003. Today the world is accustomed to seeing demonstrators at just about every major global convergence (G8, IMF–World Bank, FTAA, WTO meetings, and more), but in the early 2000s this was newer territory.

Chapter 6 is about my experiences in New Orleans beginning in October 2005, when I helped build Common Ground Relief, a community-based effort in wards and parishes devastated by Hurricane Katrina. Our rap was solidarity, not charity, and our practice was redistributing everything we could. Chapter 7 will look at the Gaza Freedom March in 2009 and the G8 protests in Germany in 2007, both of which show the tactical importance of occupations and taking space. Chapter 8 will take us to the streets of Manhattan in 2011, when On May 12th, the mobilization that came before Occupy Wall Street, sent a strong signal that bailing out banks while people were losing their homes was fueling a people's uprising.

Chapter 9 takes us to Ferguson in August 2014, when years of pent-up anger poured into the streets, fully righteous in acts of courage against police violence and murder. In chapter 10, I share my unforgettable, transformative experiences at Standing Rock, where Indigenous communities and their allies stood at the front lines, using their bodies, hearts, minds, and spirits to stop the Dakota Access Pipeline.

Today it feels like we are facing an onslaught of challenges coming from all directions, and the immensity of it can be overwhelming. In response, I propose that we have the courage to resist belief systems of hate; to shut down the power centers of greed; to topple the unjust structures that oppress. We must do the demanding work of creating something radically new. We must take the painting off the wall, turn it upside down, then put it back on the wall. This might sound ambitious—impossible, even—but in the following pages I will show that this type of work has happened in the past, is happening right now, and will continue to happen so long as we continue to take action. I want to share my experiences with organizers, dreamers, protectors, and everyday people who know that what's happening in their community, school, workplace, or world just ain't right, and have chosen to do something about it. Welcome to the ranks of those who seek to disobey.

CHAPTER 1

Election Night 2016 and the Power of Decentralized Networks

*Another world is not only possible, she is on her way. On a
quiet day, I can hear her breathing.*

—ARUNDHATI ROY

O n the night of November 8, 2016, I sat with three friends in
the back room of a bar at the Prairie Knights Casino on the
Standing Rock Indian Reservation in North Dakota. We were
at Standing Rock to stop the Dakota Access Pipeline (DAPL), known
through prophecies as the Black Snake. I had been there since October,
joining with tribal elders and activists from all backgrounds to do everything we could to stop treaty violations and prevent the environmental
destruction that would put local communities, the lands, and the water
at risk. Deep down, we knew that if Republican presidential nominee
Donald Trump were to be elected, he would green-light the project.[1]

As a lifelong organizer and devoted rabble-rouser, I tend to avoid electoral organizing, having seen firsthand that lasting changes and shifts in
power are so often brokered in the streets rather than in the halls of power.
And yet elections have consequences—some more than others. Each generation is infused with the politics of the day, and our descendants live under
the weight of policies that were put in place before they were born. This is an
understanding that underlies Indigenous wisdom, which teaches about living
in alignment with the natural world, walking in right relation, and imagining,
with each choice we make, how the Seventh Generation will be impacted.

As the night dragged on, a knot filled my belly. The murmur of voices
around me talked about Hillary's sure victory; smoke filled the air, and as
the poll results came in, I knew she had lost. I ordered a whiskey, Jameson

on the rocks, and picked up a cigarette, though I very rarely smoke. I lit it. I knew this was a self-destructive strategy, but it quieted the grief and shock that were emerging.

Part of me wondered how we could have elected this white supremacist, this misogynistic bully of a man. But have we not done this before? Today we are witnessing yet another resurgence of the White Wing—white supremacists who are empowered to enact their visions and embed them further into our laws and policies. As I sat at that bar in Standing Rock, I was surrounded by the descendants of the Indigenous people of this land who suffered under the first American supremacists, those westward-expanding men and women who cemented a legacy of colonization, including land theft, ecological destruction, slavery, and genocide.

This is what is real, and history was repeating itself. Colonization can be recognized today in extractive industries and in the displacement of people through gentrification. Racism is alive and well, and slavery continues in the criminal injustice system. The #MeToo movement continues to expose the patriarchy woven into the fabric of the nation, while capitalism creates poverty and destroys the environment, all to the benefit of white people and the 1 percent. The KKK, neo-Nazism, lynchings—these all continue today. As the reality of a Trump presidency set in, I knew we had a hard and dangerous road ahead. It was the same road we have been traveling since the founding of this nation. Trump felt like the last desperate gasp of the Anglo-colonial empire rearing its ugly head as the foundations around it crumbled. A cornered animal is dangerous, and here we had a cornered animal with money and a strong constituency. The far right had been primed during the eight years of Obama's presidency with hundreds of millions invested in media like Breitbart and Fox News, while industry groups like the American Legislative Exchange Council (ALEC) crafted extreme legislation behind closed doors, doing away with hard-won social justice victories. It was—and still is—terrifying.

Breathe, Lisa, I told myself, *you know this is nothing new*. Years of observation have shown me repeating patterns, pushes and pulls in our culture. I have lived through numerous administrations. I have fought for nonviolent social change since the 1970s, and I have trained tens of thousands of activists to replicate these strategies. Over the years I have told people that my job is to create a crisis for those in power, because crisis is the leading edge where change is possible. On the night of the election, I knew that our protest movements would be called upon once again to create crisis. In today's United States change via crisis is essential, and it doesn't come easy. "If there is no struggle, there is no progress," Frederick Douglass wrote. "Those who profess to favor freedom, and yet depreciate agitation, are [people] who want crops without plowing up the ground."

Memories of life under Ronald Reagan resurfaced. It was a similar time when we saw right-wing forces coalesce around a radical conservative who sought to restructure our economy and world. Jesse Helms and the Christian Right unleashed attacks against women's reproductive rights. They went after queer people and went after poor people, whom they infamously called the "welfare queens." They went after the immigrants who had come here as a result of Reagan's wars in Central America. We saw giant tax cuts for the rich. It was a very difficult time, but it forced us to organize, and it forced us to learn how to organize *better*.

Changing the world is a lot of work. For some, the injustices we're fighting are a matter of survival. For those who are more privileged, we often get to choose which "issues" we will engage with. In either case we must understand that a war is being waged upon the people and the planet. Are you going to fight for justice? And if so, how? What is the story you will tell your grandchildren about what you did?

In the years since Trump's electoral college victory, we have witnessed waves of street protests, school walkouts, teacher strikes, mass mobilizations like the Women's March, airport actions to thwart the Muslim ban, and an uprising against the nomination and confirmation of Brett Kavanaugh to the Supreme Court. We've seen people rallying for climate justice, disrupting fossil fuel extraction, and a rising, youth-led movement against gun violence. We've seen a sanctuary movement grow to protect and support immigrant communities facing raids, deportations, border assaults, and the imprisonment of immigrant children. We saw the first two Native American women elected to Congress—*and* the first two Muslim women! We've seen the emergence of new groups like Indivisible and a rebirth of the Democratic Socialists of America. We saw the Blue Wave and record-breaking get-out-the-vote efforts. We saw millions of people rise up to save the Affordable

Care Act, not once but three times. People who have never before called their representatives picked up their phones. I have been thrilled at what I've seen. So many have taken to the streets—students, immigrants, queer folks, women, people from all walks of life, all over the country. Yes!

But I have also watched people falter, feeling doubtful that their actions matter, or concluding that voting is the only way to make their voice heard. The powers that be take advantage of these doubts, capitalizing on every moment that the people aren't paying attention. Street actions and pressure on Congress prevented the repeal of the Affordable Care Act, but then people took their eyes off the ball and the individual mandate, one of the main pillars of the ACA, was dismantled as part of the 2017 tax bill. We took to the streets to protect the children ripped from their mother's arms as part of the family separation policy, but then we took our eyes off the ball and the policy was quietly, and unofficially, reinstated.

Taking to the streets is essential, but mass marches are just one of the many tactics at our disposal. At some point, showing up at a march begins to feel ineffective because it's being done over and over again without the level of impact that we hope for. Marches must be coupled with strategic direct actions and mass community network building if their impact is going to last.

Some believe that if it gets really bad, everyone will wake up and act. But it rarely happens that way. People tend to keep going along, believing that going along is in their best interest, or that challenging authority is too risky, takes too much effort, and won't have an impact anyway. But these people are wrong. My experiences over the past four decades as an organizer behind historic civil disobedience and social disruption campaigns have shown me that deep and loving resistance results in concrete, positive change. And when we don't achieve the change we hope for, we build new relationships that infuse our work over the long haul. The stories I tell throughout this book show that it's vital to resist *continuously*, and also to resist *strategically*.

One of the challenges with today's movements is that online-based activism has become, for many, the only point of entry into the movement. A pattern of participation has emerged: Twitter and Instagram feeds or posts on friends' Facebook pages call attention to a social problem or an impending legislative action—like a vote on the latest gun control legislation—and people are inspired to call their member of Congress or attend a local protest. These acts are done in isolation, usually in response to major events, and are not typically followed up with ongoing efforts or participation in local groups. We can also get easily overwhelmed by how many problems there are, and become depressed and demobilized.

In their book *Rules for Revolutionaries*, Becky Bond and Zack Exley, the lead digital strategists for Bernie Sanders's 2016 presidential run, explained how their experiences during the people-powered campaign showed them the largely untapped potentials of on-the-ground organizing in the digital age. "When the center of the organizing world moved from small community, labor, or campaign organizations to mass 'internet organizations' with huge loose memberships, real organization building seemed to disappear," they wrote.[2] They described how the success of the Sanders campaign was fueled by combining internet recruitment with old-fashioned, bottom-up organizing, such as convening local meetings to build local groups or talking on the phone and going door-to-door rather than sending mass emails. And these were the conclusions of the campaign's *digital* strategists!

Strong national movements that persist over time are outgrowths of local groups capable of quickly organizing local actions. The internet and social media have opened up a ton of tactical options in the areas of communication, recruitment, mobilization, and strategic actions, but this can't replace on-the-ground community organizing, mobilizations, and actions. Any effort at social disruption requires offensive tactics both on the ground and in the air. We rarely change things when we're on the defensive. We need to build relationships and structures that grow our capacity to stay on the offensive to protect our communities in these dangerous times.

Nonviolent Direct Action and Horizontal Networking

As an organizer, my primary strategies have included horizontal, network-based community organizing; strategic, creative nonviolent direct action (NVDA), including civil disobedience; and the creation of crisis as a means of bringing about change. While history has shown that direct action delivers the goods, many fail to understand how to integrate it into their work. Many nonprofits, NGOs, and labor unions shy away from direct action and civil disobedience because they're not interested in taking the risk, or they might be apprehensive for legal, moral, or strategic reasons. But sometimes the problem isn't a matter of will, but simply not knowing how to do it.

Direct action is an umbrella term referring to actions that directly confront power, shifting power from the oppressor to the oppressed. In her book *Direct Action*, my friend and longtime activist L. A. Kauffman defined *direct action* as an all-encompassing term covering a set of actions with the common goal of inciting change:

> "Direct action" can refer to a huge variety of efforts to create change outside the established mechanisms of government—it's a slippery and imprecise term, much debated by the movements that use it. Protest marches, boycotts, and strikes all are, or can be, forms of direct action; the same is true of picket lines, sit-ins, and human blockades. . . . Those who have taken part in direct action know that it's a profoundly embodied and often personally transformative experience.[3]

Direct action is a way of life and a lens through which to view the world. It is not about asking permission, but rather doing what needs to be done to accomplish your goal as effectively and efficiently as possible. It means working together, democratically, to take care of the problems we face, instead of waiting for others to make the change. Direct action is empowering, in the purest sense of the word. It allows people and communities to assert their power, to exercise their freedom, and to draw on their own wisdom to transform their lives.

Anyone who has participated in direct action or protest, even if you're a one-timer who held up a sign at the Women's March, knows that it is inspirational and life affirming. While there are many pathways to transformation, I have found that nonviolent direct action and civil disobedience are the most rapid and radically transformative for people.

When I train activists, I talk about shutting things down to open things up. Creative, nonviolent action is all about *space*—physical, emotional, mental, and spiritual. We can reclaim it, transform it, occupy it, liberate it, shut it down, open it up, shift it, or just be present in it. There is an art to knowing when to take it and how to shape it, and to acting without hesitation at the precisely opportune moment—because if you do not, the opportunity may not come again, like the opening of a door.

This book is filled with stories of joyful, courageous direct action. I approach these stories with a set of assumptions about how the world works and how the world *could* work if the goals of our movements are to be realized. My primary analytical lenses include understanding the power dynamics behind colonization, white supremacy / racism, patriarchy, and capitalism. All of these worldviews or belief systems are embedded into our dominant culture in the US. I analyze movements vis-à-vis an understanding of how power relations are constantly contested. I have also developed a growing appreciation for the science of complexity and systems theories, which seek to understand how large-scale social phenomena emerge and exist according to rules and patterns found within organic living systems. This is a process called *emergence*, which women's rights activist adrienne maree brown explores in her important book, *Emergent Strategy*. She writes that emergence is "another way of speaking about the connective

The People's Institute for Survival and Beyond

My analytical lenses are integrated throughout the book, but I'd like to pause for a comment about the increasing—but still lacking—awareness among white organizers like myself regarding the importance of an anti-racist lens. As a white female organizer who came into the movement during the early '80s, I have always thought I was aware of the racism and sexism that run deep in our culture, but my understanding of white supremacy in particular continues to evolve and deepen. I had the honor of first working with the People's Institute for Survival and Beyond (PISAB) in the late 1980s in Washington, DC. I worked with them again at Common Ground in New Orleans after Hurricane Katrina, and again beginning in 2013 with my work on Undoing Racism Austin. PISAB's Undoing Racism and Community Organizing workshop helped me develop my anti-racist lens, forever changing how I view the world and do my work.

I have also become keenly aware of how white supremacy and facing down oppressive powers can create trauma, so I have been working to integrate somatic healing strategies into my practice—essential, I believe, for all movement work.

OUT OF THE TOOLBOX
Direct Actions

Nonviolent direct action and civil disobedience are radically transformative for people. Actions become moments of connection often infused with beauty, love, and hope. Great actions inspire and transform both those participating and those observing. These are some of my favorites, but this list is not comprehensive. For more ideas, look up "198 Methods of Nonviolent Action" by scholar and nonviolence advocate Gene Sharp. Actions are limited only by our imaginations; sometimes we strive for seriousness, sometimes for tactical frivolity.

The Classics

Occupying spaces like boardrooms, parks, and capitol buildings

Shutting down government buildings, corporate meetings, bank lobbies, offices, hotels, conference centers, malls, train stations

Office jams (delegations)

Blocking intersections

Strikes

Pickets

Sit-ins

Unpermitted marches

Boycotts

Going to jail

Using Our Bodies

Flash mobs, flash dances, dance parties, body sculpture, freezes, swarms, earthquakes, human surges, human waves

Die-ins, sick-ins, art-ins

Snake marches, black blocs, pink and silver blocs, flying squads

Wildcat or breakaway marches

Human perimeters

Making Noise

A cacophony of resistance occupies spaces and attracts attention! Use drums, whistles, pots, pans, horns.

Local singers and musicians singing in the right place at the right time

Portable speakers blasting music or sounds

Chant sheets and song books

Marching bands and choirs (Infernal Noise Brigade, Brass Liberation Orchestra / BLO, samba bands, and the Rude Mechanical Orchestra have been some of my favorites!)

Chin-chinas—can shakers with popcorn kernels or BBs inside

Art, Ritual, and Media

Banner drops

Ceremony, rituals, and prayers

Flags (great for tactical communications)

Candlelight vigils

Giant puppets

Torchlight marches

Billboards

Social media campaigns using your opponents' sites

Posters, to be taped, stapled, pushpinned, or pasted all around town

Ring of fire—signs strategically placed around your target's home

Light boards and projections. My first light board was back in 1988, Christmas lights on plywood attached to the back of a pickup truck. Our message: NO US MILITARY AID TO EL SALVADOR. We drove around the White House during the annual Christmas tree lighting ceremonies.

Contestorias—a performance telling a story with images or words painted on sheets that can be turned

Newspaper wraps (full-sized phony newspapers wrapped around the actual papers)

Culture-jamming memes and parody news

Street theater productions (puppets, props, improv)

tissue of all that exists—the way, the Tao, the force, change, God/dess, life. Birds flocking, cells splitting, fungi whispering underground."[4]

One of the most important outcomes of strategic direct action is that it can bring a situation to the *edge of chaos*—a term I learned when reading about complexity science. It's at the edge of chaos where the deepest changes can emerge. In the dominant culture, the words *chaos* and *crisis* often connote violence and destruction, and are used to engender fear. But to me, the edge of chaos is not inherently violent. I have found that violent situations are usually counterproductive, generating fear and demobilizing people. By contrast, nonviolent actions that build strategic crisis can make people feel powerful while exposing the power brokers, convincing them that things have to change.

Imagine a business owner whose workers get fed up and go on strike. Day after day, he sees his employees picketing outside his building, leaflets denouncing his business practices, and negative coverage in the media. Local intersections are blocked to protest his corruption. He is losing money, and his reputation is being tarnished. He is now facing a crisis, and it starts making sense for him to concede to the protestors' demands before he is put out of business.

The edge of chaos and crisis needs our respect, not our fear. The edge of chaos is the space where an old order comes apart or decays and a new order emerges. But we must also have a vision and a plan for what can replace the status quo. This is the liberation part of strategy—creating what will be and practicing it in each moment. Thinking back to the business owner ready to negotiate, those who have gone on strike must be clear about their demands and have a plan in place for how, and when, their demands can be fulfilled. The workers have been successful in shaking up the status quo, and this requires two parallel strategies: dismantling structures and processes of oppression, and creating structures and processes of liberation. In other words, if we repeal, we must also have a plan for replacement, or else a whole lot of folks will be SOL.

There are many ways to organize direct action, but I have found that action is most effective when it takes place within a strong, moderately dense, linked network of participant groups. This is a model of social movement organizing that involves self-organized local groups in a network using working groups, clusters, caucuses, assemblies, or councils as needed. These smaller groups are structures that serve as anchors or hubs in an ever-evolving network. Broadly speaking, this approach is called horizontal or network-based organizing, and it advocates for decentralization and shared power.

In recent years scholars and activists have been increasingly aware of how networks are leveraged to create social, cultural, or policy-level change. In their 2006 essay "Using Emergence to Take Social Innovations to Scale," organizational behavior researchers Margaret Wheatley and Deborah Frieze write, "In spite of current ads and slogans, the world doesn't change one person at a time. It changes as networks of relationships form among people who discover they share a common cause and vision of what's possible. Change begins as local actions spring up simultaneously in many different areas. [But] if these changes remain disconnected, nothing happens beyond each locale."[5]

Wheatley and Frieze explain that when these small local actions become connected in a network, each individual action or event becomes more powerful. They call this synergistic quality *emergent phenomena*, and argue that emergence within networks explains why specific events in history had a larger impact than might have been expected. When the Berlin Wall came down in 1989, this individual action was hugely impactful because actions around the world, supported by a decentralized network of linked groups, had been supporting the goals of the people of East Berlin.

I've seen the power of networking in a wide range of movements: the anti-nuclear and AIDS movements of the 1980s, the Global Justice and environmental/climate movements that coalesced in the early '00s, and more recently Occupy Wall Street, Black Lives Matter, and the Indigenous sovereignty movements. All of these developed strong, agile networks as a model of organizing, with groups working collectively, building strong relationships and communities, escalating action, fueling a crisis that affects local, national, and international players and policies.

Whatever a person's point of entry is into a movement, once they take on the struggle for justice, their lives begin to change. Abbie Hoffman, my early mentor, once wrote that "Democracy is not something you believe in or a place to hang your hat, but it's something you do. You participate. If you stop doing it, democracy crumbles."[6] This process of engaging in consciously liberating action is when we feel most alive, inspired, and connected. As we take action, personal transformation takes root.

In this way I see that nonviolent direct action is not just a strategy but a way of life. It is how we can step into our power to create and change our conditions as we respond to injustices that come upon us. It is a way to undo the dominant cultures of oppression. Once we understand that we don't have to obey or believe in what the external authority says is true, we begin to trust ourselves and our communities more, taking responsibility for our own lives, together creating the world we believe is possible.

Rise Up Texas and the Power of Networks

In July 2013 a network called Rise Up Texas / Levanta Texas was born when individuals and groups came together in an effort to confront the right-wing assault on reproductive health in Texas. This is a great example of a local network that rose up to make a change using direct-action. There's no doubt in my mind that this group wouldn't have been possible without the groundwork that had already been laid by the smaller groups that linked together to create the network.

On June 25, 2013, Wendy Davis, a Texas state senator from Fort Worth, staged a filibuster against one of the most egregious anti-abortion bills in the country, SB 5. The ALEC-crafted legislation, if passed, could have resulted in the closure of thirty-six of the forty-two abortion clinics in the state by requiring doctors performing abortions to have hospital admitting privileges within thirty miles of the clinic, among other restrictions. The proposed changes were extremely disturbing for Texans, where access to abortion and other reproductive health services had already been limited, with at least fifty-three clinics closed statewide between 2011 and 2013 thanks to a concerted effort by anti-abortion activists and politicians.[7]

On the evening of the filibuster, I decided to head over to the capitol. When I entered the building, I was shocked to see that women were everywhere, on the ground floor and on every floor encircling the rotunda above. The Senate chambers were full, and they had closed off the entrances. I wandered over to the capitol extension, where the hearing room was packed with people watching the legislative proceedings on big screens. It was getting close to midnight when the Republicans finally maneuvered to start a vote to end the filibuster. The crowd began to roar "Let her speak!" as the Republicans did all they could to shut Davis down. As if a whistle had been blown, the crowds throughout the building surged to the doors of the Senate chambers. This was the closest thing to an insurrection I had felt in years.

Inside and outside the chambers, we roared! We would not back down. Our voices, thousands of women's voices in every hallway, stairwell, office, and rotunda, were chanting. It felt like the whole building was vibrating. The clock struck midnight mere minutes before the Republicans began the vote to pass SB 5. Midnight was the deadline, so the vote was invalid. But the Republicans, who had owned the state legislature for two decades and grown accustomed to abusing their powers, were not about to let the opportunity slip away. Lieutenant Governor David Dewhurst tried to change the official time stamp so that the final vote appeared to have occurred before midnight. The trick didn't work, and in the early-morning hours, we learned that the bill had not passed.

In this moment of victory, Cecile Richards, the then president of Planned Parenthood, called us women to the rotunda and urged us to go home. I thought this was a mistake—there were thousands of women here who would have stayed and occupied the capitol building. Many of us were worried that in the coming days, the Republicans would hatch a new plan to get their bill passed. The energy was palpable, and it felt like a critical, irreplaceable moment to create a crisis. Unfortunately, the moment passed.

Three days later Governor Rick Perry called for another special session to secure the passage of SB 5, now called HB 2. I tried to get in touch with Richards to propose the idea of organizing massive trainings to prepare for the upcoming special session, including plans for acts of civil disobedience if needed. I felt strongly that large acts of civil disobedience, such as plans for sit-ins or occupying the capitol, could have a positive outcome and prevent the passage of this bill. I was ultimately unable to connect with her or other leaders in the mainstream movement, but meanwhile I was getting calls from friends—local organizers in Texas—asking what they could do to help. I was thinking, *Damn, the will of the people is demanding to be heard, we need to do something right away.*

Knowing from past experience that if you don't do something yourself, perhaps nobody else will, I decided to act. I organized a meeting of local people and groups, contacting many of the younger women I knew as well as the old-timers. Over seventy people came to that first meeting at the headquarters of the Workers Defense Project, a nonprofit organization in Austin that works to achieve fair employment opportunities for low-income workers. In attendance were individuals from groups including ADAPT, Austin Democrats, NARAL Pro-Choice Texas, the Texas State Employees Union, the Tejas Web, Casa Marianella, Planned Parenthood, and more.

The first question was, "Who will be most impacted by this legislation?" Women as a group would be impacted, especially women of color, poor women, and trans people—all of whom have less access to reproductive health services and thus poorer health outcomes. We all agreed that we wanted to center and uplift these voices. What emerged from this meeting was a shared power network that was explicitly anti-racist, understanding the intersection of oppression. Our chief goals were to take nonviolent direct action to stop HB 2 and to build a sustainable, anti-racist grassroots power base in Texas.

We quickly established and split into working groups that could each take on separate tasks, including a strategy group, a training group, and a media group. We decided to call ourselves Rise Up Texas, and within a day we had organized mass trainings, formed affinity groups, and established *spokes councils*—larger meetings where the smaller affinity groups come together to coordinate mass actions.

Days later, when the special session began at the capitol building, we were ready. We had a giant banner filling the rotunda. We organized meditations, sang songs in hearings, made altars with baby shoes, dressed in costumes, carried dramatic signs and banners, and used specula as props. We entered offices, hearing rooms, and legislative chambers. If they did not listen, we burst out in song: "We're Not Gonna Take It" by Twisted Sister. Leaders in the Democratic Party and mainstream groups were not happy with us, but we did everything we could to keep communications open so they had the opportunity to anticipate our actions and fold them into their own plans. The Democratic Party in Texas has been trying unsuccessfully for years to diversify, and here was an opportunity to engage with members of their constituency who would directly suffer under this legislation. They did not heed our call, unfortunately, but I hope that the very act of witnessing us left the door open for leaders in the party to learn about the power of action, especially when those most impacted by the policies are leading.

OUT OF THE TOOLBOX
Organizing Basics

Building power requires people to be active. Our goal is to get people in motion in a variety of ways, and building relationships is the foundation of our work, whether you're going door-to-door, starting a new organization in your community, or making phone calls. Relationships make us feel connected and remind us we are not alone. Relationships are the basis of community and accountability. We can often see in others what we cannot see in ourselves, so relationships are like mirrors that allow us to learn and grow.

A basic tool in organizing for reaching out to new people is called a *rap*. Here are my tips for that first conversation:

BEFORE YOU BEGIN. Take a breath to settle yourself.

INTRODUCTION. Tell people who you are and why you want to talk with them. Ask if it's a good time and if they have a few minutes.

QUESTIONS. Ask questions to learn what they care about and their interests. Ask if they know about the issue at hand, and whether their family has been affected. Ask what they think and feel about it. What do they want or need? Mirror back what you hear.

DISCUSSION. People's responses offer openings to go more deeply into the topic, bringing up points you want to make and relating them to what people care about to fit their concerns. You can share your experiences and why you care.

COMMITMENT. Ask people to do something concrete. Include several options for what they can do. See if they need support in carrying out the action.

CLOSE. Clarify the next steps and what you will do to follow up. Express appreciation and gratitude.

Each conversation is an opportunity to assess the person you're talking with and whether they're someone you think will become active. You might also find you have a lot in common and find yourself at the beginning stages of a new and lasting friendship.

We knew that the larger reproductive rights movement around the country needed to see us fighting back. We set up a communication system that allowed for coordination between each smaller group, including working group email lists, public meetings, and mass text loops. We used Facebook and Twitter for publicity and mobilization. A corporate media strategy, led by women of color, garnered a huge amount of national and international media attention. Our efforts culminated in acts of civil disobedience that disrupted the proceedings and the vote process itself, with sixteen people arrested during our demonstrations against the House bill.[8]

In the end we did not stop them from passing this legislation. Abortion clinics all over the state have closed, though the impact was mitigated by a 2016 federal Supreme Court decision that blocked the measure. Despite our losses, there is a unanimous feeling among the members of Rise Up Texas that this was a partial victory. A strong network was established, and the relationships continue to this day. Since 2013 we have seen the creation of a radical doula movement grow across the state with organizational roots in Rise Up. Some of the Texas-based reproductive rights groups, including NARAL and the Lilith Fund, have begun anti-racist processes in earnest. La Frontera Fund emerged from this work, and it continues to support reproductive justice initiatives to mitigate the impact of these bills, especially in border communities.

The experience of demonstrating against the bill, in and of itself, has been a catalyst for change. Hundreds of women and gender nonconforming people went through a transformative experience that forever influenced the course of their lives, opening up the potential for radical change. Rise Up activist Rocio Villalobos wrote in 2014,

> Since the summer of 2013, we've seen record participation and widespread support from people all across Texas whose vision differs from the draconian, anti-democratic, misogynistic political tricks we saw come out of the capitol . . . Since last summer, Rise Up / Levanta Texas has been working on becoming a sustainable and fixed presence in Central Texas that consistently advocates and works towards reproductive justice . . . Just as important has been our ability to connect with other activist groups and individual organizers working

around these issues in other red states that face similar, if not copy-cat, legislation to what we now have to contend with.[9]

The groundswell of activism that I saw around the HB 2 proceedings, and the irreversible, positive changes that resulted, are familiar to me. Over the years I have seen the energy that emerges when groups of people with common goals come together. Each individual action connects us to a growing network of others who are willing to build relationships, build communities, and take strategic collective action to improve our conditions.

Complexity Science and the Edge of Chaos

In the summer of 2013, I visited my dad at his cabin home in upstate New York, and he handed me a book called *Complexity: The Emerging Science at the Edge of Order and Chaos* by M. Mitchell Waldrop. I loved the title, the cover design, and the solid hardcover binding. It had my dad's notes scribbled throughout, and before long my notes were scribbled alongside. This book opened up a whole new world to me. My dad was like that, opening new worlds of possibilities.

Complexity science is a cross-disciplinary field that explores the natural order of the complex systems that exist at every scale, from cells and bodies to families, economies, ecosystems, institutions, and cultures. The more I learned about complexity, the more I saw that it described and explained the dynamics I have experienced in organizing social movements. It gave me a new lens through which to understand why and how change happens, as well as a rich language to describe the repeating dynamics of growth and change. We can understand the whole world through complexity: Humans are complex systems, coalitions are complex systems, and social movements are complex systems.

Complexity science has its roots in mathematics and physical sciences like biology and physics, but insights from its study are increasingly used in the social sciences. International development expert Ben Ramalingam has been working for years to apply complexity science to improve international aid efforts. He writes that, "The tools of complexity science and chaos found their early articulation within the physical sciences. However, once developed, scientists started to see similar processes everywhere—not just in the atmosphere, but also in the turbulent sea, in the fluctuations of wildlife populations, in the oscillations of the heart and the brain, in the movement of stock markets, and in the movement of traffic."[10]

A key insight of complexity is that a system's starting conditions will determine how it responds to new input. It also teaches that the interactions among small, interconnected, and interdependent parts (networks) are affected by new inputs (information); thus, sharing information is the fuel for change. Complexity science teaches that the richness of change is enhanced when there is diversity among the networks and the interactions—in the context of social movements, this means moderately dense relationships and using multiple strategies. It teaches that change is not linear but cyclical, and that the edge of chaos is where the deepest changes are possible, as the system releases what does not serve it while new ways of being emerge. Change emerges when small, replicable actions increase and form a tipping point where change happens fast.

Complexity helps explain why techniques—like horizontal organizing and bottom-up power structures—are effective. According to Ramalingam, "Complexity has appealed most to those who feel that top-down, command-and-control and reductionist approaches can be inappropriate in many real-world situations."[11] The insights of complexity show that in many situations, systems are stable yet also dynamic when energy is disbursed in clusters rather than centralized.

In this way complexity undermines the theoretical foundations of capitalism, militarism, and even nonprofits that rely on the assumption that amassing centralized, hierarchical power is the ideal form of organization.

Looking at our social movements as complex systems, we see that periods of chaos or instability are necessary. We can even embrace, cultivate, and create them. With the right resources and planning, we can be poised to take action as opportunities open and influence the direction of change, even if we are not in control of the outcomes. We can proactively bring situations to the edge of chaos, which is understood as the place where a system is neither stable nor in complete chaos. Ramalingam writes, "In human organizations, the simplest example [of the edge of chaos] is of a system that is neither too centrally controlled (order) nor too unorganized (chaos). The key question for many thinkers, who suggest that the edge of chaos is the place of maximum innovation within human systems, is how complex systems get to the edge of chaos."[12]

I have come to believe that crisis is necessary to bring about fundamental or radical change. I see the edge of chaos as the moment or space that precedes deep shifts in power. There are times when conditions in a society are ripe for change. When ideas are breaking through and spreading, the change becomes unstoppable. As Victor Hugo once wrote, "Nothing is more powerful than an idea whose time has come."[13]

I am clearer now on the importance of what most people, even activists, tend to avoid—the step of intentionally creating a crisis for the decision makers and power brokers who oppress and exploit us. In his "Letter from a Birmingham Jail," Martin Luther King Jr. wrote,

> You may well ask: "Why direct action? Why sit-ins, marches and so forth? Isn't negotiation a better path?" You are quite right in calling for negotiation. Indeed, this is the very purpose of direct action. Nonviolent direct action seeks to create such a crisis and foster such a tension that a community which has constantly refused to negotiate is forced to confront the issue. It seeks so to dramatize the issue that it can no longer be ignored. My citing the creation of tension as part of the work of the nonviolent resister may sound rather shocking. But I must confess that I am not afraid of the word "tension." I have earnestly opposed violent tension, but there is a type of constructive, nonviolent tension which is necessary for growth.[14]

I like to envision the point of crisis that Dr. King famously referenced as a place that exists on the edge of chaos. This place between order and disorder, equilibrium and instability—this edge of chaos—has been taken up by enthusiasts across disciplines and vocations to describe "a region of bounded instability that engenders a constant dynamic interplay between order and disorder."[15]

One of my concerns with today's social movements is there's too much of a focus on data—money raised, phone calls made, and so on—and not enough on developing strong, networked local organizations creating actions that exist at the edge of chaos. Calling members of Congress and contributing to organizations like the ACLU that wage battle in the courtrooms are

Lisa preparing people for action against the Brett Kavanaugh confirmation in the Hart Senate Office Building, October 2018. T-shirt design by Laurie Arbeiter. *Courtesy of Kisha Bari.*

important actions, but these must be continuously combined with actions that "create such a crisis and foster such a tension that a community which has constantly refused to negotiate is forced to confront the issue."

Today it often feels like we are, in fact, poised at a moment where great change is possible. Ideas once shunned by the mainstream are now openly embraced—health care for all, a wealth tax, real gun control, pathways to citizenship for every undocumented person, and voting rights for felons, among many other proposed policy changes. We must actively seize this moment rather than sit back and passively hope that a Democratic president will make all of our dreams come true.

No matter which strategies we explore, we will get pushback from those who benefit from the continuation of colonialism, white supremacy, patriarchy, and capitalism. The best option I see is for us to stay focused on organizing our communities, healing, and building collective power to face what might come at us. We must continue to forge more connections within our movements and use a diversity of strategies—electoral organizing, corporate campaigns, media outreach, and support for lawyers in the courtrooms, yes, but also building local coalitions/alliances/networks in our own communities that are able to organize direct actions like sit-ins, shutdowns, office delegations, blockades, occupations, and uprisings in places of power. The more connected we are and the greater the variety of tactics we use, the greater the possibility of something better emerging from this troubling moment in history.

CHAPTER 2

Shutting Down the CIA and the Power of Bottom-Up Organizing

On the morning of April 26, 1987, I rolled out of my town house in the Mount Pleasant neighborhood of Washington, DC, with three others crowded into my Subaru Brat. It was cold, dark, and foggy as we slowly snaked down Rock Creek Parkway, making our way to the Memorial Bridge. I drove with caution, remembering the loosened lug nuts on my tire just a few days before.

We were just passing the Kennedy Center when I noticed a police car behind me. We made it to the bridge and had almost crossed into Virginia when I saw two more police cars up ahead. The car behind me flipped its lights, and sure enough, I was being pulled over. We had no choice but to wait and see what they had planned for us.

Finally an officer approached and said I was speeding. This wasn't true—I had been extremely careful about my speed, knowing that I might be followed. I provided my license, and then we waited and waited. It became clear that their orders from above were to delay us, as we were key organizers of the planned action at the CIA.

After thirty minutes the officer came back and let us go. We crossed over into Virginia and headed out to the Chain Bridge Road, where we hit traffic coming from all directions. *Shit.* Rush hour. Thankfully, we made it to the designated staging area at Langley Fork Park just in time. It was still cold, with the early-morning light just breaking through. We were there to shut down the CIA, and with all the hard work that had gone into planning this action, I had an inkling that we would pull it off.

———————

That morning in 1987, thousands of demonstrators succeeded in blocking the entrances to the Central Intelligence Agency's headquarters in Langley, Virginia, to protest that agency's involvement in President Reagan's "dirty wars." His administration had been covertly supporting the rebels in Angola and the Contra groups in Nicaragua, who were trying to topple Nicaragua's newly formed Sandinista government. During the 1980s, organizations throughout the US had joined a "Pledge of Resistance" against the conflicts in Nicaragua and elsewhere in Latin America. The Pledge, I believe, was an ideal model for horizontally organized movements, one that I still advocate for today. Shutting down the CIA was the biggest, most complex call to action the Pledge ever put out, and to my knowledge this was the first and last time the CIA has been shut down.

My involvement traces back to Boston in the early 1980s, where I first learned about the Pledge and the structures and processes of horizontal organizing. The Pledge had support from many national religious organizations and leaders, along with solidarity groups, political groups, labor organizations, human rights groups, and policy groups. Everyone was involved, everyone was united, everyone was organized, and that's part of why it worked. The Pledge created a space to build a culture of solidarity and love. The work was rooted in training, art, prayer, and strategic action. Over forty thousand people signed the Pledge in the first three months alone. By the mid-'80s there were over one hundred thousand signers and groups in over eighty cities.[1]

My work with the Pledge had a powerful impact on me. I saw a whole new model emerge that included self-organized local affinity groups functioning within an interconnected national network. The organizing structures that the Pledge built in those years enabled us to take bigger risks because we knew a whole community of people was standing with us. We were learning to self-organize, to practice direct democracy, and to stand strongly in our power by saying *no más*, no more killing, no more illegal wars, no more murder, no more money, no more advisers, no more secret deals, not in our name. It was during these early years with the Pledge that I learned the power of nonviolent direct action and civil disobedience to create legislative and political victories large and small.

Learning to Organize in Boston: 1985

In the spring of 1985, I packed my belongings up in my Subaru and drove from New York to Boston, where I had taken a job as a legislative coordinator for Citizens for Participation in Political Action, CPPAX, a group that worked on a range of social and economic justice issues. CPPAX focused on the legislative and electoral arenas; little would I have guessed that working for them led me on a path away from electoral politics.

Boston was a straight three-hour shot on Interstate 90 from my dad's house in Chatham, New York. Five hours to the south, on I-95, was my mom's house in Hawthorne, New York. I was only twenty-three, and while I had been independent in many ways, it was nice to know family was not so far away. I found a room to rent in Dorchester, in South Boston, in a house owned by two lesbians. It was a great space, a big room with hardwood floors, a tall ceiling, and big windows looking out on beautiful trees. It was painted a light yellow, giving everything a softness when the sun came in.

The CPPAX office was just off Tremont Street, the heart of historic Boston. There were all kinds of people in the area and all kinds of hustle and bustle, from the Massachusetts State House across the Common to the nearby shopping district. If you continued east on Tremont, you would enter an area where the Federal Building, City Hall, and Faneuil Hall were all located. These were interspersed with other places of interest, including an army recruiting station and an office of the CIA. I would soon learn the importance of knowing the geography of offices of the government, where marches, sit-ins, and delegations might be organized.

CPPAX was on the fourth floor of a worn-down building that housed lots of other political groups. When I walked in on my first day, I was a bit overwhelmed by how much clutter was everywhere in the huge space—boxes of papers, posters, pamphlets, brimming file cabinets, and more. There was some order to the chaos, and you could tell that years of intense commitment to the work emanated from this place. CPPAX was a pretty significant operation. It was a merger of two citizen action groups, the Massachusetts Political Action for Peace (Mass PAX), and the Citizens for Participation Politics (CPP). Dick Cauchi, the executive director, was a funny little man with perpetually rolled-up sleeves, always ready to focus on the tasks at hand. I was going to be a good fit, I thought. I liked the scrappy, grassroots feel.

By the age of twenty-three, I already had eight years of intense organizing experience under my belt, but there was still so much to learn. I had always loved organizing. When I was ten years old, my mom took me to a protest in our neighborhood calling for a traffic light to be installed at a busy intersection. I have a vague memory of how great it felt being out there with other people, trying to make a change.

Neither of my parents was especially political. I like to joke with my mom that the traffic light rally caused me to choose my path in life. As a sophomore in high school, I founded an underground student newspaper called *The Free Thinker* that ran a range of articles on everything from student rights to advocating for changes in the counseling department. As I remember it, things started to change at school as a result of the paper, and I started to change, too. As a senior, I was elected president of the Student Government Association. During that year we painted murals around the school, held student-principal breakfasts, knocked on doors in the neighborhood urging passage of the school's budget, and organized a student walkout to fight austerity measures. I learned that even in institutions as small as a local school district, key people in power conspire to exploit the system in ways that create harm. This was a scary and upsetting reality, but I was learning. There was injustice, and people working together could make a difference.

I continued to organize as a student at Skidmore College, a small liberal arts institution of the ruling elite in Saratoga Springs, New York. With the support of the Progressive Student Network, I was elected president of the College Government Association, much to the apprehension of the administration. I was an outlier, on full financial aid, and ignorant of what a preppie was. My parents divorced when I was young, and my mom struggled to raise three kids on her own. She had left her family support system behind in Georgia, and she worked multiple jobs, eventually becoming a secretary at a small real estate office in Thornwood, New York. When I was eleven she married Joe, a bus driver for a local school district. During those early years, I spent many weekends in New York City with my dad, a photographer and director working in advertising at McCann Erickson. But he went near-crazy in the cutthroat world of advertising, leading him to live in a cabin he built in the woods of upstate New York by the time I was a teenager.

Part of my parents' divorce agreement was weekend visitation, child support, and paying for our college education. Well, my dad did well with the first one, but fell well short on the others. At Skidmore I had no khaki pants, loafers, or Lacoste shirts in my wardrobe. In between board of trustee meetings, I was cleaning toilets and making beds as a union housekeeper. But my leadership and organizing on campus could not be dismissed.

During this era the Reagan administration was cutting millions of dollars in student financial aid and restructuring the money from grants to loans. I organized with the New York State Student Organization to stop these cuts, taking a busload of students to DC to lobby. Skidmore was also looking at ways to save money and decided to close the nursing school. Working with the nursing students, we forced the board of trustees to change their decision, allowing everyone enrolled to complete their degrees. To this day Skidmore maintains their nursing program through a partnership with NYU.

In 1982, when I was a senior, Abbie Hoffman, the famous revolutionary who started the Youth International Party (also known as the Yippies) and was later put on trial as part of the Chicago 8, spoke at Skidmore about a community organizing internship at Save the River.[2] I applied right away. Abbie wrote back and said A-plus, come on up! The program never materialized, but after I graduated I packed my car and drove on up anyway.

Save the River in Clayton, New York, is in the heart of the Thousand Islands. Johanna Lawrenson, Abbie's partner, had a cottage on the river that was built by her great-grandmother. When the Army Corps of Engineers released its devastating plans to retool the St. Lawrence Seaway, Abbie, Johanna, and their friends founded Save the River, fought back, and won.[3]

In 1983, the year I came on board, the same environmentally destructive plans for the seaway were resurfacing. We acted fast, organizing the Canadian government, the governors in the Great Lakes regions, and the entire New York State congressional delegation to oppose it. And we won.[4] Congress had embedded the project in an omnibus waterworks bill, which is very hard to change, but we defeated the $2 billion boondoggle, to the surprise of many.

During this fight Abbie and Johanna had been traveling to Nicaragua, coming back with stories of a revolution. This was all new to me. I had already seen the amazing powers of organizing, but very little of my previous work had to do with foreign policy, and at this point in my life I didn't understand the true immoral depths of war and greed. In 1984, shortly before moving to Boston, I traveled to Nicaragua with Johanna and Abbie, helping to organize a delegation of seventy journalists and learning what revolutionary love looked like. I was also reading *Bitter Fruit*, the award-winning book about US involvement in the 1954 coup in Guatemala, and this shattered any remaining illusions I had about our democracy. I was learning that these covert war activities were in fact happening all over the world, and in the 1980s they were very active in Central America and southern Africa under the direction of the Reagan administration.

These wars had vast humanitarian and political impact. In South Africa the CIA was instrumental in the arrest of Nelson Mandela in the early 1960s, and for years they supported the South African regime with intelligence, advisers, and weaponry to maintain the apartheid system.[5] The CIA was also deeply involved in the Angolan Civil War. There was so much bloodshed in these senseless proxy wars that played out as the Cold War between the US and the USSR continued. Involvement in these foreign wars also secured US access to human and natural resources to be exploited by US corporations.

In Nicaragua the leftist Sandinista government had taken power in 1979. From the moment Reagan took office, he sought to undermine them. He increased military funding, supplied weapons, sent US advisers to Central American countries, and began a series of National Guard training exercises. It became evident that the administration was building an infrastructure to support a possible invasion of Nicaragua, which prompted Congress to pass the Boland Amendment in 1982 prohibiting the federal government, including the CIA, from providing military aid to the Contras "for the purpose of overthrowing the Government of Nicaragua."

But Reagan just kept going underground, supporting what was called a low-intensity conflict while funding the guerrilla tactics of the Contra rebel groups. The Contras had set up their main operations just over the border in Honduras, from which they launched excursions and attacks in Nicaragua. It is estimated that during these years the Contras carried out more than thirteen hundred terrorist attacks.[6] The Reagan administration was also supporting the right-wing Salvadoran military dictatorship, despite international condemnation of high-profile atrocities committed by the death squads that had been trained at the US School of the Americas. These included the March 24, 1980, assassination of Archbishop

Óscar Romero, who was shot down in his church after he spoke out about the government's violence. In December 1980 three US nuns and one volunteer were raped and murdered—Maura Clarke, Ita Ford, Dorothy Kazel, and Jean Donovan. In December 1980 the Salvadoran Army killed more than eight hundred of its own civilians in the El Mozote Massacre. Despite the horrors, the United States, first under Carter and then under Reagan, continued to spend billions of US tax dollars supporting the military regime in El Salvador.

It was in reaction to these US-funded atrocities that the Pledge of Resistance came into being. The Pledge started in 1983 at a gathering of Christian peace activists who publicized their message through *Sojourners* magazine.[7] They put out a call for legal protest, nonviolent direct action, and civil disobedience to stop a US invasion of Nicaragua. From the beginning, the Pledge, seen as an emergency response campaign, pursued a horizontal network at the grassroots level. They trained tens of thousands of people, organizing them into affinity groups that coordinated with one another in local spokes councils. These processes and structures spread rapidly across the country, with each local network mirroring the other. The Pledge had an explicit structure and tons of flexibility to meet local needs. This is what I now call a *hybrid structure*, mixing national coordination with local coordinating committees, spokes councils, and affinity groups in an emergency response network.

I learned that Boston was one of the more active local Pledge groups. It was strongly influenced by a crew of slightly older women, mostly lesbians, who had been a part of the Women's Pentagon Action in 1980. These included Cathy Hoffman, Laura Booth, and Nancy Alach.[8] There was also C. T. Butler, one of the founders of Food Not Bombs and a big advocate for consensus decision making, a process he had learned as part of the Clamshell Alliance. His book *On Conflict and Consensus* is still a definitive handbook on the formal consensus process. I was lucky to be raised up by so many great people who understand that training is essential for movement building.[9]

As it turned out, my job as a legislative coordinator at CPPAX gave me a seat at the table of the local coordinating group of the Boston Area Pledge, which was made up of numerous staff people from various Boston-area peace and justice groups, along with activists who were representing working groups. As a new member of the Pledge, I took part in a mass training held at the First Church on Garden Street, just across from Cambridge Common. This is where I learned the foundation of the organizational model that I still practice today.

Horizontal Organizing 101: Affinity Groups, Spokes Councils, Consensus Decisions

My initial training at the First Church really blew me away. I will never forget the experience. The building was humming with activity that morning. Numerous peace and justice groups had offices there, and there was a massive main hall with cavernous ceilings where the training took place. Food Not Bombs was there with food and coffee to keep us nourished. It was mostly white people of all ages: grandmothers, students, religious folks, and more. There was lots of energy, and clearly many there already knew one another.

The trainers started out by splitting us into small groups for an active listening exercise where one person spoke first, uninterrupted, while the others not only listened for words but tuned in to emotions and body posture. Next was a presentation on the conflict in Nicaragua and the history of the Pledge itself, which was followed by an activity called a Spectrogram. They had us line up, and we were presented with different direct-action tactics and asked whether the tactic was violent or nonviolent. The room shifted each time. We quickly saw where we were in alignment, and where we were not. So simple, but so effective.

The trainer then put us in two parallel lines, called Hassle Lines, and told one side that we were protestors blockading the Federal Building in Boston to protest military funding to the Contras. The other line would be people who worked in the Federal Building. One line blocked the doors; the other tried to get through. I remember I kept talking to my opponent, trying to explain why I was there, while I kept my arms open and wide to prevent him from walking forward. Up and down the line, there was movement and yelling. Afterward we debriefed and discussed de-escalation strategies like asking their name, making eye contact, staying calm, breathing, or using silence.

At this point the trainers asked us to form into small groups. If you came with friends or colleagues, you could group up with them; if you came alone, you joined the others who'd likewise come alone. I didn't fully realize it, but we were breaking into the real affinity groups with whom we would be planning direct actions in the near future.

Once in our groups, we were asked to make a quick decision about what our group would do if the police came. Little did we know that they had "spiked" each group with someone who played the role of facing higher risks, saying they had asthma or were pregnant. Later the trainers asked us to think about our decision-making process. It was a good opportunity to make power dynamics visible, including those around gender, race, and health status. Did anyone *facilitate*—in other words, take on a leadership role? Who? Were all voices heard, or just one or two? How did we make decisions? They were helping us see that humans have ways of making decisions through processes other than just voting. This process of reaching agreement without voting is a form of informal consensus, and it happens all the time in real life.

Next the trainers asked each affinity group to decide how their group would participate in a larger plan for blockading the Federal Building. The trainers provided a map of the building, showing us where the doors were and outlining the advantages and disadvantages of the site's layout. We were asked to decide how many of us were willing to risk arrest and where we wanted to enact the blockade.

Each affinity group was then asked to select a spokes person—someone who would sit in an inner circle with the other spokes people, each with their affinity group sitting behind them (in case they needed to consult) as the proposals were discussed by the spokes council. The spokes people shared their plans and we tallied numbers from each affinity group, forming a plan for a larger action involving all of the groups working in clusters at each door. We figured out how many people were needed for each door of the building, and when we realized we fell short in numbers for the back door, another affinity group switched its location.

We were all beginning to see how the affinity group process worked to ensure effective actions. Now that we had a plan, it was time to practice. One end of the room was set up with chairs to denote the various doors to the Federal Building. We gathered at the other end of the room, where we began the march. This march was the "beginning" of the mass action. As I would learn, every good direct action has an explicitly planned beginning, middle, and end.

We were all together in the march, but soon we split off, each group having its own task. We started chanting: "Stop the Bombing, Stop the War, US Out of El Salvador!" We surged forward, splitting, each group moving to a different door. We sat down in our blockades. Before we knew it, a group playing the police started to pull everyone apart. Everything got really crazy, as they had "batons" made out of rolled-up newspapers. They were hitting us hard. We linked our arms and held on. Some people got up and walked, but most of us did not. I had just learned earlier in the training about choices, consequences, and the power of non-cooperation—and non-cooperation was the choice I wanted to make! The "police" grabbed me and started pulling, but the people around me held on. It was a tug-of-war, and then the trainers yelled, "Stop!" The exercise was over.

We settled in for the debrief. We talked about how the police targeted those who are most vulnerable—people of color, queer people, or those who appeared to be organizers. We practiced ways to protect our bodies by getting on our right sides, pulling our knees up, and putting our arms over our heads. The lawyers briefed us on our rights, the medics provided information on first aid, and the organizers talked about the role of community support. I was both adrenalized and tired as we got back into our affinity groups to talk about our hopes and fears. I was starting to learn the importance of facing my fears and then acting with courage despite them. The eight-hour training closed with an announcement about the next big spokes council meeting. They were happening once every month, and right then and there my new affinity group made a commitment to attend.

During my training at the church that day, I learned about the most important parts of horizontal group organizing. These include:

AFFINITY GROUPS. Self-sufficient groups of about five to fifteen people who support one another before, during, and after an action. They are the smallest nodes in the network. An affinity group might plan their own action or they might work together with others toward a common goal in larger actions. Affinity groups sometimes remain together over long periods of time, existing as emotional support or study groups in addition to participating in actions. When affinity groups join in mass action, each group chooses a spokes person to represent them in a spokes council meeting.

Affinity groups serve as a support structure for the members and reinforce a sense of connection and belonging. They provide a solution to the isolation or separation that can come when individuals act alone. AGs also help to weed out infiltrators because if someone in your group does not abide by agreements, there is immediate accountability. The term *affinity group* was first used in Spain around the time of the civil war in the late 1930s. *Grupos de afinidad*, as they were called, were made of anarchists who self-organized and formed the core of the resistance to the fascist government, led by Francisco Franco, that was then coming to power.

CLUSTERS. Two or more affinity groups working together within a larger action. Clusters might form to take responsibility for blockading an area or organizing one day of a multiday action. Clusters might organize around where affinity groups are from (example: Texas cluster), an issue or identity (examples: student cluster; immigration cluster), or an action interest (example: street theater cluster).

SPOKES COUNCILS. The larger coordination and decision-making bodies that convene to organize mass action or network coordination. Each affinity group, cluster, or working group empowers a spoke (representative) in a spokes council meeting to decide on important issues for larger actions. A spokes council does not take away an individual affinity group's autonomy within an action; affinity groups make their own decisions about what they want to do, where, and when, as long as it fits within the action guidelines that each affinity group agrees to. A common action guideline is an agreement not to bring drugs or weapons. All decisions in spokes councils are made by consensus, meaning that all groups have agreed and are committed to the plan (or have agreed not to stand in the way of the action going forward). Spokes councils are effective because they allow for the conversations to be had by smaller groups of people. If there are five hundred involved, the spokes council discussion is being had by maybe fifty spokes people who represent the concerns of their group.

CONSENSUS DECISION MAKING. A decision-making process with roots in the Quaker and feminist traditions. Horizontal movements have used it to ensure that every group's voice is heard. During this process, everyone expresses their concerns as proposals are modified.

The first step is asking if anyone has outstanding reservations or concerns. If there aren't, we ask if there are any stand asides. A stand aside doesn't have major concerns but simply doesn't feel called to this action and therefore can't be counted on for its implementation and might not participate. If there are a lot of stand asides, you might still reach consensus, but you should assess whether it's wise to go forward with that action. Next, we ask if there are any blocks to the proposal. A group or person would block if they believed that the proposal might harm the very fabric of the community and the work. If there are no blocks, then consensus has been achieved. Consensus is not about everyone agreeing, but about resolving differences and moving forward with a plan that everyone is willing to implement.

WORKING GROUPS. Similar to affinity groups, but they function to organize the infrastructure or support needed for the movement. Typical working groups might include media, publicity, action planning, tactical communications, art/culture, finance, fund-raising, transportation support, housing, medical, legal, food, and training. Similar to a spokes council, representatives from working groups often circle up into a hub or larger coordinating group to ensure that everything needed to support the work is in place.

DIRECT DEMOCRACY. This occurs when people make decisions about things that directly affect their lives. DD differentiates itself from representational democracy, where an individual makes decisions for the group and typically uses voting as the primary means of making a decision. Affinity groups, clusters, and spokes councils using consensus are forms of organization that support DD because these structures and processes ensure that everyone participates, there are no winners and losers, and any decision to go forward is informed by the perspectives of everyone involved.

It wasn't long before I put my new knowledge to use. My affinity group's first action was blocking an army recruiting center across from Boston Common. The police surrounded us with giant horses, which was very frightening, and then they dragged us away through the horse shit. Then on May 7, 1985, we did a mass action shutting down the JFK Federal

Building to protest the US trade embargo against Nicaragua and El Salvador. Almost three thousand people were involved—our affinity group structure was working! At our earlier actions, the police had pursued a plan of not arresting us, because they didn't want to give our movement visibility. But that wasn't working anymore. On that day 559 were arrested, which inspired many of us as we felt the power of the people surge through our veins.[10] We could no longer be ignored.

During that action, my affinity group dropped a massive, twenty-by-forty-foot banner off City Hall that read, simply, NO CONTRA AID.[11] This was before the post-9/11 security boom, when it was relatively easy to get into and out of government buildings. We were terrified as we made our way through City Hall, up the elevator to the top floor, then down the hall to the stairs leading to the roof. Down below were thousands of activists rallying in the Federal Building Plaza, protesting the recent round of Contra aid funding. We were using lead fish weights attached to the bottom of the banner to weigh it down. *One, two, three—let's drop this baby!* The crowd below broke out in a huge cheer. Before you knew it police were storming the roof, and we were arrested, handcuffed, and taken to jail.

During our trial, the prosecution argued that we could have killed someone with the fish weights.[12] And you know, he was right. Ever since, I have taken meticulous care with my banners, using cardboard, sand-filled baggies, or half-filled water bottles as weights. This arrest also taught me another important lesson: The police lie. They said we broke onto the roof, and that it was marked DO NOT TRESPASS. Neither assertion was true.

Perhaps our most successful action involved pressuring the Massachusetts governor. In early 1986 the governor of Maine announced that he wouldn't allow the Maine National Guard to train for activities in Central America. Recognizing this as a timely opening, I worked with Bob Warren from the Central America Solidarity Association (CASA) to pressure Governor Dukakis of Massachusetts to follow Maine's lead. We put together educational materials to distribute at tables at public events, recruited a number of organizations to support the cause, then took over Dukakis's office in the State House, filling it with about forty of us demanding to see the governor. Since I was affiliated with a long-standing organization in Boston (CPPAX), I was a bit nervous. This was a formal

OUT OF THE TOOLBOX
Banner Drops in 10 Easy Steps

There are so many places to drop banners once we've trained our eyes to look and see: bridges, overpasses, parking garages, elevated walkways, windows, balconies, atriums, and tunnels. You can track traffic patterns on your phone to see where slowdowns occur. You can use a street view to eyeball the bridges. Is there a guardrail, are there metal beams, or is it cement? Is there a fence? Is it chain link, easy to pull a rope through? I have done a shitload of banners over the years and everyone always has a good time. If you can all eat breakfast together afterward, all the better!

MAP YOUR SITES. Use Google Maps and Google Earth to get an overview of the roads and bridges around and within your city. Better yet, drive around, looking for nearby parking garages or other ideal surfaces for tying the banners. Choose your sites and know where you can park.

GATHER MATERIAL. You'll need flat sheets, spray paint, duct tape, scissors, a knife, rope, zip ties (if there are bars or fences), and weighted materials for the bottom corners. Bring extra of everything.

PREP MATERIAL. Make duct tape grommets in all four corners. These are the holes to thread the rope (top holes) and weights (bottom holes) through. You can also purchase grommet kits, but it's not necessary. Tear four-to-six-inch strips of duct tape to reinforce all four corners of the sheet front and back. Tape on.

Once taped, cut a hole with scissors. A trick is to fold the corner and cut through the little triangle—that makes for a strong hole.

PAINT YOUR WORDS. Sketch them in with a pencil. Make sure everything fits, usually four to six words. Place the banner over a big sheet of plastic. I have also taped sheets up on walls or fences with plastic underneath, or had people hold the banner up while someone sprays.

CUT AIRHOLES IN THE BANNER. Find several places between the words to cut little airholes in a V shape. The holes help the banner resist the winds.

TIE ROPES IN THE TOP CORNERS. Usually I use twelve-foot-long pieces that I put through the top holes, giving me a double rope about six feet long on each side for tying. Plastic zip ties can also work great if the rails aren't very thick. Your tying strategy will depend on the fence or structure material—always bring extra rope!

WEIGHT the bottom corners using cardboard, newspaper, sand in bags, or half-filled water bottles.

FOLD from the bottom to the top and then like an accordion so that when you open, you can just pull the two top corners and it unfolds fast and easy!

GATHER YOUR TEAM. This is usually an early-morning job. A team of three people can hang three to five banners in a close geographic zone. For bigger actions, multiple teams will work at the same time.

DROP. Celebrate. Take photos. Get out of there and go out for breakfast!

space with cushy sofas and chairs and big windows with long, velvety curtains—not exactly the type of space that CPPAX was known to disrupt.

Dukakis of course did not come to speak with us, but we made it clear we would be coming back. A few days later we got word that the governor was very close to making a statement. I remember that Bob and I just looked at each other and smiled. Dukakis was one of the first governors to refuse to send their state's National Guard. In August of that year, at the National Governors Association meeting, a resolution was passed affirming that governors have a right to determine where their Guards can be sent.

These experiences in Boston taught me the power of movement building based on a model of self-organized smaller groups that are networked together. The system contained both centralized and decentralized parts that worked in harmony and with accountability through the spokes council and the local and national coordinating groups. At the national level, the Pledge had policy experts tracking Congress, forming a signal committee to alert the local groups of crisis situations or sneaky maneuverings in Congress. There were solidarity groups that kept us informed about humanitarian needs, handled important messaging, and provided clarity about the desires of the people in Central America. The Pledge's religious groups had a huge base that provided sanctuary to Central American political refugees. The model melded together staff members at organizations with unaffiliated activists. The Pledge could move fast; it could move big, it could move small, it could move in multiple places or one place at a time. And as I was about to learn, it could move on a large scale to shut down big centers of power.

DC and Shutting Down the CIA

In the fall of 1986, I was recruited for a short-term gig in Washington, DC, at the Committee in Solidarity with the People of El Salvador (CISPES), a solidarity organization that was part of the Pledge of Resistance coalition. I rented a great room on Kilbourne Street, right in the heart of Mount Pleasant, an activist neighborhood with many political households. Mount Pleasant was seeing the beginning of a large population shift as thousands of Central Americans were escaping US-funded wars in Central America and emigrating to the US. In DC many were moving into Mount Pleasant, which had been a predominantly African American neighborhood already dealing with years of exploitation and oppression. Tensions between Black and Brown folks grew for years, and I watched this come to a head, at least in my world, during the Justice for Janitors campaign—but ah, that is the next story![13]

I loved my new home, a three-story town house, and I quickly connected with my new roommates. All of us were in our midtwenties and political. During this time, I met Joanne Heisel, and we became partners in love and organizing. Joanne worked at the Network in Solidarity with the People of Guatemala, NISGUA, and later became a staff person at the Guatemala Human Rights Commission. Just as in Boston, I threw myself in, working long and intense hours with CISPES, developing action alerts, participating in the legislative strategy team, and working Capitol Hill. CISPES was working on a campaign to defeat US military aid to El Salvador; at the time, Reagan wanted to send millions of additional dollars to El Salvador's Duarte regime, which backed the death squads.

I also started organizing with the Local DC Pledge of Resistance. The DC Pledge was made up of creative and bold people who were willing to throw down.[14] We became a good team and fast friends. My reputation for being a good organizer was getting around, and I was meeting a lot of the key players, including those in the national pledge campaign.[15] In March 1987 I was hired by the Mobilization for Justice and Peace in Central America and Southern Africa as the national coordinator for the civil disobedience action to take place during a large mobilization being planned for April.

I was excited to be a part of a large-scale mobilization on something I cared so much about. At this point in my life, the idea of national work seemed mysterious and powerful. I often wondered: *Who are these people? How do they do it?* These illusions faded away as I saw that national work, like local work, is organized by "just people," coming from different perspectives, struggling together, doing what they thought was best to stop US wars and to support the liberation of the people of Central America and southern Africa. There were thirty-five organizations on the national steering committee, with many others that endorsed and would participate in the mass action. But there were only about ten of us on staff, all working in the cramped basement office of the Coalition for a New

Foreign and Military Policy. Leslie Cagan was the overall coordinator, working to ensure that everything was coming together.

By the time I joined the staff, the location of the civil disobedience action hadn't yet been finalized. There had been a huge debate on the steering committee about whether it would be included at all, with much of the resistance coming from the participating labor unions. It was finally agreed that groups could choose to sign on to the rally but forgo involvement with the civil disobedience action. We moved forward with discussing possible targets at the White House, the State Department, the US Capitol, and the Pentagon. We had not gone to the CIA—in fact most people had no idea where it was—but it was a timely target because its role in the Iran-Contra affair had been recently exposed and was still in the news.

I decided to go take a look around. The CIA's headquarters were in northern Virginia, in a conservative community called Langley southwest of DC. It was a wooded area south of the Potomac River. I headed out to the Washington Memorial Parkway first, where there was an exit that led directly to the CIA. As I pulled off, I saw a security checkpoint about one hundred feet ahead, with two lanes in and out. The road was lined by woods on each side and felt very secluded and exposed. I turned left to get back on the parkway, which took me straight to Chain Bridge Road, leading to the CIA's south entrance. I pulled into the tree-lined drive leading right to the gates, with a turnaround and a grassy area. I realized that if we got up to these gates, it was pretty open, with room for people on the grass. A great gathering space and photo op.

Next I turned around to see what Langley Fork Park had to offer. The park would be a perfect assembly site: There was a parking area and a spot to rally and march from, which is always super helpful when organizing an action. As I followed the road around the park, it became clear that CIA employees could also come in from the entrance of the Federal Highway Administration. A third entrance. This meant we would need three blockades, with at least a hundred people holding down each entrance.

I had gathered the information I needed and it was time to get out of Dodge. Back at the office, things were humming as the staff worked to pull everything together. By all accounts this felt like it could be big. The steering committee had put together numerous working groups, including city mobilization, mobilization and outreach, the fund-raising group, a media group, logistics and programming, and the direct-action group that I led.[16] The majority of the steering committee's attention was devoted to the rally, which would include speeches from big names like the Reverend Jesse Jackson, who was eyeing a presidential run at the time.[17] We finally had the opportunity to present our idea for civil disobedience at the CIA, and to my amazement everyone agreed!

I felt so lucky to observe and learn from the impressive people on the steering committee. At the same time, I was beginning to see that national movements overprioritize the big marches and rallies while investing too little in acts of civil disobedience. The CIA action wasn't well integrated into the overall plan. I knew that if this was going to work, it was on my shoulders. Participants from over two hundred cities were coming to DC, with more than a thousand buses reserved. I worked furiously with my intern Dylan, the civil disobedience working group, my friends in the Pledge, and the staff to put the infrastructure and coordination in place for the weekend.

Organizing people from out of town once they arrived in DC was going to be key. We planned for mass trainings on Sunday and a mass spokes council meeting on Sunday night at the New York Avenue Presbyterian Church. I have learned over the years how absolutely essential it is to have advance prep sessions and a day-of framework for a mass action. There have been numerous mobilizations over the years where people build infrastructure and then expect participants to come and figure out their own actions. There needs to be logistical planning in the weeks and months leading up to the action as well as a clear vision and plan for the action itself, including a framework with timetables, schedules, and clearly defined sites of action. Without this structure/framework, you end up with thousands of excited, well-intentioned people who have no idea what to do. The framework helps sort out who does what, and where. For example, we knew we were blockading three gates, but not everyone wanted to risk arrest by actively blockading. We planned for areas of legal protest along with blockades of higher and lower risk, with each affinity group choosing the action and location right for them.

Little by little, it was all coming together. The CIA action was the culmination of a national convergence called the March for Peace and Justice in Central America and Southern Africa, April 24–26, 1987. On Friday night there was a big concert, on Saturday over 150,000 people marched and rallied in the streets of DC, and on Sunday over 1,000 people participated in a mass direct-action training on the East Lawn of the US Capitol Building. The training was for our big action on Monday morning: shutting down all three entrances into the CIA.[18]

Interest in the CIA action exceeded our expectations. In fact, our success was starting to make the labor leaders in our ranks increasingly uncomfortable. Some were afraid of violence erupting; I was not so worried. Our action had been organized tactically, meaning everyone had agreed to nonviolence. In the typical way that liberalism works, the fears of the leadership forced us to tone down some of our language, like saying it was a sit-in instead of a blockade. I didn't get too hung up on that. No matter how you worded it, our impact would be pretty much the same.

One day at the office, we learned that someone had cut cables in the car of David Cortright, the executive director of the Committee for a Sane Nuclear Policy and a member of the mobilization's steering committee. A few days later I felt a strong shudder in my car as I drove along the Rock Creek Parkway. I pulled over. It's a good thing I did, because the lug nuts on my back left tire had been loosened and were about to fall off. I never learned who did any of this, but I do know that we cannot let our fears stop us. It's important to keep things in perspective. It's scary to think that you're on the radar of the CIA, but to me it seemed worth it when the slaughtering of hundreds of thousands of people was being funded by our tax dollars. If we want to stand up to these massive crimes, we must learn to face our fears and take courageous action.

———————

And so it happened that on Monday morning at about six thirty, I was pulled over in my Subaru on the way to the action. When we finally arrived at the staging area at Langley Fork Park, I was on the move, checking on the status of everything. People were already gathering in groups, preparing to move to their designated entrance. We got our bullhorns distributed and helped the stragglers find their group. It was a beautiful thing. Almost everyone else had arrived on the buses we organized from downtown, which got there before the traffic started. The vast majority of people were young college students angry about the war and inspired by President Carter's daughter Amy Carter, who along with

Abbie Hoffman had fought and won a campaign to block CIA recruitment on college campuses.

I helped to coordinate the blockade of the South Gate, Leslie was on point at the West Gate, and Josh took the North Gate. The buses taking people to the North Gate were stuck in traffic, so another 150 or so folks set off on foot around the Federal Highway Administration, through the woods and toward the parkway entrance. The South Gate group was a massive procession of over a thousand people. As we marched up toward the checkpoint, one big group went forward to blockade the gate while the rest of us stayed in the road leading to it. Those who didn't want to risk arrest lined the sides of the drive, holding signs and banners while singing and chanting.

Soon enough we heard helicopters in the sky, and the police moved in, a couple hundred of them with riot gear, clubs, and pepper spray. It was a good show of force. Local police, federal police, and park police were all on the scene. Soon they started arresting people sitting or kneeling in the road. I looked over to the side as I heard the crowd cheer. A small group was mooning us, each with a letter painted on their butt that together spelled out N-O—R-E-A-G-A-N. I spotted some great signs: CIA—CRIMINALS IN ACTION. Some wore photos on their shirts, or the names of people who had been killed in the dirty wars. The chanting went on and on: "Hey Hey CIA, You're Not Going to Work Today!"

A little after 8 AM, the action was in full swing and the sun came out, bringing us warmth and a big blue sky. A massive sound truck arrived at the main gate, and we listened to words of wisdom from people like Daniel Ellsberg, the former military analyst who had exposed what was really happening in Vietnam with the leak of the Pentagon Papers. Also speaking that day was John Stockwell, the ex-CIA agent who had exposed the illegal actions of the US government during its involvement in the Angolan Civil War. As these amazing people told their stories, rows and rows of people blocked the road in front of the main gates, holding signs declaring, YOU SHALL NOT PASS. *We are here to expose who you are and what you do!* Some of us had our arms linked; some sat silent in prayer. It was powerful to watch as wave after wave of people were either escorted or carried away by the police, and then packed into vans and buses and taken to jail.

For over four hours that morning, the entrances to the CIA were shut down. It might have been fleeting, but we were creating havoc in a disciplined and courageous way. Around 560 people were arrested: 355 of the 1,200 people at the South Gate; 19 of the 100 people at the West Gate; 183 of 200 at the North Gate, including our legal observers and lawyers.[19] Many at the North Gate were beaten with batons. We had a strong jail

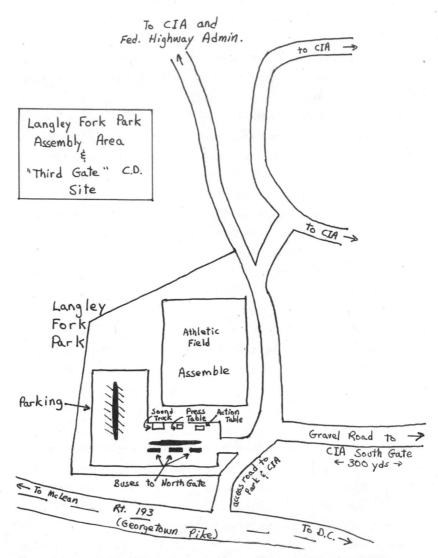

Organizing map of the CIA action assembly site. Drawn by Lisa, April 1987.

support plan in place, and we were able to assist everyone with lawyers, moral support, and loving arms on their release.

The direct action at the CIA shows that creating crisis wakes people up and opens minds. On that morning, if only for a few hours, we made it impossible for a single employee of the CIA *not* to think about the morality of their job. We paralyzed rush-hour traffic and made the front page

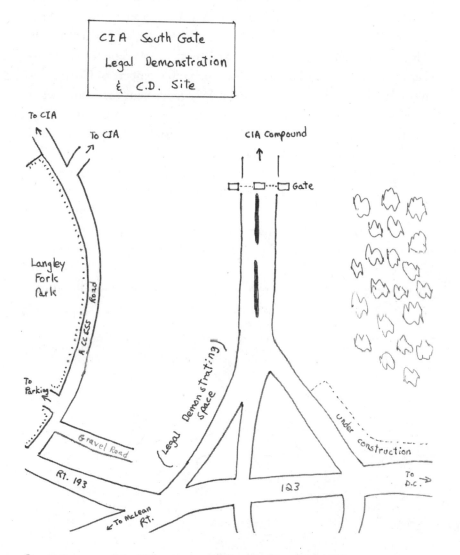

Organizing map of the CIA main gate. Drawn by Lisa, April 1987.

of almost every major newspaper in the country with headlines about the arrests. We created space for whistle-blowers and showed a new generation of people the power of nonviolent direct action by shutting down one of the scariest institutions of the US Empire.

During my years with the Pledge of Resistance, I learned that victory is often incremental, but that without our efforts, there might have been no victory at all. The Reagan administration was never able to invade Nicaragua as they desired, and I believe this was because of the continuing, unrelenting public pressure. They could not find a way around the light we shone on the truth as more and more people took to the streets. Our direct actions shifted the debate, enabling members of Congress to shift as well. Unlike the anti–Vietnam War movement that came before it, the movement around the wars in Central America explicitly used a national strategy of nonviolent direct action and civil disobedience to thwart the machine—and to some extent, it worked.

We were young and old, strong and wise, and we threw down together. We went to jail, got roughed up by police, and put our time, money, blood, sweat, and tears into the movement. Some of the relationships formed during the Pledge of Resistance era continue to this day. That is what movement building is about: a long road with many intersecting paths where we meet again and again. I like to think that today, even as I'm writing these words, new groups are forming, finding voices that will continue to rise together, chanting in harmony for decades to come.

CHAPTER 3

Justice for Janitors and the Power of Escalation

The sun was barely up, but morning rush hour was in full swing. We gathered our teams, reviewed the plan, and drove eastward onto the 14th Street bridge, the main artery into Washington, DC, from the suburbs and cities of northern Virginia. We towed a dead car on a truck trailer and positioned it across two lanes of inbound traffic. Horns blared as traffic backed up. We had shut the bridge down.

The dead car was missing its two front wheels. It wasn't going anywhere, and neither were we. Traffic was at a standstill, and with the hardest part of our task accomplished, our team rushed to the car and joyfully surrounded it. I bounded onto the roof to take in the scene: To one side, four lanes of traffic backed up as far as the eye could see. To the other, our nation's capital, with its bare trees and gleaming white buildings tinged with the early morning light. Out in front were the glittering waters of the Potomac River. Hundreds of janitors and allies were over on the DC side of the bridge, holding up banners that said DC HAS CARR TROUBLE and RISING OUT OF POVERTY, cheering us on. The sun beat down, warming us on that unforgettable December day.

We were exhausted, but our adrenaline had us pumped. It was Thursday; we had been running the streets nonstop the previous four days, from 7 AM to 9 PM, treating DC to what we called a Week of Rage. The police were angry because we had managed to run circles around them. We had captured the attention of the public, the politicians were concerned, and the commercial real estate industry leaders and building owners were pissed. A media war was under way as the previously "invisible" workers of DC's commercial real estate industry were front and center.

All week the plan had been for our escalating actions to culminate right here, taking this bridge and creating the crisis we hoped for. I could hear the sirens getting closer, and soon an array of police vehicles rolled onto the scene, blocking the bridge as well. The police charged. One grabbed me and ripped me off the roof. I went limp as a rag doll as they stuffed me into the back of a police wagon. Thirty-eight of us were arrested that morning, and news about workers blocking the 14th Street bridge quickly spread across the labor movement.[1] Labor had been losing power for years, and it was rare to see a union take such a strong stand.

Coming off that week in December, we did not convince the cleaning companies to negotiate a contract with the janitors—but we were determined, disciplined, nonviolent, and organized. We had a plan and we rolled with the punches as they came. During the course of the following year, the Justice for Janitors campaign continued to escalate its actions across DC and the nation. Within a few years of our first action at the bridge, 70 percent of the commercial real estate buildings in DC were under a union contract, up from 20 percent in 1987.[2] This was a historic victory.

The DC Justice for Janitors (J4J) campaign was one piece in a movement that gained traction in cities all over the country in the early '90s. This was a true-life story of David and Goliath. The people who were invisible by day, vulnerable at night, and poor twenty-four hours a day

14th Street bridge blockade during the Justice for Janitors Week of Rage, March 1995. *Courtesy of Rick Reinhart.*

rose up and brought some of the most powerful people in our country to the table. In an era of union decline, it was unprecedented. I saw Black and Brown people, immigrants, and women of color taking huge risks, fighting back, winning hearts and minds along the way. Many did not have legal status. Many were working for less than $5 an hour and juggled two or three jobs. They were mothers and fathers, sisters and brothers, cousins and friends. It was the wisdom of the workers that informed the campaign's radical decision to organize citywide, not worksite by worksite. The janitors and their allies struggled together even when their jobs and livelihoods were at risk. They persisted.

In 2015 Stephen Lerner, the mastermind behind the campaign, wrote, "The Justice for Janitors movement became a living example of what was possible—even against the greatest odds."[3] Decades later, our movements can still learn a ton from what went down during the formative years of Justice for Janitors. Below are stories and lessons from the small role I played.

Grassroots Girl in the Union World

During the 1980s the Justice for Janitors campaign tried to reorganize janitors into a union with little success. The campaign used a variety of strategies, including direct action, litigation, legislation, and media, but advances were few. There was some initial success in Pittsburgh, where a defensive strike fought off concessions, and in Denver, where a thousand new members came into a citywide master contract. These campaigns built credibility, but it was the Los Angeles campaign that really put J4J on the map. In 1990 the police viciously attacked a group of janitors on strike in Los Angeles. This galvanized community members who were shocked by the police violence and became a turning point that led to a massive union contract victory. The momentum that followed inspired new organizing strategies that I continue to teach to this day.

The Justice for Janitors model centers on the concept of *escalation*, where workers and their allies mobilize over a protracted period of time, engaging in creative, disruptive actions that escalate to a point of crisis for the power holders in the industry and their political allies. This type of escalation—if done persistently and strategically—results in major wins. I have used this strategy again and again with janitors, autoworkers, nursing home workers, security officers, and teachers, as well as in the struggles for global and domestic economic, environmental, climate, and racial justice.

In retrospect, my job change from grassroots organizing to union organizing in 1993 was serendipitous. I came onto the labor scene just as some badass players in DC and elsewhere were reviving older direct-action union tactics and fashioning them for a new age.

My past work prepared me well for the union world. Shutting down the CIA in 1987 was deeply inspirational to me as a budding organizer. Our collective action, aka the power of the people, shut down a huge and scary government institution. After that action I was hired as a co-coordinator at the Washington Peace Center, a grassroots group started by a Quaker activist in 1959 to protest a biological and chemical weapons facility. It became a key player in the antiwar and anti-nuclear movements. During my six years there, we shut down the Supreme Court, the White House, and the Pentagon as I continued to learn that we can face these places of power and actually affect outcomes. But by 1993 I was worn out from years of work at a job that didn't pay very well and decided it was time to seek out financial stability. I took a job as a union representative in the labor movement.

Boy, did I learn a lot.

My first gig was with the Local 25 of the Hotel Employees and Restaurant Employees Union (HERE) in DC. Labor laws are designed to make organizing against employers difficult, which is why organizing in the labor movement requires creativity. During a six-week lockout of the workers at the Madison Hotel, we organized early-morning wake-up calls at the hotel: Wake Up, Pack Up, and Check Out of the Madison Hotel! We also organized sick-ins at their high-end restaurant, popcorn and peanut pickets, and a Thanksgiving Day meal on the picket line. It was fun, and it was also effective—we nearly put the hotel out of business, convincing the owner to settle.

In 1994 I was hired by Local 82 of the Service Employees International Union (SEIU), a huge union that represents workers in the health care industry (nurses, home care workers, and so on), the public sector (state government workers, public school employees), and property services (janitors, maintenance workers, window washers, security guards, and more) in more than 150 local unions. I came on board as a union representative in the government sector. My turf included the Department of Justice, the FBI building, and the National Security Agency (aka No Such Agency). It was so weird to no longer be sneaking in!

During site visits I introduced myself to the janitors and asked how they were doing, what they liked about the union, and what their challenges at the worksite were. Much of my job involved filing grievances when a union contract was violated. In one case I remember a young woman who filed a grievance because her hands were raw and covered in a rash. This was likely the result of the harsh chemicals she used to mop the floors, but her boss refused to provide chemical-resistant gloves. After we showed him the provision for this safety measure under the Occupational Safety and Health Act and threatened action, all the janitors had the gloves they needed the next day—and the young woman's hands healed within a week.

Learning the turf, the people, the security, the systems, and the contract was a piece of work, not to mention the grievances. I was reminded about who I was and who I was not. I struggle with individual problem solving, being more attuned to tackling problems at a systemic level. I did my best to motivate and rally energy with the workers at lunchtime meetings, but in the end I really wasn't cut out to be a rep. I'm a direct-action girl.

During this time my partner Mary Anne Hohenstein, an amazing person and organizer on the DC Justice for Janitors campaign, taught me a lot about being in the union world.[4] She was part of SEIU's international team under the leadership of Stephen Lerner, SEIU's property services director.[5] I got the chance to meet and observe Stephen, and I wanted in! Stephen was the primary architect behind the J4J campaign and a brilliant and visionary strategist. He saw that progress in the movement was too slow for the janitors, who had faced draconian wage cuts across the industry. He and others at J4J were putting forward the idea that to build real power, we needed to organize industry wide in cities and nationally, not just site by site. Stephen was pursuing a "comprehensive campaign" that involved multiple strategies simultaneously—worker organizing, direct action, and legal/regulatory, financial, political, and media strategies.[6]

As I saw this group get down to crafting a plan for citywide actions, I learned more about what was at stake. This wasn't just about the janitors in DC; this was part of a nationwide crisis of de-unionization and lowered wages.

Across the US the commercial real estate industry in the 1970s tended to comprise union workers with full-time jobs and benefits who were direct employees of the buildings. When a huge influx of Central American refugees came to the US in the late '70s and early '80s, the industries saw a new workforce that could be easily exploited. The building owners moved away from hiring workers directly and instead started contracting out the work to cleaning companies.[7] This was a de-unionizing strategy. In DC the unionized African American workers were laid off or transferred to government buildings, while the cleaning contractors hired part-time Latinx workers en masse with lowered wages and no benefits in the commercial real estate buildings.

Labor laws dictate that workers can only bargain their wages and benefits directly with their employers—in this case the cleaning contractors. But it was the building owners who had the real power to set the rates, so workers were caught in a Catch-22 situation where they weren't allowed to bargain with the players who actually had the power to change their conditions. This dynamic was playing out nationally as more work was being contracted out, causing union density in many industries to decline.

The effect of de-unionization on the wages and benefits for janitors was huge. A 1990 report put out by Justice for Janitors described a unionized janitor in New York City who earned $11.29 an hour plus benefits, while a non-union worker in Atlanta earned $3.40 an hour with no benefits. The de-unionization of service industry workers was especially troubling because the economy as a whole was moving from manufacturing to service. Millions of low-wage jobs were being created, and without union representation, there were typically no benefits, no security, no protections, and little respect.

Unionizing service workers in 1990s DC seemed like an impossible prospect. At the time, only 20 percent of the industry was unionized. Most unions were created by an election process established by the National Labor Relations Board (NLRB) that requires more than 30 percent of the workers to signal their desire to unionize by signing a union card, followed by an election. A good organizer would sign up over 50 percent before filing for an election as you need more than 50 percent to win. Employer anti-union campaigns can erode your support by intimidating workers and spreading fear, so you want a solid majority to start with. The employer has the upper hand in this process because there are many dirty tricks to delay elections, and even if the election is won, it doesn't guarantee a contract. A complex industry of union-busting firms, consultants, and lawyers has emerged, teaching bosses how to fight the unions and delay the contract. In 33 percent of NLRB elections, workers still don't have a union contract two years after winning the election.[8]

We needed a better, faster way to achieve union density, so J4J advocated the card check process, an older method that was effective for industry-wide organizing in the 1930s. With the card check process, you still need to sign up a majority of the workers, but there is no election. Instead you go straight from signing the workers to demanding union recognition. Since employers rarely agree to a contract right away, they must be convinced that unionization is in their interest—and this is often done by showing them what labor unrest can look like.

One of the premises of the J4J campaign was that the individual contractors are not going to unionize on their own, but when enough companies come on board, wages and working conditions can be negotiated across the city, creating a domino effect that results in widespread unionization. Property owners have to be willing to cover the costs of increased wages and benefits, and this willingness comes from public pressure and competition from other owners who have been convinced to hire union contractors.

It was this logic that led us to Oliver Carr.

DC Has Carr Trouble

Oliver Carr, the largest building owner in Washington, had first set sights on DC when the riots following the assassination of Dr. King left the city in disarray. Today he might be known as a disaster capitalist, seeing opportunity to profit off people's pain. At one point in 1979, it was believed that Carr owned more than 10 percent of DC's office space. In 2000, when he retired, the *Washington City Paper* characterized his legacy as "tearing down everything in his path and building bland, virtually identical office

buildings that drained the life from formerly lively, diverse streets."[9] Over
the decades he bought and demolished many buildings of historic or architectural importance. Carr had helped de-unionize DC, having personally
"flipped" a number of union properties, but we felt we could get him to
switch strategies if combating the unions no longer served his bottom line.

Carr was charging high rents but paying very little in property taxes,
forcing a financial crisis in the city and creating an undue burden for
residents, including our members at Local 82. From our vantage point
this made Carr a public story, a representative of how the moneyed class
exploits the poor. Carr was conservative and anti-union, but he cared a lot
about money and was not an ideologue—it's the ideological ones who are
the toughest to crack!

In autumn '94 we began preparations for a full Week of Action. We
partnered with the HERE Local 27, which represented parking lot atten-
dants, and together we recruited from our members and supporters. Our
goal was to bargain with the cleaning contractors working for buildings
all over the city, securing a master contract that would cover all service
workers in their buildings.

The first Week of Action followed a pattern we would later replicate.
On Saturday we trained our people. On Sunday we wheat-pasted posters
all across the city and blasted our messages on the radio and in the media.
Early Monday morning we deployed teams to drop banners off bridge
overpasses and parking garages. On Monday, Tuesday, and Wednesday,
our actions at buildings across the city escalated. Thursday was reserved for
the "big" action—we always save our biggest action for Thursday because
Friday is a bad day to go to jail. In December, this was the shutdown at
the 14th Street bridge.

Most of the buildings we were interested in were in DC's K Street
corridor. We rolled out action after action, day after day. Our targets
included key commercial office buildings, offices of the cleaning contractors, government buildings, and restaurants in our target buildings.

We had three hundred workers and allies organized into three mobile
action groups of about one hundred people each. We called these flying
squads, and each was color-coded. Sometimes we marched as one big
group; other times we split up, with one group going west while one across
the street was going east. We picketed in front of parking garages and

building entrances during morning rush hour. We shut down intersections and got up when the police came. We were a powerful moving force,
creating a cacophony of resistance as we used our voices, our bullhorns,
drums, and chin-chinas.[10]

By day two we took over building lobbies. By day three the arrests began.

Our goal was to create a sense of escalating chaos in DC, but our plans
were highly organized, with detailed maps and routes decided in advance.

I was running with the red group, one hundred of us in bright red shirts
and red bandannas worn on our arms or wrapped around our heads. We
hit the streets in the early morning, surging with the morning rush hour.

We did lots of little actions that week and some bigger public ones.
On Wednesday our three flying squads gathered at Freedom Plaza for a
public rally, joined by hundreds of supporters, including a host of labor
leaders, religious leaders, students, and community activists. We had music,
balloons, bucket drums, banners, and flags. After a few short speeches, we
took to the streets, marching first toward the Willard Hotel, one of Carr's
premier properties, then to Metropolitan Square, another premier property that had a huge atrium in the center. A battle for the doors ensued.
We eventually got in and flooded the atrium, chanting at the top of our
lungs, releasing balloons and waving our flags as we danced inside!

One of the public tactics we used that week was the creation of vermin
and cockroach flyers. We researched the restaurants and eateries in Carr's
buildings and discovered that a sandwich shop at 18th and K had a recur-
ring problem with rats, so we designed a flyer with a picture of a giant rat
and an image of the actual public health record. We alerted the restaurant
in advance by faxing them the flyer and giving them a chance to correct
any factual inaccuracies. We call this telegraphing our action. As you might
imagine, they flipped out and called the building's property manager.

Another tactic was attending the parties that property managers throw
for their tenants. At one such party the property manager had a fancy
tenant picnic on the roof of a key Carr building. A group of janitors and I
arrived with our brown bag lunches and sodas and immediately spread out
and sat down at different tables. These events almost always have a stage
set up for speeches. When there was a lull in the program I made a beeline
for the mike. "Hello!" I boomed. "I'm here to talk about the situation of
the janitors in your building. They're treated unfairly and paid poverty

The Menu of Actions

Over time we developed a roll-out "menu" for escalating actions that is useful for weeklong campaigns. It was Bill Ragen, the Justice for Janitors organizing director, who called it a menu—appetizers, sides, the main course, and desserts. Here's a quick sampling of my favorites, but there are many items you can add to the menu:

Appetizer: Advance Buildup to Create Tension

Wheat-paste posters
Banner drops
Human billboards
Smaller actions at important targets (if you'll be occupying a main
    downtown office, occupy smaller offices earlier in the week)
Leaflets and social media campaigns to educate employees,
    customers, and the general public

Sides: Actions to Telegraph That We're Coming

Leaflet employees or tenants in their offices to let them know
    about the coming actions
Quick, short traffic blocks at intersections near the targets
Flash mobs
Call in to radio shows, ads in local papers, media outreach

Main Course: Actions to Create Crisis

Marches, occupying intersections, blocking traffic
Delegations (showing up at politicians' or corporate offices and
    refusing to leave)
Picket at the homes of power holders or politicians
Strikes or work slowdowns
Occupying spaces—lobbies, parks, offices
Civil disobedience

> **Dessert: After the Week of Action**
> Celebrate!
> Follow-up op-eds and media exposure
> Debrief your people to review what worked and what could be
>   improved
> Engage opponents on their willingness to make ongoing changes
> Use your successes as the groundwork for the next campaign; learn
>   from your mistakes

wages. If you're happy with how your office is cleaned, please support these janitors." At this point security was heading right for me. The janitors and I chanted "Justice for Janitors!" as we made our way out the door.

These types of actions require a good deal of research in advance, but it's well worth the effort because they negatively impact the boss's core interests: making money, doing business, and public image.

Kicking Corporate Booty 101: Weeks of Action

The [4] Weeks of Action (also called Weeks of Rage) became a template that would be expanded upon and replicated. I don't think we realized it at the time, but we were creating a new model for action. We knew that direct action and civil disobedience were core ingredients. We knew that escalation was needed, and we knew that strategic targets were essential. We wanted to create nonviolent social disruption at such a scale that we could no longer be ignored or tolerated.

The key tactics and philosophies that are integral to the Week of Action model include:

PERMEATE THE COLLECTIVE CONSCIOUSNESS. This is all about piercing the veil of distraction that keeps us focused on things that aren't important. We want to get people's attention and help them access their emotions, then mobilize them into action. Permeating the collective consciousness is about public education, and it's a great way

OUT OF THE TOOLBOX

10 Tips for Successful Wheat-Paste Posters

I first learned about this public visibility tactic in the 1980s during the Pledge of Resistance, when our national network would put up posters in almost a hundred cities overnight. *Bam!* Our message was everywhere. In the age of social media, street posters are under-utilized, which is a shame because they're great for mass publicity. There's nothing like being face-to-face with the message while you're walking down the street or driving on your way to work. Post-ers can be taped, stapled, or pushpinned, but for large jobs there's nothing more efficient than wheat paste. You can buy it online or find it at hardware or wallpaper stores. You can also cook it yourself using water, flour, sugar, and glue. Here are tips that I've honed over the years for getting your message out with wheat-paste posters:

1. If you're working with multiple posters, pre-organize them into sets, and place each set into stacks that can be accessed easily.
2. Simple, eye-catching designs with short, simple, agitational messages or questions work best. Bright color paper jumps out, but I like basic black-and-white.

to describe what goes down during Week of Action campaigns. We want to make the janitor's struggle larger than life! We want to tell stories about how this struggle fits into the larger political moment. We want to create a sense of collective responsibility. People must know there's a conflict under way, and that we are working hard to

3. In terms of size, 11×17 copies do the trick, but bigger is always better.

4. If you're pasting big posters, apply the glue with buckets, rollers, and brushes. If you're working with smaller posters, squirt bottles and sponges are easier to carry around.

5. A large, smooth surface is key. You'll need to scout locations in advance and know exactly where your teams are going.

6. Apply a layer of paste on the surface, put the poster on, and then apply another layer of paste on top of the poster. Make sure the edges are glued down; otherwise it's easy to pull the poster off.

7. Wear junky clothes and latex gloves.

8. Working in teams of three or four is ideal: one or two people to paste, one to put up the posters, and one to look out for cops. Our cop watchers yell, "Hey, Joe!" if a cop is seen.

9. My favorite time to paste is in the mid-evening, after it's dark but while people are still on the street. It can be easy to blend in.

10. Great locations to paste include light poles, electric boxes, newspaper boxes, and construction walls. Posters on bridges have a long viewing life since it's a hard-to-reach location.

change the situation and implement a solution. Permeating the collective consciousness means getting people to feel part of the fight and understand what they can do about it.

RANGE OF STRATEGIES (MIX IT UP). We want to keep our activities dynamic, creative, and varied. If our events are predictable, they become boring to the public and background noise to our adversaries. Legendary community organizer Saul Alinsky devised thirteen "Rules for Radicals" about strategic community organizing, and several of them are about mixing it up, including:

- A good tactic is one your people enjoy.
- A tactic that drags on too long becomes a drag.
- Keep the pressure on, with different tactics and actions, and utilize all events of the period for your purpose.

COMPREHENSIVE CAMPAIGNS. This is a term used in labor organizing to describe campaigns comprising a range of strategies that roll out over time. With these types of campaigns, it's important to have primary, secondary, and sometimes tertiary targets. The primary decision maker, for example, would be the building owner. A secondary target would be a board member, and a tertiary target would be a restaurant owner who rents the space in a key building. A comprehensive campaign engages a variety of strategies—legal (the courtrooms), regulatory (health and safety), political (policy), electoral, corporate (targeting the companies), financial (following the money), community organizing, and media—along with direct actions, including strikes.

In my experience, while many unions use comprehensive campaigns, many do not prioritize creative disruptions that escalate to periods of compression and crisis. They want to turn people out to rally or to vote, but that is rarely enough for change. The success of the J4J template shows that repeated, escalating direct actions that create a social crisis should be considered a necessary ingredient.

INTEREST-BASED ORGANIZING. This is an incredibly helpful way to think about strategy. Basically you look at what the boss cares about (the boss's interests) versus what the workers care about (the workers' interests). The art of change is making the boss's interests align with the workers' interests. Table 3.1 breaks down interest categories. The key is to strategically target your actions so that the power broker risks (1) losing money, (2) having trouble operating their business, and (3) having their reputation tarnished. You can chip away at each one or impact all three at the same time—at some point the power broker will see that it's in their interest to negotiate a change.

STRATEGIC ESCALATION. This is the uniting philosophy of Weeks of Action. The art of an ongoing campaign is engaging your opponent at every step. At the beginning, we inform them of the solutions to the problem and give them a chance to do the right thing. They either fix it or they don't. In the case of Oliver Carr, he responded to our first Week of Action by filing a restraining order and escalating his public support of tax breaks for building owners. So clearly he hadn't yet been moved.

We then escalate and educate, get more people involved, and come back again with another Week of Action. We give the power brokers another chance to do the right thing. They fix it or not. We escalate again, using protests and direct action. They fix it or not. And so on. At some point, if things are not improving, you are in a protracted struggle where making it more personal becomes necessary—in other words, doing actions at the churches or homes of the key players to pressurize even more. In some cases it makes sense to put them out of business and create an alternative.

The concept of escalation also applies *within* each Week of Action, where the first day is relatively low-key, then the drumbeat of action builds. We want to leave people wondering: *What's coming next?*

The key to escalation is patience. It might take several years of escalating action before the power brokers fold. Soon after my work in DC, I helped organize a campaign in Denver that took years of action but led to an amazing contract that made the city of Denver and its suburbs a majority union city. By contrast, when I was sent to Detroit in 1995 to help organize an escalating campaign during

Table 3.1. Objectives of Interest-Based Organizing

POWER OVER HOLDER INTERESTS	OUR OBJECTIVE	PEOPLE'S INTERESTS
Making money	COST THEM MONEY	Fair wages
Doing business	DISRUPT BUSINESS	Meaningful work
Image	TARNISH THEIR IMAGE	Dignity and respect

the Detroit newspaper strike, the union leaders were indecisive. The workers wanted to continue to escalate, but ultimately leadership was afraid and unwilling to take dramatic action. The strike eventually ended with no victory.

Any campaign that follows these philosophies needs workers and allies in motion, both in the streets and in the places of power. Two of the essential structures we use to organize our people during Weeks of Action are:

1. **FLYING SQUADS.** These are large mobile teams of eighty to a hundred people each. They are highly organized and tasked with carrying out disruptive actions within the context of a mass action, especially marches or strikes. This concept traces back to the early-twentieth-century labor movement, when the United Auto Workers occupied automobile plants in Detroit. Flying squads quickly take off, or "fly," from one area to another. They might be tasked with breaking off from a march and singing and dancing on one particular street, marching through a building, handing out flyers at key entrances, or blocking doors. These mobile teams are colorful, loud, and proud, whether they're on the sidewalks or in the streets! Each flying squad has its own leadership team, including a tactical coordinator, march leaders, a police liaison, a traffic team, chant leaders, and props and leaflet coordinators.

2. **DAY BRIGADES.** These typically comprise fifteen to fifty people and are tasked with daytime actions like phone banking, holding signs, picketing buildings on strike, delegations to the offices of decision makers and politicians, and attending/crashing industry, corporate, or tenant events. Day brigades were especially important during the J4J campaign because many of the janitors worked at night. The day brigades allowed them to take action on their own behalf while still going to work if they were not on strike.

The goal of all of the above is to create a sense of compression and crisis that ultimately moves the power holders to settle the conflict. Let's see how we got to that point in DC.

Congress Has Carr Trouble

After the first Week of Action, Carr played it off like we weren't a threat while relying on his underlings—the contractors—to fight for him. DC's building contractors were organized under a powerful industry association, the Apartment and Office Building Association (AOBA), which was the local affiliate of the Building Owners and Managers Association, or BOMA. In the late '80s the SEIU had approached AOBA, describing how service workers were facing rapidly reduced wages and asking for help to re-unionize the industry. Instead AOBA began coordinating an anti-union campaign that included the infamous "banning letter," which banned anyone affiliated with the campaign from entering buildings in the district.[11]

After we shut down the 14th Street bridge, the AOBA was spooked. They attacked us in the media and lobbied for more tax cuts for building owners. In February 1995 these tax cuts passed despite strong public opposition.[12] Around this same time, city services in DC were on the chopping block, including libraries and vital services like schools, firefighters, and police. Twenty-two thousand union workers across the city were facing an average 12 percent pay cut.[13] The public debate over taxes was at a breaking point, and we realized this was where we had leverage.

We began to plan for a second Week of Action, now with a new message. Instead of "DC Has Carr Trouble," we blasted out "Oliver Carr Must Pay His Fair Share!" and "Save Our City, Tax Oliver Carr!"[14]

This time around our targets included DC's city council as well as national political players. When large companies and corporations are involved, it's often political or religious leaders who can mediate the dispute. But first, they need to be made aware of the crisis.

We recruited from other unions in the area and across the country to send their people to participate in our Week of Action in March. This allowed us to increase our people power while training union organizers and members to take the DC strategy back to their own city. Numerous unions bought in. The United Auto Workers Region 1A under the leadership of Bob King threw down big, sending about twenty-five people.[15] The carpenters showed up in large numbers as well. Our capacity had doubled since December, with six hundred people organized into six flying squads doing actions every day.

This is what escalation is all about. We expanded upon what worked well in the first Week of Action, scrapped what didn't, and used the first week's success to recruit more people.

This time we took the fight to Oliver Carr directly. Instead of demonstrating at his company's headquarters, we kicked the week off with a candlelight vigil in front of his house in Bethesda on Sunday night. This was accompanied by street posters, banners, and a deeply researched white paper provided to the media outlining how the commercial real estate industry was robbing the city budget of millions of dollars in property taxes.

On Monday we started where we left off by blocking the 14th Street bridge.[16] This time we brought a long Cadillac that shut down three lanes instead of two. The police let us stay for forty-five minutes as traffic all over the city backed up. We knew this was a show of solidarity. The police were pissed about the budget cuts as well. In fact, the month before, police officers and corrections workers had disrupted a city council meeting against the budget cuts along with the janitors.

On Tuesday we shut down Pennsylvania Avenue from all directions near Carr headquarters. On Wednesday we tried to disrupt traffic on the expressway leading to Congress with a U-Haul and four fake plywood houses that we towed in, but the whole thing fell apart—we didn't have enough numbers to hold the space, plus we were down one dead car, which really did die on its way to the action. It was here that I learned the importance of getting as many people as possible in the street, knowing some will leave when the police arrive.

Our final action on Thursday was ambitious, with three simultaneous actions beginning in sync at 10 AM. The first group was a hundred janitors who occupied a city council meeting. The second group occupied the offices of Newt Gingrich, who at that time was Speaker of the House. The third group was small but mighty. We were tasked with disrupting the open session of Congress.

Many people don't realize that Washington, DC, is a colony. By law the US Congress approves the DC budget, not the city council. What's more, DC has one representative in the House, but that seat doesn't have a vote. How fucked up is that? There has been a long fight for statehood that has yet to be won. Because of this arrangement, Newt Gingrich, as Speaker of the House, had unusual authority over DC's fiscal crisis.

Janitor sit-in outside the Reeves Building at 14th and U Streets NW. *Courtesy of Rick Reinhart.*

I was a bit nervous as we approached the balcony level entrance to the House of Representatives' Chamber Gallery. This was the upper level where visitors could observe the proceedings. We entered quietly and looked down below as the congressional representatives filed in. As 10 AM rolled around, sure enough, out came Newt Gingrich. He cleared his throat and began reading the morning prayer, followed by the Pledge of Allegiance. I breathed slowly, waiting for my moment.

Gingrich called the House to order with a thud of his gavel, and right then I leaned over the railing and yelled at the top of my lungs, "Newt Gingrich, Save DC, Tax Oliver Carr!"

We pulled out our banner and held it high as all heads below turned on us. Security was rushing, climbing over the rows of seats to reach us. Funny how they act like they're in an action film when all they're dealing with is three unarmed women. A few yanks and they pulled us out of the row, down the aisle, and out the door, with us chanting the whole way. A clip of this became part of their opening footage on CNN for weeks. They sent us to DC's Central Cell Block—not a nice place—and kept us for the night. We curled up on the metal bunks, hoping to sleep despite the scurrying of cockroaches on the floors and on the walls around us. Despite these less-than-optimal lodgings, we were happy. The March Week of Action had been a huge success.

On the heels of our second Week of Action, the DC power brokers and elites knew they had a problem on their hands. We were effectively shutting down the city and halls of power. We had received tons of media coverage, and we had impacted and educated many, including tenants in

Lisa is carried away by the police during the Justice for Janitors Week of Rage, September 1995. *Courtesy of Rick Reinhart.*

the buildings. They learned our story. They saw how rough the police were with peaceful protestors, and they witnessed the janitors rising up and demanding justice.

Over the summer we kept the pressure on with building actions, public protest, and political work. In September 1995 we did our final Week of Rage. Our big action that week was blocking Route 66 on the Roosevelt Bridge, which was the inbound route to DC for wealthy communities coming in from northwestern Virginia. This was bigger than our previous blockades—at this point we'd had some practice. We set up a full-on classroom on that bridge with chalkboards, desks, chairs, and a huge school bus. The impeded commute ended up delaying votes in Congress and flights at National Airport. We received a lot of media attention, some branding us traffic terrorists as Congress held a special hearing that resulted in making it a felony to block DC bridges.[17]

It's not uncommon for a bit of time to pass before a settlement is reached, but by this point we knew the Weeks of Action had created the conditions needed for settlement. During the couple of years after our final Week of Action, we continued with smaller actions and strikes as we built and solidified the relationships that allowed contract negotiations to proceed. The power brokers had seen enough of us. They wanted it to end.

End it did. By 1998 the DC market had gone from 20 percent to 70 percent union, with increased wages and benefits for the janitors in the commercial real estate industry.[18]

A Good Strategy Needs Good Research

The success of Justice for Janitors wasn't the result of good luck and happenstance. It was the result of a solid strategy enacted with persistence and joy.

Strategy is a plan to win. It's about asking questions—who, what, where, when, how, and why. Who has the power to decide? What are their resources? What are *our* resources? Where can we find them? When are there good times for engagement? How will we engage them? Why are they doing what they're doing? And so on.

A good strategy means understanding the history, institutions, and players that created the injustice. It should roll out over time, escalating on all fronts, using a series of creative tactics that engage your targets and inspire your base whenever and wherever possible. Strategy means engaging the whole community as stakeholders in the problem. Strategic campaigns that create a public crisis ensure that political and economic forces will demand a remedy to the problem.

A good strategy creates a complex campaign. There are many players moving and engaging, cooperating and competing in the dance of power that determines whether we remain the same or change. Remaining the same, though, is an illusion. Change is inevitable, so it's important to focus on the type of change we want and put our energy toward making it happen.

In DC we were fighting to increase the wages and benefits of janitors—and then, over time, window washers and security guards. But oppression is never about a single issue or group of workers; it's about how capitalism thrives at the expense of the people. We must always connect single struggles to larger systems of oppression and keep open the possibility of larger changes.

Strategy means crafting a credible plan to win. Our people must believe it is possible. People don't activate because of problems—they activate to achieve solutions. Strategy is outlining the options, understanding the possible consequences of each, then making choices about how to engage your opponent, which tactics to use, and when to use them.

In other words, strategy means a hell of a lot of research.

Looking back on my years in organizing, it was the Janitors campaign that taught me the power of strategic research. Research often gets short shrift in grassroots organizing, which is unfortunate because it can make the difference between winning and losing. It's not rocket science, but it must be done methodically and in advance.

Research is all about figuring out who/what has the power and how to leverage them. If you want to move a big rock, you will need a big pole. When the rock is a corporation or a regime, there is rarely one pole that will move it. We need a lot of poles, which is just fine, because we are many.

When I begin my research, it all begins with *power mapping*, which is done in four steps:

1. Write the entity (company/institution) or person with the most power to make your desired change in the center of the paper/board/screen. Draw a circle around it/them.

2. Around this central person or company, add the names of other people/
   companies that could have power to convince your central entity to
   change their behavior. Draw lines connecting your circles. You might
   organize these entities in quadrants—work, political, social, and personal.
3. Along the lines, write down how the connected relationships can
   be used, and what new information can be brought into that relationship. Generally this will be a positive incentive, aka a carrot, or
   a negative incentive, aka a stick, to convince the central entity to
   change their behavior.
4. Develop messages and tactics for each secondary or tertiary target,
   assessing the best time line for each. In every tactic you choose, highlight how the central entity with power is responsible for the problems
   and what they need to change.

Power mapping can be combined with *interest-based organizing*,
discussed earlier. This type of organizing assumes that your opponent is
trying to protect (1) their money, (2) their ability to conduct business, and
(3) their image/reputation. You'll want to create and prioritize a list of
leverage points in these three areas. Here are factors to consider for each:

MONEY/PROFIT. Research each avenue your target takes in making
   money. This includes looking into the company's investors, lenders, and shareholders, the banks they're borrowing from, their main
   competitors, suppliers and vendors, customers and clients, legal problems, scandals, health and safety concerns, the CEO/worker pay ratio,
   debts, plans for future growth, and so on.
DOING BUSINESS. Map out the inner workings of how the company
   does business. Look at the board, management, departments, staff, and
   business locations—offices, plants, stores. Look at the government
   agencies and oversight organizations. Look at meetings, conferences,
   and trade shows. Look at the organization of the workplace and where
   workers are unhappy. Look at relevant labor laws, discrimination laws,
   and zoning and planning laws.
IMAGE/BRAND. Reach out to coalitions and allies to help impact the
   company's image. Think about nonprofits, policy groups, associations,
   civic groups, humanitarian groups, religious leaders, and educational

groups. Plan social media campaigns. Affecting a company's image
and bottom line via social media campaigns such as #GrabYourWallet
can be very effective. Tell your story in street posters, fliers, radio, TV,
op-eds, features, talk shows, and so on. Leverage the target's legal problems in your public relations work. Culture-jam the brand by engaging
sponsors, promoters, ad agencies, social media, and more. Every tactic
you use needs to consistently expose/portray them as the bad guy.

Organize the fruits of research into databases. A lot of what you're
doing is compiling data about individuals and organizations. You want
to track their names, phone numbers, emails, faxes (yes, some places still
use faxes!), and addresses. You'll want to compile information (family,
hobbies, politics, finances, idiosyncrasies, and so on) on everyone who
might be important, including the CEO, executive board members, board
of directors members, executive management, heads of divisions, heads of
regional, state, and local offices, heads of industry associations, political
officials, and so on. You'll also want to map the political and cultural world
of your target city or town. Many cultural gems like museums, theaters,
operas, or symphonies receive donations from your target or have key
business players on their board. They also cater to the wealthy. This makes
them ripe locations for actions. Building a calendar of their meetings,
activities, and events can help you identify key moments to take action.

Your research forms the basis of your strategy by creating lots of opportunities for engagement. A great example of this was during a 2006 Justice
for Janitors campaign in Houston, which ultimately was very successful.
Our power mapping showed us that the Greater Houston Partnership
was an industry group powerhouse representing the key building owners.
They had a campaign called Houston: A World Class City, so we spoofed
this with our own messaging: Houston: A Poverty Class City. We made
them a key target, crashing event after event, until finally they called us
and essentially said, "We want this to stop, what do we need to do?" This
campaign was a major labor victory for workers in the South.

Industry associations are major, but often overlooked, players in business and corporate relationships. Most national industry associations have
offices in each state. They are clubs for the rich and powerful, and they
host such lovely events for us to enhance!

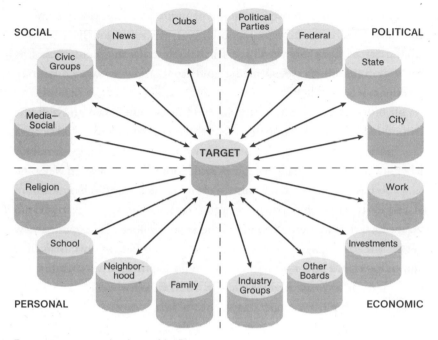

Power mapping tool enhanced by Lisa.

Power mapping helps reveal whether to pursue a big-fish or little-fish strategy. Oliver Carr was a big fish, but that's not always the way to go. In a J4J campaign in Denver, the big guy was so anti-union that we focused on the smaller employers instead, organizing them into a trigger agreement, meaning that when we organized the majority of them in the market, they all went union, isolating and eventually leading to the big guy needing to negotiate.

———

Key to the success of the J4J campaign was that we integrated creative direct-action tactics into all aspects of the larger campaign. Direct action was understood by everyone to be part of the plan to win, along with doing battle in the courtrooms, in the media, and politically. Direct actions shouldn't merely be tacked on; they should be part of the planning process from the beginning.

In other words, how do we see an entire movement or campaign through a direct-action lens? How do we bring tactics on the ground and through the air into an overwhelming symphony of disruption, allowing transformation to occur? In my opinion, it's this mind-set that's missing from many of today's movements—the willingness to augment our political, corporate, media, social media, and legal strategies with escalating direct actions.

In 1990 SEIU policy expert John Howley researched the strategy behind J4J during the campaign's formative years. He wrote, "Justice for Janitors argues that we don't have to wait for better board appointments, labor law reform, or a change at the White House. We can begin developing now the new ideas and new habits that are needed over the long term."[19]

The J4J campaign pursued escalating direct actions at a large scale to create the crisis we needed to move the power holders. It inspired a new generation of organizers and sent a message to other unions about how you can win. We believed that change could happen *now*. We chanted it every day: "*Sí, Se Puede*. Yes We Can" . . . and we did!

CHAPTER 4

The Battle of Seattle and the Power of Going to Jail for Justice

At two in the morning on December 2, 1999, I sat on a bus outside an arrestee processing center in Seattle with a mighty group of fifty rabble-rousers and dissidents. The Battle of Seattle raged in the streets as we waited on the bus, not knowing what the police had in mind for us. We'd been arrested the morning before while demonstrating in a public park, and had been chanting, singing, and sleeping on that bus for fifteen hours.

An officer came aboard and started the engine. *Finally!* I thought. But when they didn't pull forward to where the other buses were parked, I was confused. When they drove around to the back of the building, where there were no media or supporters to witness, my confusion became fear.

This was the moment we had prepared for. We had decided that our strategy was to non-cooperate with the police, which often involves going limp when they come to take you away rather than cooperating by walking along. It can also mean refusing to give your name at the station, forcing them to process you as Jane Doe or John Doe.

As the police entered the bus, we moved off the seats and formed a human chain, sitting down in the aisle, holding on to each other from behind. I was about the tenth person from the door. I sat behind Peter Lumsdaine, a tall, slender, soft-spoken organizer in the anti-nuclear movement. One by one the police came in and, with difficulty, pulled people off the bus.

The officers were frustrated. You could feel the pressure building. Peter was next; he held on to the seat leg. The next thing I knew, the policeman was unloading a canister of pepper spray directly into Peter's face. He screamed in pain as they pulled him out. It was horrible and terrifying, and I was next.

When they came for me with canister in hand, I made a quick choice. I did not hold on or go limp. I got up and walked off the bus.

This was the beginning of a five-day journey non-cooperating in the Seattle jail. I have always been an advocate of non-cooperation in our acts of civil disobedience, because that is where our true power lies—but sometimes, the cost is greater than the gain. Non-cooperation is safer when you have a community backing you, and in Seattle, we had one hell of a community, along with detailed plans for jail solidarity.

What happened in Seattle changed the world. We came sixty thousand strong to stop the World Trade Organization (WTO) from consolidating its power during their ministerial conference taking place at the Washington Convention and Trade Center in downtown Seattle. The anti-WTO protests represented a new coming-together of previously insular movements—a nascent global justice movement rising up in response to a newly globalized neoliberal world order.

Before Seattle, most people had no clue what the WTO was. After Seattle, it was a household discussion. We pierced the dominant cultural veil, and when the state came down hard against us, we rose up with beauty, courage, and grace. Our fierce ragtag community had the audacity to imagine that a shutdown of the ministerial was possible, and then did the hard work and community building that made it happen. The whole world was watching as the battle raged for days.

Seattle, for me, was about hope. We came from every movement, every direction, every age, and every race to say no to the WTO. The contemporary global justice movement was taking shape, and in the two decades since Seattle, there have been successes and failures, as there always are. In 1999 the seeds of the movement were blooming with creativity, energy, and action, and the spirit of that time has carried us a long way.

The Global Justice Movement Blooms

Some say that the anti-WTO convergence in Seattle was the beginning of a movement, but it was not. It was an outgrowth of many movements across the world that were fighting corporate globalization.

The WTO's roots go back to the 1940s, when forty-four allied nations gathered in Bretton Woods, New Hampshire, for a UN conference on monetary policy. A new system and new institutions were created, including the International Monetary Fund (IMF) and what was to become the World Bank. In 1948 a collaboration of nations negotiated a global trade deal called the General Agreement on Tariffs and Trade, or GATT. After several more decades and rounds of trade negotiation, the World Trade Organization was formed in 1994, replacing GATT. The WTO took on the role of global negotiator and administrator of multilateral trade agreements, and judge, jury, and arbitrator of global trade disputes.

The capitalists had achieved their global infrastructure, generating enormous wealth for industrialized nations at the expense of the people and the environment. In the US, corporations had been gutting the manufacturing industries and moving work overseas, creating massive job and wage losses. Business education became dominant in colleges as a massive financial services industry grew. CEO and executive pay increased, creating an even deeper wage gap.

The IMF and World Bank were putting country after country in the Global South into debt. Loans with big interest rates were conditioned on the imposition of structural adjustment policies. This meant major cuts to social programs, driving people deeper into poverty while their land, labor, and natural resources were made available on the global market. Sweatshops boomed. Farmers lost their farms. Indigenous people lost their forests, land, and water. Global pain was spreading, and we were told there was no alternative.

But was this path inevitable? We didn't think so. And we did not stay home.

Today's global justice movement owes much of its inspiration to the Zapatistas, who rose up on January 1, 1994, the same day that the North American Free Trade Agreement (NAFTA) was implemented. It was a twelve-day uprising in Chiapas, Mexico, in which many Indigenous communities banded together to form the EZLN, the Zapatista National Liberation Army, simply known as the Zapatistas.

The Zapatistas are a peasant army. In 1994 their demands were basic: land, food, health care, education, justice, autonomy. Their revolution was not focused on taking state power, as most revolutions are.

They concentrated not on defeating a single government, but rather the neoliberal corporate global agenda supported by NAFTA. Their uprising destroyed government buildings in San Cristóbal de Las Casas in the south of Mexico. It didn't take long for the Mexican army to go on the offense, bombing villages and killing many. A cease-fire was negotiated days later, but despite continued government repression, the group has continued to thrive in Chiapas while inspiring hundreds of thousands of people all over the world with their autonomous communities, poetic communiqués, global *encuentros* (encounters), and ongoing resistance.

In the mid-'90s I was in the throes of labor organizing and didn't yet fully appreciate the impact of the Zapatistas, but I was in awe of their revolutionary ways. In 1998 I was hired by the Los Angeles County Federation of Labor under Miguel Contreras, a brilliant and bold leader.[1] Miguel came out of the United Farm Workers and he knew how to fight. He was also a master at politics and was responsible for getting a number of progressive candidates elected in the city and state. The LA County Federation had over eight hundred thousand members, making it one of the biggest AFL affiliates in the country. I did a lot with the federation, but I did not succeed at changing the sexism baked into the culture of labor organizations. A male supervisor was taking credit for my work, and I became increasingly disillusioned. I found myself doing more grassroots work, the kind of organizing I learned in the '80s.

One of these actions was a protest on June 18, 1999, as part of a global Day of Action called for by the Peoples' Global Action (PGA), an emerging global network that took inspiration from the Zapatistas and was made up of movements like La Vía Campesina from the Global South and Reclaim the Streets from the Global North. People were talking about capitalism as the problem, which I found refreshing. Labor does not talk about capitalism as a problem, because they benefit from it, or so they think.

In the following months, I tapped into an emerging network that was gearing up to shut down the WTO ministerial meetings planned for November in Seattle. Like all big events and convergences, it begins with people talking to one another and generating ideas. Seattle was no different. Many players were organizing around the ministerial, but it was PGA that termed the mobilization N30—in reference to November 30, the first day of the ministerial, spawning actions in hundreds of cities around the world. The largest coalition was People for Fair Trade / NO2WTO, which organized under the leadership of Global Trade Watch, a project of Public Citizen. These were mainstream nonprofit organizations concerned about human rights, workers' rights, environmental protection, and the anti-democratic nature of the WTO. Big environmental groups like Sierra Club and Friends of the Earth were involved as well.

Flyer for the student and labor walkout during the WTO protests in Seattle.

The AFL-CIO, the largest federation of unions in the US, was another big player. Their local affiliate in Seattle was led by Ron Judd, who became a key coordinator. In June they convened a labor-community coalition to start preparing for the big march and rally on N30 while organizing with young people for a mass work and school walkout. An assortment of religious organizations convened under Jubilee 2000 to focus on human rights and the crippling effects of debt and structural adjustment policies. Numerous events, including an interfaith gathering and teach-in, were planned.

All of these organizations and sectors were hoping for a seat at the negotiating table, working with the WTO to adopt protections and reforms.

And then there were the grassroots activists and anarchists who believed that the WTO was undemocratic and illegitimate and therefore needed to be shut down. Two such efforts converged. In Seattle local organizers with the Nonviolent Action Community of Cascadia (NACC) were convening meetings that led to the formation of the Direct Action Network, DAN. This collaborative expanded with the help of a call from Art and Revolution in San Francisco initiated by David Solnit. DAN gained steam when groups like Global Exchange, the Rainforest Action Network, Ruckus Society, and the National Lawyers Guild agreed to support the effort. DAN was aligned with the People's Global Action and began organizing in earnest for N30.

The labor unions and NGOs did not imagine that the ministerial could collapse—and they were afraid of our calls to shut it down. Fortunately, there are people who have relationships between the sectors, in-betweens who help build trust. Michael Dolan, a primary organizer with the NGOs under Global Trade Watch, had a solid relationship with Hilary McQuie, an organizer with NACC/DAN, while my connection with the LA County Federation made it easy for me to connect with Ron Judd at the Seattle Federation of Labor. Ron was not afraid of direct action, and we were able to keep communication lines open.

Those of us doing civil disobedience and direct actions are often marginalized and seen as a threat to the agenda of mainstream groups. Most of this fear, I believe, is rooted in a feeling of superiority and a need for control. In Seattle the NGOs feared that our actions could affect their ability to negotiate inside the WTO, but looking back I believe that Seattle was successful because of—not in spite of—our differences in approach. The social crisis created by those of us on the outside—taking direct action or marching in the streets—lent negotiating powers to those on the inside of the ministerial who were speaking out against some of the WTO's proposed rules.

Despite our different approaches, we moved forward collectively, condemning the WTO. Our success changed the playing field, creating a new phase of relationship building that has become so important in the era of mass, transnational movements and convergences.

The Convergence Space on Denton

I arrived in Seattle ten days before the ministerial. It was cold and gray as I headed to an apartment just north of downtown where my friend Nadine Bloch was staying. Nadine is a powerhouse. She is a talented direct actionist, a visionary artist, and a boat woman who had spent a lot of time on the waters with Greenpeace. She also happens to throw one hell of a Halloween party.

This was my first time in Seattle and I had to get my bearings fast. Fortunately, union work requires you to quickly familiarize yourself with new places—and given that I love maps and have a bit of a photographic memory, new cities are easy. I knew I had to get in touch with the labor folks since the LA County Federation was supporting my work in Seattle, but I was more interested in touching base with my kindred spirits in the direct action world, so Nadine and I headed over to the convergence space on Denton Street, where DAN was setting up.

When I first saw the convergence space, it seemed to reflect the weather outside. It was a large gray building with a small door and garage bays. I always find these large convergence spaces a bit intimidating—at first. But after walking inside I realized this place was vibrant and colorful, a jam-packed building holding an emerging community that shared a vision and purpose: to shut down the WTO.

The lobby had a table covered with flyers, pamphlets, and zines with everything you wanted to know about the WTO and upcoming events. There was a white erase board with the daily schedule, making it easy to know what was happening. I headed down a hallway with smaller rooms on both sides, one for the medics/healers and another for the legal team. This led to a large open area with workshops and training spaces, plus a kitchen set up in the back and a huge art-making space in the far corner.

There were trainings going on in the meeting rooms, and I noticed a massive map of Seattle on the wall. The convention center, where the WTO delegates would be meeting, was highlighted, with black lines radiating out in all directions like a bike wheel. *Ah, a tactical map—excellent!* I would check that out later.

Nadine and I wandered over to the art space, assuming we would find my friend David Solnit there, and sure enough we did. David is an awesome organizer and longtime kindred spirit. He mixes art and action and has been doing so for decades. He was in his zone, moving through the space, helping volunteers be useful in the production of banners, flags, posters, and props like the truly *giant* puppet!

David and I gave each other a big hug; then he took a few minutes to orient me to the space before going back to puppet making. Nadine brought me over and introduced me to Hilary, one of the local Seattle organizers. Hilary was about my age, with long thick blond hair, and I could tell she was adrenalized, exhausted, and sharp as a tack. I liked her immediately. She oriented me to the big tactical map and explained the current thinking about how we would accomplish the shutdown.

The black lines radiating out from the convention center formed pie slices, as she called them, and they were labeled A through M. This is where we would take action. The goal was to block the delegates from getting to the convention center, and the idea was that affinity groups would take a slice of the pie, scout it, and then plan their blockade for that particular geographic area. I was impressed, but immediately wondered about those who weren't in affinity groups or who would arrive the day before N30. I brought forward the idea of incorporating flying squads. Flying squads, which are usually made up of eighty to a hundred people, could include the folks who arrived later and give them something useful to do. I also knew from Justice for Janitors that flying squads not only support actions but can be mobile blockades themselves.

Hilary asked me to join the direct-action tactical group, and we quickly amended the plan to add two public gathering sites and flying squads. I also joined the trainers groups and started leading action trainings the next day. We consistently reviewed the action scenario and encouraged affinity groups to visit the pie slices, hone their plans, then come back in the evening to participate in the spokes council meetings.

The convergence space was a hive of people creating an alternative world. There were daily trainings: nonviolent direct action, legal, jail solidarity, medic, communications, and media. There were educational events and art workshops. Food Not Bombs and Seeds of Peace were providing hot meals every day, and the comms team was setting up a system of tactical communications with everything from central dispatch to on-the-ground mobile systems.

It was wild. I remember walking through the space and seeing a scruffy young man with a head of thick black hair and a giant beard hunched over a little box with all kinds of wires. He looked up and said, "Hey, Lisa." I said, "Do I know you?" He replied, "Yeah, I'm Dylan, I was your intern when we shut down the CIA!" It was crazy running into him and learning that he was still in the movement after all those years. Later he became one of the founders of the Prometheus Radio Project in Philadelphia.

During the nightly spokes council meetings, hundreds of people sat on the floor, divided into affinity groups with their spokes person in front sitting in an inner circle. These meetings sometimes continued well after midnight, and our numbers grew each night as N30 got closer. We knew that with these large numbers and our agreement to non-cooperate if arrested, there was a good chance that a lot of us would be going to jail.

Going to Jail for Justice 101

I have spent over forty years going to jails all over the country, and I've learned that all jails are set up to break your spirit. It doesn't matter what state it's in or whether it's maximum or minimum security, the people who support this system—the police, the guards, or the literal executioners—disconnect from their humanity in order to do the job they believe they're supposed to do.

The system continues to find ways to make life for inmates harder. Prisons have been privatized and felons are often moved out of state where loved ones can't visit. Contact visits have been replaced with phones and a glass window, and now they're moving to video screens. Solitary confinement has become widespread, and it's used on children and low-level offenders. People who support "tough on crime" policies tell themselves that our jails are filled with violent criminals, but the truth is the majority of people in US jails have not been convicted of a crime but are awaiting trial because they can't make bail.

The United States holds a higher percentage of its population behind bars than any other country in the world, with El Salvador, Russia, Thailand, and Turkmenistan close behind.[2] Yet for many, this reality is nothing but a shocking statistic on the page. If you're white or affluent, incarceration might not affect your family at all. This is why I encourage white or otherwise privileged people to make the choice to go to jail for justice. The experience shows you what it's like to lose your privilege. How easy it is to be criminalized. When they treat you like a criminal, you feel like one. You start questioning yourself, thinking of yourself as a criminal just because they say so. Experiencing this dehumanizing process can make white people understand more about what has been happening to Black and Brown communities for generations. Once you see for yourself how the state enacts violence and robs people of their freedom and dignity, you can never unsee it.

Going to jail for justice is more possible for people with privilege. It is also a risk or sacrifice that many of us, under the right conditions, can make. If you decide to take the risk of going to jail, it's important to be prepared mentally, physically, and spiritually, and ideally to go as part of a group. Part of our success in Seattle was that close to six hundred of us went to jail with a collective plan to non-cooperate. We were well supported, and the legal organizing in Seattle spawned a new generation of legal activists, political lawyers, and legal collectives like the Midnight Special Law Collective.

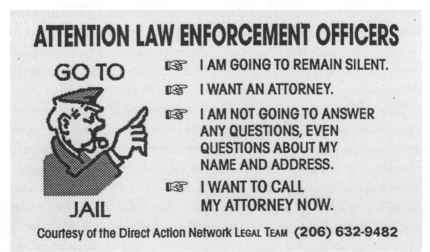

Arrest information card distributed by DAN during the Seattle WTO shutdown.

The trainings began the week before the ministerial. The DAN legal collective, headed up by Katya Komisaruk, a radical lawyer and activist, was advocating for a jail solidarity strategy and providing daily Know Your Rights and Jail Solidarity trainings.[3] *Jail solidarity* means looking out for one another and working collectively when we are arrested. We can refuse to cooperate from the point of arrest through the courtroom proceedings. Many of us agreed in advance not to bring IDs or money during the action, and that if arrested, we would not give our names.

These plans were in accordance with the philosophy of non-cooperation, which can be defined as the antithesis of cooperation. In the context of civil disobedience, *cooperation* means doing what the police tell you to do, like providing the required information or allowing yourself to be photographed and fingerprinted. It means eating jail food and showing up for your court dates, paying fines, or doing community service if offered. Systems of oppression are maintained through cooperation; we can take their power away by refusing to cooperate and withdrawing our consent from an unjust system.

Non-cooperation is doing what your conscience calls you to do. It is a personal choice and a political strategy. Non-cooperation might mean staying linked up with others when the police approach. It can mean not providing your fingerprints and turning your head when they take your mug shot. Sometimes it means not eating their food and going on a hunger strike. It could mean refusing to go to court or pay fines. If you're willing to assume the consequences, there isn't much they can do to stop you.

Non-cooperation doesn't apply just to protests or civil disobedience. I often say that nonviolent direct action is not just a strategy but a way of life. It means choosing a life where you're fully conscious of what you want, what is just and unjust, and what you're willing to do, or not do, to oppose systems of oppression. It means taking responsibility for the consequences of your actions. Direct action and non-cooperation are acts of conscience and an exercise of your power.

Your race, gender, class, age, ability, ethnicity, faith, or citizenship status will affect your options and the consequences of your choices. Taking action in community makes a huge difference. The consequences of your choices could include losing your home, job, friends, and even your life. It takes a lot of infrastructure, training, planning, and legal/political coordination to help ensure the greatest possible impact from the sacrifice we make by going to jail.

OUT OF THE TOOLBOX
Support Before, During, and After Arrest

The most important strategy for going to jail for justice is working within a group. Below are some checklists for organizing in preparation for a civil disobedience action. I don't know where these originated, but they have been used in many actions, and I have updated them a bit.

Support Before Arrest
Be part of a group, or at the very least have a buddy who will support you once you're in the system. Make sure you know:

Which jail people may be taken to
The people in your group by name, description, and contact information
Who the attorneys are
Who wants bail and who does not
Who needs to be contacted on behalf of the arrestee (friends, family)
What medical or other special needs your people have
Who might be more vulnerable (those with a disability, trans people, POC)

Witnessing acts of civil disobedience and non-cooperation can affect those who do harm or are complicit in harmful institutions, who at some level may ask, *Why am I doing this?* It also affects others who are watching/witnessing. When a person sees you putting your body on the line, or when they witness police abuse or violence, they begin to question what is happening, and why.

Whether the individual plans to non-cooperate, and in what ways

That the arrestees have a legal number to call written on their body

Support During and After Arrest

Have a pre-designated support person write down the name of everyone who is arrested, along with the time of the arrest. Write down the officer's name and badge number, and record any instances of police misconduct.

At least one support person should stay at the place of arrest until all members of the group are arrested.

At least one support person should go to the jail where the arrested are taken and bring food, blankets, and whatever else might be needed.

Be prepared to advocate for your people, asking for information throughout the process.

At least one support person must call the emergency contact for each arrested person, if needed, contact the attorneys or legal support operation, and liaise with each arrested person's affinity or other group.

Someone must be tasked in advance with caring for the kids, pets, cars, plants, and so on, for those in jail.

Make sure there are arrangements for pickup upon release.

Before engaging in actions that might result in arrest or harm, it's advisable to do some research. Who is the local district attorney, and what are their politics? What is the local history with protests, surveillance, and police brutality? What are the local laws? Is there legal support, such as pro bono lawyers, paralegals, public defenders, legal observers, and legal volunteers who will help?

Going to jail for justice amplifies the message because the media is more likely to cover arrests, especially if many are arrested together. Non-cooperating, like refusing to give your names, can amplify the story further. But not everyone is willing or able to non-cooperate. Cooperative arrests are easier and less risky, and in large numbers it's still effective even if it's just symbolic—meaning we're not really putting a wrench in the gears.

Civil disobedience has become more popular today, with many nonprofits and labor unions choosing this tactic. They tend to highlight the *civil* part of disobedience, cooperating with the system by negotiating the arrests with the police. This is an approach that I understand and have participated in myself, but I believe that advance negotiation, often leading to on-site or quick release, can undermine our power and the lessons that can be learned by going to jail. The legacy of going to jail for justice is about taking risks, sacrificing your privilege, and creating disruption to inspire fundamental or radical changes, whether those be the liberation of a country, as in India, or the liberation of a people, as with the arrests of the US civil rights movement.

My first major experience with non-cooperation was back in Boston in 1986, when I was part of a group arrested at the Federal Building in solidarity with eight West Germans who were taken hostage by a US-backed Contra rebel group in Nicaragua.[4] During processing we refused to give our names, instead saying we were West German Hostage #1, #2, and so on. Eventually we were transported to the Massachusetts Correctional Institution–Framingham, a state prison.

We arrived at Framingham shackled at our hands and feet—a bit unnecessary for peaceful protestors. They took us into a side room, where we were told to take off our clothes. The strip search began, with the squatting and coughing. The female guards were ruthless. That is one of the things about jails—the guards have the power to do harm with no judge or jury in sight. I was handed a pair of underwear, a jumpsuit, a toothbrush, toothpaste, and a towel, and moved to a waiting cell, where I was left by myself.

Along with most people, I hate being confined. You are turned into a caged animal—cattle. More than once in my life, people have told me that I'm like a caged tiger or stallion. This is what I like to remind myself when I pace back and forth behind bars—I am not cattle waiting for the slaughter, but a powerful animal waiting to be free.

To my relief, the others joined me and we were eventually moved to the same cell up on the second floor. Some of the women had seen us on TV and were excited to talk with us. Over the next few days, we had great conversations with women in the common room, many of them political in their own way. We were visited by our lawyers, who told us the district attorney was playing hardball. We talked that night and decided to give our names on day five.

On the night before the fifth day, we wrote out the chorus to "Like A Mountain," a song written by Naomi Littlebear Morena: "You can't kill the Spirit / She is like a mountain / Old and strong / She goes on and on and on . . ." We slipped a piece of paper with these words under every cell door, and when everyone was locked in that night, we started singing as loud as we could through the crack at the bottom of the door. Another voice joined in, then another. All the women started singing, raising their voices in song. Chills moved through my body and tears came to my eyes. We sang and sang, despite the guards ordering us to shut up.

The next morning when they released us, we said goodbye to a group of cheering women. You can't kill the spirit.

My white privilege made this all relatively easy. There are many people who can't be arrested without fear of violence and retribution from the police, and they can't simply give their name and be free.

Shut It Down

On the morning of N30, I woke up around four o'clock, unable to sleep. I ate a good breakfast and downed a quick cup of coffee, then bundled up in my blue winter coat and black hat, with a couple of layers underneath in case I was arrested. Layers are good as jails tend to be very cold, and if you are just being processed before release, you typically wear your own clothes.

Nadine, Hilary, and I were rolling as a team that day. We set off around six, heading to Victor Steinbrueck Park, about ten blocks from the convention center near the waterfront. Hundreds of people were already there. One of my jobs was to inform the crowd of the plan, so I climbed on top of a van to be seen and heard. Our goal was to assemble into large flying squads that would "fly in" wherever one of the pie blockades needed assistance. I wanted everyone to have a shared vision of our mission. In my experience, the more people hold a common vision, the greater the possibility of it happening.

As people streamed into the park, the police harassed us in any way they could. One of the funnier moments was when a group showed up with a giant prop carrot. The police were beside themselves. They were not used to dealing with giant carrots, so they searched that entire group and wouldn't let any of them into the public park. Last time I checked, giant carrots are not against the law.

Information started to come in that the blockades were being deployed. The police were reportedly trying to push through, so we knew it was time to fly! I jumped back on the bullhorn and said, "We are ready, let's roll!" We moved up Virginia Street and turned right on Pike Place, then left onto Pike Street, which would take us straight to the convention center. This was a big commercial area of Seattle with popular stores like Nordstrom and Gap.

The back half of our march broke off to support the blockade on the west and south sides of the convention center. Since our numbers were so big, we decided to bring more folks to the north, near the Paramount Theatre, the location of the opening ceremonies. Once there, we saw that the police had surrounded the theater's entrance with metro buses and a net fence, which we pushed right through.

It was about 8 AM, and from what I could tell, we were effectively shutting everything down. In every direction I looked, there were blockades in place. Some people were making human chains by linking arm-to-arm, while others locked down to "sleeping dragons," which are tubes constructed for people to put their arms into and lock onto a bar secured inside, forcing the police to cut you out. These tactics were developed by deep woods activists struggling to save old-growth forests. Seattle was the first time I was aware of them being used in an urban setting.

At this point the police were starting to retaliate, so Nadine, who was pregnant, moved to a safer location not far from the action where she could help with reconnaissance. Hilary and I were buddies for the rest of the morning, moving from site to site. (At the next action we did together, Nadine already had her daughter, and Hilary arrived pregnant, so it was her turn to stay out of the fire.)

A festive atmosphere was taking hold as we swarmed the area. Ladders appeared out of nowhere and people climbed on top of the buses. There were puppets and flags and giant cardboard ears of corn. Everywhere, people were dressed like butterflies and turtles. I stepped away from the group and took a few minutes to walk around, in awe of what was happening. People were free. No one was in charge. And it was working!

I was struck by how otherworldly it was. There was a giant puppet of Death and another of a beautiful brown-skinned woman who stood tall in power. I turned the corner to find a giant inflatable whale moving slowly above the crowd. The Infernal Noise Brigade, a radical Seattle marching band, passed by in full formation, all wearing furry black hats and black jackets. The drum major in front had a green wooden gun that she was twirling with great joy. The sound was incredible. As I continued to move, I came across an intersection with a bunch of young women hula-hooping their hearts out in front of a line of police. A giant inflatable Earth was being tossed around by the crowd behind them. There were all kinds of creative signs like CLEAR CUT THE WTO and WORLD TERRORIST ORGANIZATION and DON'T TRADE OUR FUTURE!

A lone tuba player was set up on a corner playing with a great set of lungs. *Hope he stays out of the tear gas*, I thought as I caught a whiff of it lingering in the air.

On another corner, some young folks were tossing newspaper stands into the streets and banging on them like drums. Down the street, a group of cheerleaders had climbed up on a cement wall and were doing a set of radical cheers: "My Back Is Aching, My Bra's Too Tight, My Booty Is Shaking from Left to Right, Sound Off Revolution!" There was a queer bloc: "We're Here, We're Queer, Get Used to It!" Others could be heard shouting "Down, Down, WTO!" Around another corner there was a PGA march of people from the Global South, including farmers from many countries, chanting and holding up signs. I had been in a lot of protests and mass actions, but never before had I seen this array of movements coming together with a common cause.

I made my way back to the front of the Paramount Theatre, and within minutes we heard that the opening of the ministerial had been delayed because delegates could not get in. A roar of celebration could be heard from block to block.

———————

A little after 11 AM, all hell broke loose as about thirty anarchists from Eugene, Oregon, formed a black bloc—dressing in black clothes, hoods, and masks—and began their campaign of corporate property destruction.[5] I was not in the immediate area, but the word quickly spread. They smashed up the banks, Starbucks, McDonald's, and a Gap. People tried to intervene and stop them, to no avail. This became one of the lingering controversies of the Battle of Seattle, sparking the historical debates on violence and nonviolence and leading to the emergence of Diversity of Tactics . . . but more about that in the next chapter!

As Hilary and I continued to walk the perimeter of the convention center, we came to a blockade with the delegates trying to get in. Our people were linked up, standing strong and fluid, moving forward or back with every push from the delegates, repeating as a group: "WTO Is Closed for Business!" We joined the line and had conversations with the delegates, urging them to recognize the impact of the WTO on the people and the planet. Some delegates continued to push, but most gave up and walked away.

We headed back into the streets and saw that the tension was increasing. There were police everywhere dressed in black-padded clothing with protective vests, helmets, clubs, and a variety of lethal and nonlethal weapons. They did not hesitate to jab people with clubs. In one intersection they tried to push people to the sides of the street, but everyone just sat down, chanting, "No Violence, No Violence." It was then that the police pulled out big red canisters of pepper spray and unleashed it on everyone sitting down. People tried to protect their faces by turning away, but it was too much, and many screamed in pain.

The labor march was beginning soon, so I headed over to meet them. They had rallied probably forty thousand people to the northwest of the convention center and were starting to march.[6] It was cold and wet, but the energy was electric. As they got closer to the action zone, the sounds of concussion grenades exploding in the distance increased the leaders' fears. The next thing I knew, the lead contingent turned off the march route. *Shit!* I tracked down the organizing director of the AFL-CIO, who told me they were looping back to the rally site because the streets were too dangerous. But as I headed back out, I saw that many in the march had decided not to turn around, instead braving the sea of conflict.

A little after four thirty the mayor declared a state of emergency, imposed a curfew, and called in the National Guard. Smoke from the afternoon of tear gas, concussion grenades, and fires settled into a gray haze as darkness fell. The police had run out of tear gas and were bringing in more from surrounding cities, but the concussion grenades continued, as did the firing of rubber bullets. The dance of power in the streets continued as dumpsters were set ablaze, creating a new source of light and smoke. It was going to be a long night.

Back at the convergence space, the medics were busy decontaminating people and taking care of injuries. Despite the state's onslaught, we had prevailed. The opening ceremony was canceled, few delegates got in, and it was unclear how the ministerial would move forward.

Non-Cooperation in a Seattle Jail

The next morning remained cold and damp. Many at the convergence space had been tear-gassed, pepper-sprayed, or beaten by the police, but we were proud of our success. We learned that many of the delegates were simply staying at their hotels this morning.

The mayor had imposed a twenty-five-block no-protest perimeter around the convention center, but we headed downtown anyway with about five hundred people. We were still a colorful crowd with our remain-ing flags and banners. It was quiet out, with very few people on the streets, so we were pretty obvious. Before we even hit the twenty-five-block "line," the police were on us.

We made a quick tactical call—a smaller group broke off and began a street blockade to distract the police while the rest of us continued into the no-protest zone. David and I were essentially leading a snake march, meaning we had no predetermined route but were trying to get back to the convention center. As police amassed here and there, we veered this way or that. It was clear we couldn't get anywhere close to the convention center, so we headed over to the Westlake Center, a commercial area with a public park in front.

We got there before the police did and occupied the space. When the police arrived, about 150 of us sat down, some in small circles, others linking up to form a massive glob. Some of the police had on their riot gear, and as I sat with some friends, I noticed that several city buses had pulled up on the street nearby.

We chanted our hearts out as they dragged us apart. When they came for me, I went limp and was carried to a bus that had two sections joined by an accordion-like material in between. They drove us over to a mass processing site at the Sand Point Naval Base and parked the buses out front. We sat and waited, watching as more buses arrived. As it would turn out, we waited for fifteen hours.

Fortunately, many of us were able to slip out of our handcuffs. We got to know one another, sang songs, and shared stories. The police wouldn't let us use a bathroom, so we organized pee circles by holding up a banner in our handcuffed hands, creating a visual block for the person peeing. We had brought ziplock bags for this very purpose. I often wonder if this is where the police get the false idea that we have bags of urine to throw at them.

When the police boarded the bus and pepper-sprayed Peter Lumsdaine, I had that moment of self-doubt that often comes during civil disobedience. *Why am I here? Will they spray me, too?* At that point of exhaustion and sleep deprivation, I was not interested in finding out. My change of mind brought some shame, but I was not prepared for a direct chemical assault.

Once inside the processing center, I found myself in a huge gymlike room, with women on one side and men on the other. Across the way I could see Peter writhing in pain. He continued like that for hours. It was a slow process because hundreds of us were refusing to cooperate. Jane and John Doe forms were being filled out, including my own.

After many hours, they loaded us back onto the buses and transported us downtown to the main jail, where we were packed into cells. The walls were bright white, the floor cold and gray. The guards threw mattresses on the floor, but even then you were lucky to get a little corner for yourself. I had been up for at least twenty-four hours and just wanted sleep, but there wasn't anywhere to lie down. In the corner was the toilet—made of metal with a sink and water fountain built in. This was the universal jail toilet, and I was quite familiar with it.

I looked across the cell, and there was Starhawk sitting on one of the beds. We didn't know each other, but I immediately recognized her. In the 1980s I had attended one of her workshops in DC; it had planted a seed within me that was still growing. Now here she was sitting across from me in an orange prison jumpsuit. I was a bit in awe and somewhat intimidated—she was a well-known, powerful witch who had been working magical direct action for years. She was an attractive woman with

OUT OF THE TOOLBOX
So, You Want to Get Arrested?

If you have made the decision to risk arrest, you'll want to plan ahead. Here are some tips for a safe stay in jail:

Get a good night's sleep and eat a good meal beforehand.

Put a protein bar in your pocket and eat just before arrest. You may not see food for a while, and it will not be good!

Start hydrating the night before.

Leave all jewelry behind.

Depending on the plan, either have an ID or not.

Wear comfortable clothes and dress in layers.

Know that you will be searched and your property will be taken from you.

Make sure you have nothing on you that could be construed as a weapon.

Have no drugs on you unless it's medicine. Bring medicine in a prescription bottle.

Don't take your phone, but if you do, make sure your passcode lock is on.

Have a legal support number written on your body with a permanent marker. I tend to write it on my belly or leg.

Have a little bit of money on you for transportation just in case.

Make friends in jail. Stretch, sing, cry, meditate, play games, or sleep—it might be a long time!

Advocate for yourself and your group. Once a woman needed a tampon and they wouldn't give her one, so we started chanting "No Tampons, No Peace!"

Don't let them criminalize you. Remember that you are fighter for justice, and for that you can be proud!

shoulder-length hair that was wavy, with a hint of gray. Her magnetic energy and charisma beamed out despite her looking very tired.

I went over to introduce myself, and it turned out she had observed me doing trainings at the convergence space. We shared stories about our lives and discovered we had a lot in common, including our histories of going to jail for justice. This was the beginning of a decades-long friendship that continues today.

Much to my dismay, I was moved to another cell, but fortunately there were kindred spirits all around. Our organizing was paying off. There were hundreds of us refusing to give our names, and the jail was packed! We had taught people how not to talk to police, what it's like to be booked, and, of course, practiced the magic words, "I am going to remain silent. I want to see a lawyer."

The legal team in Seattle was stellar. We knew our rights, which gave us confidence and power. Yes, we had a First Amendment right to protest. Yes, they can search you or your car if you're pulled over. If you are arrested, they do *not* need to read your Miranda rights, so don't expect it! This is one of the greatest myths about being arrested. They *are* supposed to read them before interrogating you, however.

The basic idea behind solidarity strategies is that we use our numbers and our non-cooperation to overwhelm the system. Jails are often at or over capacity, so it's a burden to lock up a large number of us. They need your information to process and prosecute you; without giving your name, they're shit out of luck. There is a high financial cost to keeping everyone in jail, especially peaceful protestors who are getting media attention.

Inside and outside the jail, our people demanded our lawyers be let in. We were all taken to a huge room for a meeting with the lawyers, who gave us a report on what was happening outside. The battle in the streets was continuing, with ongoing protests and in some cases police assaults and mass arrests. People had surrounded the jail and set up a 24/7 encampment out front, making it clear they weren't leaving until we were all free. But the district attorney wasn't making any substantive offers, instead intending to hold us until we gave our names, and then prosecute us all.

At this point, we needed to decide how long to hold out. I thought we needed to wait. With enough numbers, jail solidarity strategies can pressure the system into collective bargaining. If only a few are arrested, they might want to make an example and throw the book at everyone, aiming for convictions on charges like disorderly conduct or failure to obey an officer to chill future actions. But with mass arrests, our intent is to force them to charge and treat us all the same, eventually dropping or minimizing the charges.

Despite the extensive trainings on jail solidarity, jails are scary, and generally people want out. We supported those who decided to give their information while the majority of us decided to stay at least three more days.

Each day came and went. The prosecutor was not budging, but the city was in a crisis. On the fifth day they started to release us without our names, only a jail number. They finally called my number—turns out they had me gendered as male. I was released.

When I went to get my property and clothes back, I discovered that my phone's SIM card had been removed. It was then that I decided to take my oversized jail clothes, the extra-large brief panties, and the jail handbook as souvenirs. I stuffed them into my backpack along with the insurrection banner I had with me on the bus. I still have them to this day.

Outside the jail, there was a huge group waiting for us with hugs and love. It was sweet to be free.

In the end the majority of charges were dropped without us having to go to court. Only six of the six hundred arrested went to trial, and one was convicted, receiving community service and a small fine.[7] That is how non-cooperation works!

––––––––

The Battle of Seattle marked a shift in movement organizing, both in the US and around the world. In the immediate sense, the shutdown succeeded in delaying the ministerial and emboldening the delegations from the Global South, who withdrew their consent. Any hope for an agreement unraveled and the talks collapsed. More important, the Battle of Seattle put the power brokers in the WTO and in governments around the world on notice: The people would not allow them to move forward without resistance. Mainstream NGOs still wanted a seat at the table to fight for protections for the people and the planet, but the direct action-ists earned their respect, developing important relationships as we built a movement to disrupt whenever and wherever we could.

The Battle of Seattle also marked a new era of police brutality against peaceful protestors. The police unleashed a terrifying assortment of military-type "nonlethal" weapons including tear gas, pepper spray, projectiles, concussion grenades, sound bombs, and armored vehicles. While police violence has always existed, the militarization of police was growing.

The anti-WTO protests spawned the growth of new organizations and collectives: the Continental Direct Action Network, the Independent Media Centers, and the Radical Cheerleaders, to name just a few. Efforts to build a larger, more cohesive movement became possible as the Teamsters and the Turtles, the AFL and the Anarchists found common ground. Models of intergroup cooperation developed. We were on the offensive, targeting the capitalists in the WTO, the IMF, and the World Bank; at the summits of the G8, G20, and World Economic Forum; and in transnational trade deals like the FTAA.

Conversations about racial divides in the movement came to the forefront. Some of that debate was initiated by an article, "Where Was the Color in Seattle?" by Elizabeth Martínez, an American Chicana feminist. This conversation was long overdue, opening up the challenges and opportunities that exist when we try to work across the racial divide. Martínez's article spoke to the lack of people of color attending the Seattle protests and the whiteness of the DAN convergence space and the labor union rally. But it also spoke to how empowering Seattle was for many of the people of color who did participate in the direct actions.

This conversation spread to many corners of our movements. As we looked to the new millennium, we organized to incorporate anti-racism work into spaces that had been dominated by white people while fostering new allegiances and alliances between white communities and communities of color. This was particularly true in 2000, during the Democratic National Convention protest in Los Angeles.

In the end the direct-action movement in Seattle took everyone by surprise. From the state and feds down to the organizational allies, nobody believed we would actually shut the WTO down. Nobody believed we had that power. But in the words that were chanted again and again by the Chicano/a students of the Movimiento Estudiantil Chicano de Aztlán, a local student group on the ground in Seattle: "Ain't No Power Like the Power of the People, 'Cause the Power of the People Don't Stop!"[8]

CHAPTER 5

The Global Justice Movement and the Power of Creative Nonviolence

T he Battle of Seattle was only the beginning. A new generation had an embodied experience of the power of the people and the potency of civil disobedience to create a crisis for the ruling elite. The World Trade Organization's ministerial meeting in Seattle had collapsed, and the seeds of an emerging anti-capitalist movement were planted all over the world. From Prague to Quebec and from Calgary to Cancún, people showed up in the streets to resist the emerging neoliberal world order. The WTO, the IMF–World Bank, the World Economic Forum, the G8—as these transnational, pro-corporate, anti-democratic gatherings pursued policies that enriched the few at the expense of the people and the planet, we were there in the streets, using our voices to say, *Hell no, shut it down!* The movement was deemed "anti-globalist" by the press, but we rejected that framing, instead calling it the Global Justice movement. We grew into a mighty force of diverse cross-sector collaborations, using a multitude of strategies that took action at a scale unseen in decades.

I had the privilege of participating in most of the global summits during this new decade. Some called it summit hopping; I called it movement building. With each summit we learned how to work together across nationalities, languages, tactical orientations, and political beliefs. Our social movements went global, and discussions intensified around flashpoint issues, including the histories and dynamics of racism and patriarchy, questions of violence and nonviolence, revolutionary versus reformist strategies, local work versus global work, and how to interact with the increasingly influential corporate media and militarized police.

After September 11, 2001, the War on Terror pursued by President George W. Bush against the so-called Axis of Evil had a huge impact on the trajectory of the Global Justice movement. We were no longer on the offense against a capitalistic world order, but on the defense against the shock and awe military actions of the US government as it toppled regimes in Iraq and Afghanistan, causing widespread civilian deaths and regional destabilizations. This reckless action led to the rise of ISIS and a resurgence of other violent fundamentalist groups in the region. In the US the codification of the Patriot Act and the creation of the Department of Homeland Security—which included the Bureau of Immigration and Customs Enforcement (ICE)—had a chilling effect on our movements as we witnessed increased targeting of Arabs and Muslims and a new wave of infiltration by law enforcement into social justice movements.

In the context of the wars in the Middle East and the corresponding militarization of US law enforcement agencies, the tactical practice of nonviolence in the Global Justice movement took on even greater importance. Many of us felt that creative nonviolence was essential to building a broad global coalition of resistance to match the scale of the unfolding horrors in international war and policing. At the same time, other sectors of our movement doubled down on the stance that fire must be fought with fire.

This age-old debate about tactics continues today. I don't have all the answers, but I hope that by sharing my experiences during the Global Justice movement's formative years, I can help shine a light on the issues and the most constructive pathways forward.

Los Angeles and Prague: Policing Against Protestors

The birth of the Global Justice movement led to a metamorphosis in my own work and career as I grappled with the understanding that my time in the union world was ending. I left my job at the Los Angeles County Federation of Labor and returned to grassroots organizing—and there was so much to accomplish! On the heels of Seattle, three major mobilizations revealed the potentials and challenges of the emerging anti-capitalist movement.

The first of these, a convergence in DC around an IMF–World Bank meeting, was an attempt to repeat what was done in Seattle. While we had great impact—forty thousand participated, and government and corporate offices closed—we did not shut down the meeting. This convergence stands out because it showed that the militarization of the police against peaceful demonstrators was being formalized. The police raided people's homes, raided and shut down our convergence space, and even searched and confiscated our puppets. The police offensive was intimidating, but this didn't quite prepare us for what happened several months later, during the Republican and Democratic National Convention protests in July and August of 2000 in Philadelphia and Los Angeles. The police raids, infiltration, and brutality at the RNC led to over 400 arrests, putting us on the offensive in Los Angeles.

I was super proud of the work we did in my home community of Los Angeles to protest the Democratic convention.[1] We were a multiracial group that understood the importance of nonviolence in a city full of marginalized and vulnerable people. We had a crack team of lawyers and we fought back against the police efforts to control us.[2] Our actions built up for several days before the culminating events on Thursday, the final day of the DNC. We held a twenty-thousand-person march and rally followed by a concert outside the Staples Center, where the convention was being held, with Rage Against the Machine as the headliner.[3]

By the time Rage took the stage, the crowd was huge, a sea of happy people feeling the power and inspiration from the week of actions. I was hanging around backstage when I heard about some trouble at a fence close to the Staples Center. I walked over to see for myself, and there I found some young anarchists hanging out. One had climbed the fence and was waving a flag, at times haranguing the nearby line of law enforcement. It didn't seem like much of anything, but it became the excuse for what happened next. I made my way back to the stage, where Ozomatli was performing. Suddenly the power went off. The cops had pulled the plug. Next thing we knew, there was a loudspeaker announcement that this was an unlawful assembly and everyone had to disperse. WTF! We had fought hard to legally win this space, and now with helicopters overhead they were shutting us down.

We convinced the cops to put the sound back on so we could make announcements about exiting safely in the dark. Ozomatli would drum everyone out of the area—"Follow the drums, please!" This was working great until the crowd funneled through a small exit created by cement barricades put in place by the police. As this area filled with people, the officers opened fire with rubber bullets, while at the other end of the concert area, a line of riot police on horses were flushing us out from behind. Trying to avoid the horses and clubs, some of us headed to Olympic Boulevard, but once we reached the street, a line of police shot at us with "nonlethal" projectiles. It was in this area that one of our attorneys, a brilliant lawyer named Carol Sobel, was shot in the face with a rubber bullet.

It was just unbelievable how they opened up on us. Over 150 were hurt that night; a few were trampled by horses. A journalist covering the event had recently returned from a war zone, and he commented that it wasn't until coming home from war that he got shot.

The DNC protests had been organized in large part by the D2K Coalition, which focused on legal protest, and the Los Angeles Direct Action Network, DAN-LA, which embraced and advocated nonviolent direct action and civil disobedience; this made the actions of the police seem all the more egregious. We used the same nonviolent action guidelines used in Seattle, which first circulated sometime in the 1970s. They have been passed on through the generations to those committed to disciplined nonviolent direct action. The guidelines are tweaked or amended for individual actions, but the template is generally what appears in the Action Guidelines sidebar.

Action Guidelines

All participants in this action are asked to agree to these action guidelines. Having this basic agreement will allow people from many backgrounds, movements, and beliefs to work together for this action. They are not philosophical or political requirements placed upon you or judgments about the validity of some tactics over others. These guidelines are basic agreements that create a basis for trust, so we can work together for this action and know what to expect from one another.[4]

1. We will use no violence, physical or verbal, toward any person.
2. We will carry no weapons.
3. We will not bring or use any alcohol or illegal drugs.
4. We will not destroy property (except barricades put in our way).

Despite the nonviolent philosophy of the demonstrators in LA that night, we had put ourselves at risk simply by exercising our constitutional rights. Law enforcement had a new methodology—barricade marches and protests, making it difficult to enter and exit, while mobilizing an overwhelming number of officers and arming them with all kinds of new weapons. They were sending us a message that a new era of militarized policing was being normalized.

———————

In September 2000 I experienced the troubling dynamics between law enforcement and demonstrators in an international context. I traveled to Prague to support a large mobilization planned around the IMF–World Bank meeting there; this was my first major European action. My friend Starhawk had facilitated a grueling eleven-hour planning meeting for this mobilization the month before and told me all about it. The European activists were more philosophical, engaging in extensive political discourse, spending hours discussing this and that. In our organizing in the US, activists are very practical, planning logistics with lots of detail.

The Europeans' prolonged discussions in fact led to an excellent plan that has been replicated many times over. The challenge in Prague was that tens of thousands of activists were arriving from all over the world, speaking different languages and practicing different styles of activism. The Europeans are more likely to embrace what I call smashy-smashy tactics of a black bloc, which include property damage like destroying bank machines, breaking windows, burning cars or dumpsters, turning newspaper boxes into drums or projectiles, building barricades, and fighting back with rocks, bottles, sticks, or Molotov cocktails when the police attack. The majority of demonstrators in Prague (and at most mobilizations) don't want to get caught in the line of fire, so the question becomes: How can those who feel called to be part of more confrontational actions employ their tactics without putting others at risk?

The elegant solution was the creation of geographic zones divided by risk and demarcated by color. In Prague the smashy-smashy group was called the blue march. They would be prepared to confront the Czech police aggressively in their efforts to get to the summit location, accepting whatever water cannons and tear gas came their way. This group was primarily made up of Germans, Poles, Greeks, and Brits. Then there was the yellow march, led by

Ya Basta, an Italian group of mostly men who all wore white overalls. They practiced *offensive nonviolence*—meaning they would engage police lines by protecting themselves with shields and other gear and then try to push forward. The pink and silver march, led mostly by Spaniards, comprised folks preferring creative nonviolent actions. All of the groups planned to get to the IMF–World Bank meeting site, each taking a different route, with the goal of disrupting the meeting, demanding the dissolution of the IMF–WB, and drawing public attention to their harmful policies. The meetings were held at the Prague Congress Centre, a large, contemporary building complex that seemed completely out of place with the city's beautiful old architecture.

I arrived at the summit with my partner at the time, Mary Anne. After settling in at our hostel, we headed over to the convergence space, a huge warehouse covered in graffiti below a medieval bridge. Once inside, I was immediately struck by the different energies and the diversity of perspectives and experiences among the demonstrators. There were large delegations from Spain, Italy, Greece, and England, plus smaller groups from Poland, Holland, Finland, Sweden, Belgium, Germany, the Netherlands, Turkey, Austria, Ireland, and the US. I learned that there were no direct-action trainings, so I quickly volunteered to offer some. These were wild, with my words translated into seven languages simultaneously.[5]

On the first Day of Actions, S26, we held a huge rally at Namesti Miru, a public park, before marching toward the Congress Centre divided into our three colors.[6] The yellow group, practicing offensive nonviolence, used shields of netted balloons and tarp-covered, inflated inner tubes to push against police lines while blaring techno music from their sound truck. The police beat the shit out of those inner tubes. The only way to the Congress Centre from this direction was to cross a bridge, and the police showed up there in riot gear, with tanks and tear gas and huge signs in multiple languages saying we could not pass. It was fascinating to watch the Ya Basta march charge forward with their inner tubes and balloons, but despite their persistence and valiant effort, there was no way they were getting across that bridge.

We left the yellow group and headed on down to the blue group, where the black bloc had been tearing up the old cobblestone sidewalks for ammunition. Local residents were angered at the damage to their streets, and I was very upset about this as well. We were guests in this community, and destroying someone's home never garners support. A battle was raging as the police attacked with water cannons, tear gas, and concussion grenades—extraordinarily loud successions of *boom, boom, boom*, rather than the single loud *boom* from US concussion grenades. There were already several ambulances on the scene taking people away.

I had had enough. We made our way over to the pink and silver bloc, which was uplifting and beautiful as people in crazy costumes with giant pink spires, wigs, and wings danced their way through the streets. It was the pink bloc that actually succeeded in penetrating into the Summit Zone.

The next day we learned that the World Bank ended their meeting early and had canceled the next day's meetings. That evening we traveled in small groups to the Charles Bridge, a major tourist attraction in Old Town, where we marched, rallied, and danced. This was a successful display of festive, nonviolent action, bringing a different image of resistance to the world while educating people about the police brutality that our people were experiencing in jail. In total about nine hundred were arrested during the days of the convergence, two-thirds of them Czech.[7] As with most mobilizations, we heard horror stories of beatings and sexual harassment in jail. During mass street convergences, the police are pissed and frustrated, and they take their anger out on the people they arrest.

I came home from Prague with mixed thoughts about the aggressive tactics I had seen and feeling frustrated with the black bloc. From a tactical perspective, I couldn't see how their actions helped anyone. Their rocks were no match for the weapons of warfare held by the police, so it all felt inane and ineffective. But at the same time, it was all of our tactics combined that contributed to shutting down the city and thus the IMF meetings.

What were the options in the face of tear gas, guns, tanks, and water cannons? In Prague I learned that many of my "nonviolence" rules didn't make sense when you're defending yourself from serious bodily harm. We taught people not to run at protests, as this can create fear and pandemonium. But when the police are literally attacking you unprovoked, running can be the only option you have to get out of harm's way. Prague was also the first time we definitively documented a police infiltrator initiating property destruction. A man dressed in black bloc gear threw a rock into a McDonald's window and was then seen going back behind police lines. I gained a deeper understanding of how vulnerable the black bloc was to infiltration, which I feared was a serious vulnerability for our movements.

Quebec and Genoa:
Creative Nonviolence and Diversity of Tactics

After Prague, I knew that learning to work together at the international level would be a major challenge. A philosophy of nonviolence had always been dominant in US protest culture going back to the civil rights era, but a critique of nonviolence was gathering steam. The next major global convergence would be a Free Trade Area of the Americas (FTAA) meeting in Quebec in April 2001, and as plans were made for a mobilization against this, a formation called Le Convergence des Luttes Anti-Capitalistes, aka Le CLAC, emerged.[8] They developed a set of explicitly anti-capitalist principles that included a diversity of tactics.[9] The idea of Diversity of Tactics (DoT) was defined in April 2000, in the form of a communiqué by the Anti-Capitalist Bloc that read, in part:

> We believe that the most effective protest is each group autonomously taking action and using tactics that they feel work best for their situation. We do not advocate one particular tactic, but believe that the greatest diversity of tactics is the most effective use of tactics. We are critical of ideologically motivated arguments that oppose this. This is why we do not believe that it is organizationally principled for any one group to set the guidelines for the protests or claim ownership of the movement.[10]

The discussion surrounding DoT was rooted in the understanding that when the state increases its violence, your own tactics need to escalate as well, and that calls for nonviolence can marginalize and criminalize those taking riskier actions. People also argued that rigid adherence to nonviolence is the work of the privileged, rooted in ignorance and naïveté surrounding the authentic struggles of liberation movements.

But I was disturbed by the emergence of the Diversity of Tactics framework. I had seen the consequences of breaking windows and fighting with the police. It felt as though a small segment of our movement just wanted cover to fuck shit up (aka property damage), and I believed that in contrast with DoT guidelines, nonviolence guidelines were more strategic. They allowed us to put forward a political and historic position that was defensible and use a wide range of tactics. I wanted to shut down the

FTAA and educate the public about its harmful policies, not deluge the public with images of people breaking windows or fighting with police.

But I was smart enough to know that condemning and marginalizing the black bloc and others was not useful. Instead, in the streets of Quebec, I simply advocated and practiced what I believed was the best way forward.

In April 2001, tens of thousands of us from across the hemisphere arrived in Quebec, a radical province that did not want this summit, hoping to prevent the damage that the new trade agreement, the FTAA, would create. Quebec is a beautiful city, full of old stone buildings, with an upper and lower city connected by stairs and a grand, meandering stone wall. In advance of the convergence, Starhawk had put out a call to her community of activist witches, and about seventy-five responded. This group, comprising mostly middle-aged and older women, became the Pagan Cluster. After their debut in Quebec, the Pagans would continue their work all over the world.

I have never been a religious person, but I consider myself spiritual, and I felt an affinity with the Pagans' Earth-based spirituality and connection to the elements of earth, air, fire, water, and spirit. We were in Quebec specifically on behalf of the water, which would be further polluted, privatized, and monetized by the FTAA's proposed trade policies. Our goal was to deliver the Cochabamba Water Declaration to the FTAA's delegates. This was crafted by Indigenous leaders in Bolivia who, the year before, had successfully defeated the privatization of the municipal water supply in the city of Cochabamba by the Bechtel Corporation.[11]

Late on Friday morning, the first day of the meetings, I headed out with the Pagan Cluster, carrying blue cloths over our heads to denote a living river. Not far from us Le CLAC was marching to the huge security fence at Boulevard René-Lévesque, clear in their intent to take it down. They brought tools to weaken the fence, then pushed and pulled on the gates. This multimillion-dollar fence was the largest domestic security operation in Canadian history. It was ten feet tall and two and a half miles long, with chain links and poles embedded in concrete barricades. They had fenced the delegates in, trying to prevent them from seeing, feeling, or hearing the opposition to the FTAA. It also prevented us from blocking delegates like we did in Seattle. A group that satirically called itself the Deconstructionist Institute for Surreal Topology made a giant catapult and launched teddy bears that sailed over the fence, breaching the perimeter, landing softly on lines of riot police.

The teddy bear offensive is a perfect example of how creative, nonviolent actions are so powerful despite—or perhaps because of—the contrast with the guns and riot gear of the police. At the website *Beautiful Trouble*, organizer Dave Oswald Mitchell reflected on how the stuffed animals became a sensation in the Canadian media, writing,

> The catapult action was not just good theater, but also effective activism. It attacked, both physically and symbolically, the fence that kept civil society away from trade deal negotiations that would impact everyone. In the end, the protests were a success: the Summit was a public relations nightmare for the Canadian government, public sympathy swung toward the protesters and the hemisphere-wide trade deal was never signed.[12]

Soon after the teddy bears took flight, the main gate at René Lévesque was breached. I was in awe and thought this was our moment to go in—but nobody moved. We, as a whole, had not prepared for this. People don't tend to risk a likely arrest without a common vision, plan, training, and preparation. A Diversity of Tactics framework makes this type of organizing more difficult because it is clouded with secrecy—no one who plans to engage in property destruction is going to talk about their plans. By contrast, mass civil disobedience that works is open, transparent, and collaborative, as it had been in Seattle.

As the police started dumping tear gas all around to scatter the crowds at René Lévesque, the Pagan Cluster made its way to a security gate at Côte d'Abraham, one of Quebec's main thoroughfares. We formed a giant circle and asked everyone to take hands as drummers went to the center and started a rhythmic beat. This became a spiral dance, where Star, who was leading, disconnected one hand from the circle and moved slightly inward, winding around inside the larger circle. The spiral then wrapped around again and again while the chanting and drumming raised the energy we needed to release our intention—in this case, a prayer for the water—out into the world. Hundreds joined our dance as we flowed through the streets with tears on our cheeks, not only from the tear gas, but from the deep love we had for the Earth and one another.

That night, when I returned to the streets after a break for dinner, the air was thick with chemicals, and my ears attuned to a strange sound, unlike anything I had heard before. We followed the sound down the steps, along a stone wall that harked back to an earlier time of castles and fortresses. We came upon thousands of people gathered beneath an underpass. In every direction, they were banging on metal guardrails and poles, the sound reverberating off the walls and the road above like an echo chamber. Tear gas clouds hung in the sky as the sounds created a vibration that filled our bodies. We joined in, banging metal as hard as we could. *We were drumming down the foundations of the old order.* This moment gave rise to a chant—"We Are the Rising of the Moon, We Are the Shifting of the Ground, We Are the Seeds That Take Root as We Bring the Fortress Down." This powerful chant and image was used again during the G8 summit in Calgary, Canada, a year later.

The following day a great wind blew tear gas into the security zone, forcing a shutdown of the ventilation systems in the building where the FTAA meetings were held as demonstrations in the streets continued. All told, between sixty and eighty thousand took to the streets. For forty-eight hours Quebec City was a stronghold of resistance that withstood the national security state, thousands of brutal riot police, forty-eight hundred canisters of tear gas, water cannons, rubber bullets, and hundreds of unjust arrests. I was awed by the incredible innovation and creativity of our movement and the support offered us by the local residents, who provided their water hoses to wash our faces. We were more determined than ever to show the effectiveness and joy of creative, nonviolent direct action.

Police around the world were sending the people a message: We were not safe to dissent. Law enforcement protected the governments and their economic and geopolitical agendas, not the people. Nowhere was this more clear than in July 2001 during the convergence in Genoa, Italy, for a G8 summit. This is perhaps the most brutal mobilization I had yet attended.

Tools of the Police

The police have a wide array of tools at their disposal to command and control people. While some are considered nonlethal, we know the people can be harmed, injured, or killed by many of them.

VOICE. The first tool of control is the use of their voice with aggressive and loud commands. In this situation, it is important to calmly ask, "Am I being detained?" If you are not, walk slowly away.

BATONS. If batons are held horizontally to push you, use your hands as a soft shield, or turn your back if you're wearing a backpack or cushy coat. Banners and signs can also help break the impact. Simply sitting down is a great way to shift the energy and thwart their ability to push you. If police are using the batons to jab, use a pack, sign, or banner as a shield. If they are swinging the batons and you're not wearing protective gear, you may want to get the hell out of there or cover your head with your arms. If you are hurt and can't get away, curl into a fetal position and protect your head, stomach, and genitals. Lie on your right side to protect your liver.

PROJECTILES. These include rubber, plastic, or wooden bullets, beanbags, paint balls, concussion grenades, and more. If the police open fire, turn your back to protect your face, throat, and stomach. Depending on the situation, you may choose to slowly walk away, sit down, or run. These nonlethal projectiles can be lethal and several protestors have been seriously hurt, especially when hit in the face or eye area. Some have been killed from impact.

AUDITORY WEAPONS. Concussion grenade explosions are loud and scary; they can also harm our bodies and damage our hearing. LRAD machines (Long Range Acoustic Devices) send a high-pitched wave and are used to disperse protestors. Earplugs can help with both of these, but construction earmuffs provide greater protection.

HORSES. Police horses are used to scare people and disperse crowds. Police may move them alongside you or drive them into the crowd. They are big, strong, and frightening. If you're in a large, organized group and trying to hold the space, one technique is to sit down and sway with everyone's hands in the air like a moving human carpet. This scares the horse into rearing back. If you're in a small group, it might be necessary to move to another location when the horses show up to avoid being trampled. Never go behind a horse, as they can kick you. Watch your feet, which can be injured if they step on you. If you're sitting, pull your legs in close.

DOGS. Dogs are used for many things by the state. In the streets they're used for fear, capture, or crowd control. If the police bring dogs near you, it's important to keep your hands, arms, and legs close to your body. Move slowly away from them. Do not give them anything to sink their teeth into. Their leashes are longer than you realize, enabling them to lunge. Do not make eye contact with the dog, but make eye contact with the cop, and in a clear voice tell them to restrain the dog.

PAIN COMPLIANCE. These are physical techniques to force compliance through pain, kind of like torture. These are used if you're linked up with other protestors and refusing to move. Officers will apply pressure where the nerves are close to the surface, like under your ears or jaw. Or they might bend your fingers or manipulate your body in the opposite direction than it's meant to go. Depending on the situation, you might let go, or you may choose to stay and risk what might come.

CHEMICAL WEAPONS. The two most frequently used are tear gas and pepper spray. They can vary in strength and intensity, so there's no predicting what you'll get. Tear gas canisters are shot from big guns or thrown like grenades. Pepper spray comes in both small canisters and big fire-extinguisher-sized versions that douse crowds. Both of these have similar effects on the eyes, skin, and respiratory tract. They make it difficult, if not impossible, to see. Tear gas has you crying while pepper spray has you moaning with burning pain. Both cause difficulty breathing and create a feeling of agitation and pain. Protective gear like masks or goggles can help mitigate harm. Be careful about bringing contaminated clothes into your home.

WATER CANNONS. These are used to keep crowds from moving forward, and the pressurized water may contain chemical agents. If you're paying attention, you can often track the trajectory of the water in order to get out of the way. Tarp banners can be used to mitigate the water's force. Remember that in cold weather, getting wet can cause hypothermia.

LIVE AMMUNITION. In today's age I'm as concerned about unstable people with guns as I am with the police. Gun violence is a scourge on our communities. If you're in a situation of live fire or hear gunshots nearby, get low to the ground and look for cover. Keep breathing and stay focused. If someone has a gun that you can see, where is it pointed? If it's pointed up in the air, move quickly to find cover—cars, utility boxes, walls, anything you see that might shield you. If it's pointed at you, move slowly, with your hands up, backing away, scanning for cover, and calmly asking the person to put the gun down. If there are other people around you or nearby, call for support. Someone else providing a distraction can create the time you need to get to a safer or protected space.

As in Quebec, the government fenced off a large chunk of the city in a massive circumference around the G8 meetings. Unlike in Quebec, a fascist government was running the show. Prime Minister Silvio Berlusconi's police forces stooped to new lows, inviting fascists to infiltrate the black bloc as police used the actions of these infiltrated groups to justify a brutal crackdown. Hundreds were beaten. Carlo Giuliani, a twenty-three-year-old Italian, was killed, shot at close range by the police.

During the planning phases for mobilization, the more mainstream NGOs and labor forces embraced direct action, calling for actions at all the gates in the security fence. This massive front of resistance frightened the powers that be. I believe the Italian government understood that the Global Justice movement was evolving in its relationships of trust, opening space for greater collaborations. In response, the police were heavily armed and poised to attack. You could feel it.

The first Day of Action, we saw a brutal police response as they used tear gas and clubs to push us back. Carlo Giuliani was killed and hundreds of people were beaten. The scariest moments occurred on Saturday, three days into the mobilization. With the murder of Giuliani, the city was on edge. That morning I headed over for a cup of coffee at the Genoa Social Forum convergence center on the beach, a big area with a tent and picnic tables. Suddenly there was a large thud overhead, then another—tear gas canisters were being shot *into* the tent. Our only route out was to move toward the water. Once at the edge of the sea I took deep breaths, inhaling the salty air.[13]

A big march was scheduled to come our way right around that time, marching down a hill and toward the beach. The police weren't going to attack the march—were they? This was a mainstream, permitted march with labor unions, NGOs, and everyday citizens protesting the G8. Concerned, Star and I cut over to the road and up the hill. Within minutes we spotted the approaching march. As it came around the corner, the masses paused. They saw the tear gas below. Their hesitation allowed them time to pull out bandannas and goggles, and forward they went.

The death of Carlo Giuliani had not scared the people away. Instead, even more came out. Estimates put the march alone at over three hundred thousand.[14] It was massive. Star and I joined in, and down the hill we went. The police mobilized, forcing us off our planned route and onto some side streets. At one point, we passed the apartment we were staying in and ducked inside to get some water. We looked out the window and saw the riot police below, physically attacking and pushing the marchers. We closed the windows just in time as they unleashed clouds of tear gas.

That night, we attended a meeting to discuss plans for the following day. Around midnight we heard screaming from outside. Looking out the third-floor window, we saw hundreds of police crashing into our building from the doors below. *Shit*. There was no way out.

A group of us found a small space to hide in. We heard a helicopter outside and yelling from below. We didn't speak the language and couldn't understand the shouting, but we knew there was a lot of testosterone in our midst and we did not want to be caught in a bloodbath. We sat silently, waiting. All we could hear was screaming and yelling. When a policeman eventually found us, I just looked him in the eye and said in English, "We are going to trust you." I have no idea if he understood me, but my intent was to let him know he was not to harm us. Thankfully, he did not. He led us downstairs into a hallway to sit on the floor with many others.

There was a member of Parliament in our building, along with lawyers and members of the media. The police were only able to go so far, and eventually they left. Across the street, at the Diaz School, they were not so lucky.

The Diaz School was a three-story brick building the city had provided as a sleeping space for out-of-town demonstrators. The police broke through the gates and attacked the ninety-three people sleeping inside. They just beat people bloody, breaking arms and ribs, smashing teeth and noses, destroying cameras and other media documentation of police actions. We watched in horror from across the street as the police walked or carried person after person out. At one point we thought we saw body bags, but it was people in their sleeping bags, so hurt they couldn't leave on their own. Waves of despair and powerlessness washed over us, leaving trauma in its wake. In the weeks and months after this, I had no choice but to learn more about trauma as I myself was trying to heal. This is when I first became convinced that we need to incorporate more healing work into our movements.

We learned much later that the police had notified a nearby hospital to expect many casualties. It was a gut-wrenching day that many will never forget. Eventually fifteen police officers went on trial in the Italian courts for their actions during the G8, but after years of appeal, the statute of limitations on their crimes kicked in. In 2015 the European Court of Human Rights ruled that Italy was guilty of torture and gratuitous violence for its actions that night.[15]

The Power of Nonviolent Direct Action

When people ask about my approach to nonviolence, I like to say that I'm committed to strategic nonviolence, believing it is the most effective way to dismantle what does not serve us while building a better world. I am not a pacifist; I believe that our actions must have a confrontational edge, but I believe we can achieve that edge without an intent to do physical, emotional, mental, or spiritual harm. There are many nonviolent tactics that can be incredibly disruptive and effective, like highway blockades with bodies or boulders, as they do in the Global South. I also acknowledge that in the face of violence from the state, nonviolence can require incredible courage, sophisticated strategy, and creative, flexible tactics.

This stance has been shaped by my exposure to the dangers activists encounter when they're in the streets. I've watched police aggression toward public demonstrations evolve after September 11, 2001. I have witnessed the government develop its playbook against large mobilizations in coordination with the Department of Homeland Security and other federal agencies. At the anti-FTAA mobilization in Miami in 2003, the police turned their guns on labor union members and elderly activists. At the mobilization surrounding the G8 meetings in 2004 in the predominantly African American town of Brunswick, Georgia, the governor mobilized at least ten thousand law enforcement agents, including the National Guard, into a town of fifteen thousand people.[16] With this massive crackdown, only about three hundred G8 protestors traveled to Georgia.

It was abundantly clear that the Bush administration saw that summit as a training ground for the new Department of Homeland Security to practice domestic occupation.[17] From the hundreds of undercover agents wearing their humorously conspicuous squeaky, out-of-the-box leather sandals to the Humvees patrolling the streets, you couldn't miss the overwhelming force deployed to suppress the community of Brunswick and the First Amendment rights of ordinary people. The military occupation of Brunswick cost US taxpayers $35 million. Meanwhile, we "scary" protestors hosted a shrimp boil, held a candlelight vigil for those who have died as a result of G8 policies, and educated the public about the twenty-two toxic waste sites in Brunswick—all of which closed in advance of the G8 so that politicians didn't have to smell the consequences of their policies.

Ultimately, I'm not sure that violence and nonviolence is a framing that serves us. It positions the issue as emanating from within our movements, when in reality the violent side of the equation usually emanates from law enforcement or the military. I think a more useful frame is one that looks at questions of government-mandated violence and self-defense against that violence with an understanding that self-defense is a choice we make to stand up for what is right. I prefer to talk about self-protection—how we protect ourselves by training and preparing for potential violence, developing our awareness, learning how to protect our bodies, and knowing what we can and cannot endure. Some communities have defended/protected themselves or their members by establishing safe houses, building barricades, burning tires, throwing rocks, shutting down roads, occupying buildings, land, or factories, showing up in large numbers to march, establishing human perimeters, or collectivizing money and resources. Some have taken up arms. Others, like the Black Panthers, used guns more to send a message rather than send bullets.

In the global context, we will always see a diversity of tactics as people of color, poor people, and oppressed people respond to the state violence that harms them. I have learned to stop carrying judgment and acknowledge that taking the moral position that nonviolence is the only way is, in and of itself, oppressive. If I am not the one with skin in the game, who am I to say? And then there are the many fine lines and gray areas between defensive and offensive tactics. Is throwing a rock at an Israeli tank violent? Is picking up arms to stop an impending foreign invasion violence, or is it self-defense or protection?

I have also learned via my trainings that everyone has different ideas about nonviolence. What might be considered violent in one situation may not be considered violent in another, and what some people see as violence, others see as self-defense. At the end of the day, I like to stick with what my lived experiences have taught me while listening to the experiences of others, and here's what I have seen: You can create a hell of a lot of social disruption and change using nonviolent tactics alone.

In my heart I also believe that violence is a tool of the state, and in the words of Audre Lorde, "The master's tools will never dismantle the master's house." I have seen how the world pays attention when buildings burn and windows are broken, but I have also seen how it frightens people. Dismantling structures of oppression is part of what we're all in this for—but if we dismantle structures of oppression using tactics that are grounded in fear, how do we simultaneously build something better?

When I work with people who practice aggression in their dissent, I try to walk that line of not marginalizing or judging them while also showing a different way. I communicate the possible consequences of their actions and my concerns for the vulnerabilities they create. I have found that it is usually young white men who are most drawn to aggressive tactics, and I say to them, "Do you really want to take their bait?" In almost every situation over the past twenty years where people have been caught planning a risky or violent action, it turned out that a government infiltrator was in the mix urging them on. This occurred most infamously during the 2008 Republican National Convention protests, when three young white men, in two different situations, were arrested for constructing Molotov cocktails. During their trial it became clear they did not intend to use them, and it came out that an agent provocateur with the FBI had been goading them forward.[18]

Recently the public debate surrounding the anti-fascist "Antifa" has been prominent. Antifa are anti-racist, anti-fascist militants who use a range of tactics, including physical engagement if needed, to confront white supremacists and racists. After the election of Donald Trump, the actions of Antifa were more conspicuous as they faced off with the violent white supremacists emboldened by the mainstreaming of their views. The far-right media, of course, hypes Antifa; often by fabricating stories and spreading falsely captioned images.

We know that the media is obsessed with these images of protestors dressed in black, whether it be Antifa or the black bloc. We can't control this, and we need to understand that people really buy into this criminalization campaign. Over the years I have witnessed the huge effort the government puts into criminalizing our movements and the massive investments corporations put into silencing and maligning us via relentless media smear campaigns.[19] These investments against social justice movements show me that our resistance truly threatens their power. And what threatens them the most is not the black bloc, but a resistance filled with beauty, joy, and love.

Down, Down WTO:
The Power of Creativity in Cancún

It was getting hot and humid on the afternoon of September 10, 2003, the opening day of the World Trade Organization Ministerial Conference in Cancún, Mexico. Thousands of us opposing the WTO gathered to march as altars to various deities were built with flowers, herbs, and seeds. The smell and smoke of copal, a traditional Indigenous incense, filled the air, as did the sound of drums. Many Indigenous people, particularly Mayans, offered ceremony, making prayers for the land and for a good outcome for the people. I felt a deep sense of love well up inside.

This march of thousands departed for Kilometer Zero, a major traffic circle with a fountain and grassy area that marked the beginning of the road to Cancún's Hotel Zone. This is where the Mexican government had built a fence to divide the site where the WTO's ministerial meetings were held from anti-WTO demonstrators. As we marched, the landscape changed from green spaces with tropical trees, bushes, and grass on both sides of the road to scattered restaurants and shops. We approached Kilometer Zero, and the march began to surge.

The security fence was eight feet high and chain-linked. It had steel supports and was abutted by an additional structure of four-foot black barricades. Behind all of that were the riot police. I felt uncertain about what we could face from the Mexican police, especially given their brutal beatings of demonstrators in Cancún during the World Economic Forum protests in 2001.

The sea of demonstrators chanted "Down, Down, WTO" as we swarmed the fence. Usually you'll see the black-clad youth destroying fences, but a group from the Korean delegation, mostly farmers dressed in floppy sun hats and tan vests over white T-shirts, pushed and pulled. One of the Koreans climbed the fence and held up a banner, WTO KILLS FARMERS. I saw him turn and look down . . . then something happened as he came toppling off the fence and into the arms of his friends below. The crowd was yelling and there was a huge commotion as they carried him out. He was taken to a hospital, where he soon died of a self-inflicted knife wound to the chest.

We all soon learned that the man was Lee Kyung-hae, president of the Federation of Farmers and Fishermen of Korea. He had a long history of fighting the effects of the WTO's trade policies on Korean farmers, including hunger strikes and a previous attempt to take his own life. He had been relentless in the struggle to expose how the WTO pressured South Korea to open its agricultural market to foreign products from multinational corporations, leading to the rapid devaluation of Korean crops, widespread debt, and the loss of land of local farmers. In giving his life, Lee Kyung-hae brought to light the suicide epidemic among South Korean farmers.

The evening of Brother Lee's death, many of us joined the Korean delegation outside the hospital, sitting down in the road for a candlelight vigil, honoring his life and reaffirming our commitment to fight the WTO. We still had a week of actions planned, but there was now an obvious shift. From that day forward, there was an ongoing encampment at Kilometer Zero, where Lee had fallen. Our actions took on a new solemnity and urgency. The world order represented by the WTO was suffused with greed and a lack of care for human rights, dignity, and local self-determination. In fighting the WTO, we would practice a fierce, loving resistance.

The Global Justice mobilization in Cancún, Mexico, is a relatively untold story, though the ministerial conference there collapsed, just as in Seattle. At that time in the US there was a debate about local versus global activism, with some making the argument that international summit-hopping was just for the privileged few. Many chose to stay home. This was unfortunate, because local organizers in the Global South could have benefited from material support from the Global North, and organizers from the Global North could have benefited from the wisdom of the Indigenous resistance.

I became involved via my participation in the Root Activist Network of Trainers, or RANT, a small trainers collective founded in 2000 by Starhawk, Hilary McQuie, and myself. Star and I attended an international planning meeting in Mexico City in November 2002 that included representatives from eighty-nine Mexican organizations and fifty-three international ones from sixteen countries—Mexico, El Salvador, Honduras, Guatemala, Nicaragua, Costa Rica, Brazil, India, Thailand, the Philippines, Holland, Great Britain, Germany, France, Belgium, and the US.[20]

There was a general consensus that agricultural and environmental policy, including GMO policy, protection of forests, and energy extraction, should not be governed by the WTO. The call to defend the water, forests, and food sovereignty—defined as the right to eat, produce, and decide agricultural policies locally—was very strong.[21] An overall strategy was articulated that included support for developing countries to resist the World Trade Organization, breaking consensus between the European Union and United States on key issues, national civil society campaigns, and mass mobilization and street protest.[22]

Starhawk and I traveled extensively to support the mobilization.[23] We worked with a group of youth from Mexico City who formed the Global Alliance S9. Their slogans were "We Say No to Institutional Violence" and "We Support Legitimate Self Defense." We did a big training with them, and Star and I still remember the dirty, sweat-filled wrestling mats we slept on in a gym. RANT raised over $10,000 to pay for buses to take them to Cancún. These students were inspiring and experienced, sophisticated organizers. We also met with organizers and local activists in Cancún, many of whom were working with a global network of NGOs called Our World Is Not for Sale, along with Puente a Cancún (Bridge to Cancún), a collaborative of Mexican, Irish, and US activists. La Vía Campesina, the international peasants movement, was a big player, bringing thousands of campesinos to the mobilization.

Cancún mirrors many problems and realities that the neoliberal world brings, especially the extremes of wealth and poverty. This land, on the northeast tip of the Yucatán Peninsula and historically inhabited by Mayan people, was mostly undeveloped prior to the 1970s, when the Mexican government decided to develop this lush, tropical region as a tourist destination. Today it is comprised of Cancún Centro, a city center on the mainland, and a resort area along a narrow strip of land that juts into the Caribbean. The former is a poor working-class city while the peninsula is a playground for the rich.

In advance of the mobilization, we rented a four-story white building near Parque de las Palapas, the main city center park, to house our art making, meetings, and legal support, along with a nearby house for the medics and a big space for the media center. Another location, Casa de Cultura, had large meeting spaces and was where La Vía Campesina contingent would be sleeping. Together we partnered with a group of young punks from Mexico City to construct a model eco-village in the open fields to the north of Casa de Cultura.[24] (In advance of the summit, they had given us a tour of their permaculture projects in the south of Mexico City.) In the fields we constructed solar showers, a solar oven, an educational display, and ingenious handwashing stations that used collected rainwater and a bike pump with funnels for basins that recycled that water back into the soil. This was real infrastructure that supported La Vía Campesina during their stay in Cancún while educating the thousands of people who came through that space about low-cost, simple systems to reproduce in their own communities.[25]

Brother Lee's death took place on the first day of the ministerial. On the second day we went forward with a powerful, youth-led, fiery night march filled with the clanging of pots and pans. It was called a *cacerolazo*, which was first used in Chile in 1971 during protests against food shortage. When this march approached Kilometer Zero and the memorial under way, it went dead silent as everyone raised their fists in the air.

We were more determined than ever to get into the Hotel Zone. The unique geography of Cancún made it easy for the government to keep us out; there were only two roadway entrances to the narrow strip of beach, one coming from the airport to the south, the other from the mainland to the north. It was nearly impossible for us to figure out an effective action from the south, and the government erected not one but two security fences to the north. The first, at Kilometer Zero, was breached the first day. The second, more elaborate fence was about a third of a kilometer farther down the road. We did not think we could break that fence or actually get to the ministerial itself. We were wrong.

————————

It didn't seem realistic to enter the Hotel Zone en masse, but a smaller, disruptive action seemed possible if we could get into the zone. Our planning meetings were exhausting. Ideas arose, then fizzled out as the tactical impossibilities were discussed. Then a plan emerged—Operation Ballpark! What if we went into the zone as tourists? We could enter in small groups of just two or three, dressed the part, then converge around the Hard Rock Cafe and blockade the road next to the convention center. We would do this at dinnertime, when the ministerial's delegates would be out and about at nearby restaurants.

Early that evening Star, Juniper, myself, and our friend Brush drove in our rental car down Boulevard Kukulcan, easily passing through the checkpoint. We watched as the beautiful jungle scenery gave way to hotels, sparse at first, then densely packed. We parked near the Hard Rock Cafe and got some ice cream—great cover, and one of Star's favorite things. Looking around, I saw others from our group milling about, staging as tourists, getting out of taxis, browsing at souvenir shops. So far, so good.

Abruptly, as planned, a group of young folks bolted into the road. Taking their lead, the rest of us flowed into the streets. Out of inconspicuous tourists' bags we pulled drums and bags of seeds. Some drummed and chanted, some sat down across the road, some danced in a spiral around two fruit trees, calling on the elements of earth, air, fire, and water to be with us. We called on spirit to help in the healing of the environment against the ravages of globalized corporate industry. The road was blocked.

I called our media team to let them know we had taken the road, and they called some of our friends inside the ministerial, including Antonia Juhasz from the International Forum on Globalization who joined us in the street. She and other representatives with mainstream NGOs were credentialed to attend the meetings. Soon the media arrived and the sidewalks filled with onlookers. The police stood at the periphery, not making a move. As the evening grew dark, we gathered in an impromptu spokes council to decide our next move. Luke Anderson, a writer and organizer from California, urged everyone to acknowledge that we had achieved our goal and that it was wiser to be part of another action tomorrow than to go to jail. Part of the art of action is knowing when to end an action, and to me, this was a clear ending point. Much to our surprise, the police offered two luxury buses to transport us back to wherever we wanted to go. Those without cars took the buses back to Kilometer Zero.

That night, we gathered together and worked late with the Koreans, discussing plans to tear down the second security fence. I was skeptical, but the Koreans were confident it could be done. They were unyielding, carrying a fierceness I can only describe as the spirit of Brother Lee working through them. They presented the plan of using ropes to tear down the fence, and a Mexican woman proposed that the women should go first, cutting the fence to weaken it before the ropes. I was thrilled. We had been dealing with a lot of sexism, part of the Mexican culture and also deeply rooted in some of the international male organizers, including some from the States, who had arrived in Cancún full of arrogance, assuming leadership in pretty unskillful ways. There had been growing frustration among the women.

We presented our plan to the delegates assembly at La Casa de Cultura the next morning, and much to our surprise they all agreed. I raced to the nearest hardware store and bought every bolt cutter they had, along with wire cutters and heavy-duty pliers.

By 10 AM we were ready. Thousands of us marched toward Kilometer Zero, including thousands of Indigenous people in their beautifully woven clothes. The Koreans wore their tan vests and floppy sun hats, the students sang and banged on drums, and the Infernal Noise Brigade, from Seattle, brought great energy to the march. Several pushed the giant puppet my friend Gan Golan had built of Chac, the Mayan god of rain, thunder, and lightning, and we asked for Chac's support as we traveled the road that led to the ministerial.

At Kilometer Zero we paused to honor Brother Lee, then walked toward the new fence that had been erected 100 meters closer to the Hotel Zone. The women coalesced into formation, row upon row of us wearing bandannas around our foreheads or as masks. We had learned from the Zapatistas that masking your face is a way to be seen. Before reaching the fence, we linked arms, feeling happy, excited, and free. There was a crack of thunder and a brief rain poured down, cooling us all. The gods were with us! We were in our full power as we chanted "Bella Ciao," an Italian anti-fascist song of resistance. Years later, I realized how appropriate it was in light of Lee's suicide.

One morning I awakened
O bella ciao, bella ciao, bella ciao, ciao, ciao!
One morning I awakened
And I found the invader.

Oh partisan, carry me away
O bella ciao, bella ciao, bella ciao, ciao, ciao!
Oh partisan, carry me away
Because I feel death approaching.

And if I die as a partisan
O bella ciao, bella ciao, bella ciao, ciao, ciao!
And if I die as a partisan,
Then you must bury me.

Bury me up in the mountain
O bella ciao, bella ciao, bella ciao, ciao, ciao!

Bury me up in the mountain
under the shadow of a beautiful flower.

And all those who shall pass!
O bella ciao, bella ciao, bella ciao, ciao, ciao
And all those who shall pass
Will say to me: "what a beautiful flower."

This is the flower of the partisan
O bella ciao, bella ciao, bella ciao, ciao, ciao!
This is the flower of the partisan
Who died for freedom.

The fence was just ahead, and it was formidable. Massive sections of thick, chain-linked metal were reinforced from behind with eight-foot boxes of steel and topped with barbed wire. Behind that were barricades, then battalions of riot police. I passed the tools out to the women and, singing our hearts out, we cut and unscrewed. The police did nothing, perhaps having confidence in the steel wall between us. Little by little, section by section, we weakened the chains and the links. As we worked, the men behind us kept pushing forward, wanting to break through the fence before it was ready to come down. Other men held the impatient ones back until we had completed our work.

Next it was the Koreans' turn. Several of them came forward and tied the rope to the fence, then stretched the long ropes out into the crowd. When the ropes were tied tightly to the fence and secured in everyone's hands, the man at the front yelled, "*Pull!*"

And pull we did, hundreds of us together. We stopped to rest, then the command came again: "*Pull!*" On the third try, a section of the fence broke loose. The ropes were untied as the black bloc swooped in to pull apart the freed section of fence. The Koreans retied the ropes to the next section, and again we pulled. Section by section, we pulled the fence down, and each time a section broke loose, the black bloc hauled it away. I took a break to follow them, curious, and discovered they were using the fence pieces to build a barricade on a side road behind us, where police were mobilizing on our flank. *Brilliant!* I rejoined my friends on the rope and kept pulling on cue until the fence was down.

Pulling down the security fence during the anti-WTO protests in Cancún.

The road was wide open before us, along with hundreds of riot police with their water cannons, tear gas, and Darth Vader suits, plus the brown-clothed, unarmed peasants the police had conscripted to add to their numbers. There was a moment of stillness, as nobody, police and demonstrator alike, had planned for what would happen next. We all sat down, forming rows as the Koreans lit candles in the road. We held this space for about an hour, then the Koreans led a chant, "Down, Down, WTO," as we all rose together, drumming and singing. We marched back to Kilometer Zero, marching with joy, giving all we could to say "*No Más*, No More, the WTO Must Go."

The ministerial itself was several kilometers away. We would not get there, but we didn't need to. We had opened the way, a political space that the state had closed.

The next morning news came that the Kenyan delegates, representing the desires of the Group of 22 developing nations, refused to go along with the WTO's agricultural deal.[26] They walked out, and the ministerial collapsed—again. There would be no deal. It was an overwhelming sight to behold as our beloved community at Kilometer Zero broke out in joy, hugging, singing, crying, and dancing.

In Cancún, we demonstrated peacefully and powerfully with our humanity, our creativity, and our hearts. Unlike in Prague and Genoa, the police did not attack, and therefore there was no violence. We voiced our opposition to the WTO through action, and the delegates inside the ministerial were emboldened to step away from deals that would have continued to do harm to their people and their lands.

A few months later, in November, we mobilized again against the FTAA at a summit in Miami. This led to the final unraveling of the deal we had first protested in Quebec.[27] Bolstered by our street actions and emboldened by the growing collaborations and solidarity within the Global Justice movement, delegations inside the negotiating rooms from Central and South America said no. The FTAA was finished for good.

These lessons from the Global Justice movement are needed now more than ever. With the rise of right-wing populism, many are afraid of violence, and fear leads to confusion and division. It is the empire's most powerful tool for social control. We may be afraid, but we can still act. We don't all have to agree on the best way forward, and we can work together with respect and agreements. There is no one way; there are many ways. This is what the Zapatistas have taught us: "One no, many yeses." Our solidarity despite our differences in the midst of courageous, creative, and collective action is the sweet spot where the greatest changes are possible.

CHAPTER 6

Hurricane Katrina and the Power of Solidarity

I n the days and months after Hurricane Katrina made landfall near Gulf Coast communities in Louisiana and Mississippi on August 29, 2005, the scale of the devastation and suffering was difficult to comprehend. Over thirteen hundred were dead. There was no power or running water. Hospitals, schools, grocery stores, and gas stations were destroyed or closed. Street and traffic signs were gone while debris and destruction littered the streets. When I drove through the city for the first time a month after the hurricane, the term *post-apocalyptic* kept coming to me. That's exactly what it looked like.

Adding to the first human-made disaster of the broken levees was a second human-made tragedy that unfolded as white supremacists, both residents and law enforcement, exercised their racist hatred by shooting Black people who were evacuating, all while the media and government officials strummed up largely inaccurate reports of civil unrest. In Algiers Point, a predominantly white community, signs appeared proclaiming, WE SHOOT LOOTERS. Along with these signs came rumors of dead, bullet-ridden Black bodies lying on the streets in dry neighborhoods. These rumors have since become documented fact.[1]

Amid a city that had broken down, the government's response was militaristic and, in many cases, inhumane. Checkpoints were everywhere. They were alleged to protect people from downed power lines and dirty water, but in many cases they prevented rescuers from reaching victims and residents from returning to their homes.[2]

On the ground after the disaster, I saw the racial divides that plague our communities play out in the incredibly tense context of post-disaster relief efforts. Much of what I saw makes little sense unless you understand the power dynamics between white communities and communities of color. There is a long history in this country showing that when white people need help, resources and support are on the way. When it is Black and Brown folks with their lives on the line, help is hard to find. We saw this again in 2017, when the response to Hurricane Harvey in Houston was such a stark contrast with the response to Hurricane Maria in Puerto Rico.[3]

Amid the post-disaster horror, there was also awe and beauty as people rose up to provide support. One such effort was the Common Ground Relief and Collective, founded in the predominantly Black community of Algiers. Common Ground was a massive effort, moving millions of dollars of resources while building a parallel social infrastructure within a system that had collapsed. We were responding to whatever was needed—food, medical attention, cleaning supplies, water, home gutting and repair, tools, roof work, tree work, legal assistance, access to computers, bikes and transportation, and more.

Providing relief to hurricane victims seems like a no-brainer, but in the post-Katrina context, the overwhelming military presence and racist fears prevented resources from reaching those who needed them most. Over time it became clearer that the powers-that-be did not want displaced residents who were Black to return to their neighborhoods.[4] This is part of why Common Ground was so important. It sought to rebuild neighborhoods, not abandon them. Our rap was solidarity, not charity, and it became a living example of what bottom-up, people-powered relief efforts can look like.

Common Ground Relief: Power of the People

In the days leading up to Katrina, I was in the ditches of Crawford, Texas, working on Camp Casey with Cindy Sheehan, the antiwar activist whose son, US Army Specialist Casey Sheehan, was killed in action in Iraq. Just before Katrina hit, my work at Camp Casey had morphed into planning the Bring Them Home Now Tour, a powerful, difficult, wild ride. Three RVs of vets and military families traveled across the country and converged in Washington, DC, for the massive National Anti-War March.[5] When I finally got back home to Austin, my partner, Juniper, was planning another trip to New Orleans. She had already been down twice and evacuated with a friend of ours when Hurricane Rita hit just weeks after Katrina.

Juniper, aka Lauren Ross, is an environmental engineer who works on behalf of the water. We fell in love amid the tear gas in Quebec City during the 2001 FTAA protests, and in 2002 I moved from LA to her hometown of Austin. Over the years Juniper has thwarted nuclear and coal-fired power plants, opposed oil and gas pipelines, and exposed problems with developers' plans. I think of her as a silver bullet. After Katrina, she was on a mission to collect and test soil and water samples from the impacted areas. New Orleans is surrounded by oil and chemical plants, several of which flooded when the levees broke, turning the waters flooding the city into a toxic stew. Juniper eventually combined her data with EPA data and provided New Orleans residents with a map of levels and locations of the toxins.

I was exhausted after the Bring Them Home Now Tour, but it wasn't a hard decision to go to New Orleans. It just made sense.

On the morning of October 4, we left Austin early, aiming to miss the morning rush-hour traffic in Houston. We rented a huge pickup truck to accommodate the sampling equipment plus a bunch of food and camping gear. It was a cloudy, gray day, and everything was eerily quiet. As we approached the city, I could feel the tension in my belly. These were hallowed grounds. By October, the death toll from the hurricane was reaching twelve hundred. More than a million had evacuated, and hundreds of thousands would become permanently displaced. The rescue effort and search for bodies wrapped up the day before I arrived, and the military occupation was well under way.

Not long after we passed the airport on Interstate 10, we saw a checkpoint ahead. Two lanes were created by a series of orange traffic cones with police cars parked horizontally across all the other lanes, blocking each one, their red-and-blue lights flashing. Off to the side of the road I saw three military vehicles with armed soldiers nearby. Police were carrying shotguns, questioning drivers. As we waited in line we said our prayers—*Let us in!*

When our turn came, Juniper showed the officers her license and explained our water and soil sampling project. It took a while, but after a few questions and instructions about the curfew, we were free to proceed—thank you, white privilege.

Night had fallen. With the electricity out, all was dark. We merged onto US Route 90, toward the West Bank. I had a weird feeling—checkpoints, curfews, the West Bank—where was I, Palestine? But the Superdome was

to our left, orienting me back to reality. Massive sections of its roof had
been ripped off, exposing the orange underlay. We were quiet as we drove
across the bridge, the murky brown waters of the Mississippi flowing
strongly below. We exited into Algiers, a neighborhood that suffered wind
damage but did not flood. Piles of debris and trash lined the streets and
lawns. The health hazard was increasing, as was the odor. The humidity
and mosquitoes made the situation worse.

We passed a stretch of public housing projects, then crossed under a
bridge into a neighborhood with block after block of small homes, many
with children's bikes and toys strewn around the yards. As we turned onto
Atlantic Street, I saw the levee there at the end. This levee had successfully
held back the waters of the Mississippi, saving lives in Algiers. Elsewhere
in New Orleans, more than fifty levees were breached.

Finally we pulled up at our destination. We were at the home of Malik
Rahim, the co-founder of Common Ground Relief. We arrived to a bustle
of activity.

———————

There was a big truck parked outside Malik's home and a stream of mostly
young people unloading it.[6] You knew you were in the right place because
of the large hand-painted sign on the front porch that said COMMON
GROUND RELIEF with the logo of a fist holding a hammer. I joined in,
carrying boxes through a tent-covered area that was a makeshift distribution center with pallets of donated goods on each side and an aisle down
the middle. To one side was food and water; to the other side were cleaning supplies like Clorox, mops, and sponges, and necessities like towels
and toilet paper. Near the tented area in the back was an outdoor kitchen
where a crew was cooking dinner—beans and rice. The backyard next
door was filled with tents where many of the volunteers slept.

After unloading the fresh delivery of boxes, I connected with my friend
scott crow. I had met him and his partner, Ann Harkness, during the 2000
Democratic Convention protests in Los Angeles, and we became closer
friends when I moved to Austin.[7] Scott took me around and introduced me
to Malik and some of the other volunteers—Suncere, Sean, Jenka, Brian,
Toby, Kerul, Tyler, Emily, and Alan, to name a few—and Malik invited me
into his home, the house he grew up in.[8] Kitchens are always the heart of a

house, and it was no different here, with people sitting all around the table and a pot of coffee brewing. Off the kitchen was a small space converted to an office where volunteers were tracking the donations coming in. Every room was packed with people. Malik's home was the first Common Ground distribution center, but as the operation expanded there would be many more.

Malik Rahim, though soft-spoken, is a force to be reckoned with. He is a gentle man with gray hair and a beard who garners immediate respect. Like many poor Black men, in his youth Malik joined the military and served during Vietnam. He later formed the Louisiana chapter of the Black Panther Party and was part of the infamous Desire housing project shoot-out. He then worked on prison reform and housing issues. Malik sees service to the community as a cornerstone of organizing, and it was this approach that led to the impact of Common Ground.

During the hurricane, Malik and his partner, Sharon Johnson, hunkered down in their home in Algiers. After the storm passed they watched as white racists from nearby Algiers Point and Gretna were brutalizing and even killing Black people. Malik personally saw several dead bodies in the street that he believed were shooting victims.[9] Groups of white men were walking by his house, taunting and threatening him.

The existence of this all-white militia has since been documented by eyewitness testimonies and video footage. A. C. Thompson, a ProPublica reporter who investigated the Algiers Point shootings for eighteen months, characterized the formation of the militia as a white community treating hurricane victims like criminals:

Facing an influx of refugees, the residents of Algiers Point could have pulled together food, water and medical supplies for the flood victims. Instead, a group of white residents, convinced that crime would arrive with the human exodus, sought to seal off the area, blocking the roads in and out of the neighborhood by dragging lumber and downed trees into the streets. They stock-piled handguns, assault rifles, shotguns and at least one Uzi and began patrolling the streets in pickup trucks and SUVs. The newly formed militia, a loose band of about 15 to 30 residents, most of them men, all of them white, was looking for thieves, outlaws or, as one member put it, anyone who simply "didn't belong."[10]

Wayne Janak, a member of the militia, boasted about the shootings on tape in the documentary *Welcome to New Orleans*. "It was great!" Janak said, of shooting Black people. "It was like pheasant season in South Dakota. If it moved, you shot it."[11]

The police were shooting storm victims, too. Four days after the hurricane, a group was crossing the Danziger Bridge—traveling from a Black neighborhood to a white neighborhood—when police officers arrived and started shooting them, killing two and seriously injuring four. A decade later, five officers pled guilty to the subsequent cover-up.[12]

A week after Katrina, Louisiana governor Kathleen Blanco boasted about efforts to "protect" storm victims who actually needed food, shelter, and water, saying, "I have one message for these hoodlums: These troops know how to shoot and kill, they are more than willing to do so if necessary, and I expect they will."[13] By two weeks after the hurricane, there were fifty-one thousand Army and Air Guardsmen in the Gulf region.[14] Many of these men and women saved lives and brought food and supplies—but others were tasked with guarding and patrolling the neighborhoods.

Amid this charged situation, Malik and Sharon put out a call for help to activists around the country. The people of Algiers needed assistance— and not just because of the roaming vigilantes. Resources to help Algiers rebuild its wind-ravaged homes were not forthcoming. One of the activists who heeded the call was scott crow. He, along with Malik and Sharon, started discussing plans for a radical relief effort. It was at the suggestion of Robert King, a freed member of the Angola Three, that it came to be called Common Ground Relief.[15]

Malik and scott filled me in on the operation. There was a meeting every morning and lots of work to be done going door-to-door, asking what the residents needed, sorting supplies, working the distribution center, tarping roofs, clearing debris, providing medical assistance to residents, or prepping food. Volunteers had set up a pirate radio station, and two political initiatives were under way, the first to help residents resist evictions, the other providing prisoner support and documenting police abuse. In the evenings we would discuss the day's activities and anticipate future needs.

Later that evening, I bade farewell to new and old friends and left to set up a tent in the backyard of a nearby house, where the Pagan Cluster was invited to stay.[16] This house was used as a storage space for the Voodoo

Robert King, Lisa, Malik Rahim, and scott crow outside King's house. *Courtesy of Ann Harkness.*

store on the corner. We were lucky to have a functioning bathroom inside, but going in required respect and a bit of courage. There was no electricity, and the space was loaded with magical tools, herbs, and figurines.

As Juniper and I settled into our tent, I felt the exhaustion from the two months working at Camp Casey overtake me. I was overwhelmed by how raw everything around me felt, and I fell into a deep sleep.

We got up early the next morning while it was still cool and headed out to collect water and soil samples in Plaquemines Parish, an area with a number of rural fishing towns that was directly hit by the hurricane when it made landfall. There are simply no words for what we saw there. Houses were flattened or shattered. Pieces of people's lives were strewn about, covered in mud. Coffins floated in the water alongside the road. Electrical lines were down with the poles bent, and trees were snapped like toothpicks. We drove as far as we could, but with debris blocking the road, we turned around.

Over the next several days, we drove all over New Orleans collecting water and soil samples. From parish to parish, neighborhoods were destroyed and desolate. Here and there were distribution stations set up by the military where you could get ice, water, food, and Clorox, which was

believed to mitigate the mold. FEMA was providing ready-to-eat meals—
MREs—to troops, police, and rescue workers. Residents could sometimes
get them in emergency centers. I'll never forget my first MRE—it was roast
chicken, mashed potatoes, green beans, and a peach cake. The ingredients
were in a chemical packet that served as a heating element; you would seal
everything inside for about five minutes and voilà, it was cooked. As weird
as these were, they were better than the Salvation Army's food, which was
usually two slices of white bread with a piece of ham or a hot dog and chips.

On the day we went to the Lower Ninth Ward, we were unsure we
would be able to get in. This area, along with neighboring Chalmette and
St. Bernard, was inundated when the levees broke. At the time of Katrina,
the Lower Ninth was 98 percent African American, a close-knit community of homeowners who had been there for generations.[17] Henry Irvin,
a longtime resident of the area, recalled in 2015 that "before Katrina,
I could tell you the name of everyone all the way from the bridge on
down."[18] After Katrina, stories were told about the Lower Ninth that did
not capture the truth. Many thought of it as a poor neighborhood with
"hoodlums." Really it was an area filled with hardworking people, many
of them living below the poverty line, some of them middle-class and
professional people. It was an area where the Black community had been
able to accumulate some modest amount of financial security because
people owned their homes and passed them on to their children.

In nearby Chalmette, a white community that had been similarly
ravaged, people were let back into their homes just a month after the hurricane. FEMA trailers could be seen everywhere there, but not in the Lower
Ninth. In fact, the residents of the Lower Ninth weren't allowed back in until
December.[19] The National Guard stood by with their guns, "guarding" the
neighborhood from its own residents. The more time that passed, the less
likely residents could recover what belongings might be left. Over time, a
picture emerged of a governor and other key politicians who wanted to raze
the area to the ground, not rebuild or even develop it—but more on that later.

To get to the Lower Ninth, we needed to cross one of two bridges. The
Claiborne Street Bridge was still closed, so we entered via the St. Claude
Street Bridge. Passing through military checkpoints, we were able to get in
thanks to our white skin privilege, the hard hat on the front seat, and our stated
scientific purpose. Soon we saw the houses that were twisted and splintered,

moved from their original locations, some clear across the street. We saw mud, debris piles, and sitting water in every direction. It was like a wall of muddy water had smashed, twisted, and turned everything in its path. A pack of dogs ran toward us, then changed their minds and went the other way.

We moved from block to block, taking samples, standing in shock and disbelief. It was here in the Lower Ninth that the criminal failure of the levees really hit me. The levees were supposed to be maintained by the US Army Corps of Engineers, which had ignored systemic flaws for years leading to the disaster. A 2006 report deemed the maze of levees in New Orleans "a system in name only."[20] The result of this negligence was homes submerged in rushing waters in seconds while people still slept in their beds. I saw rows of homes with holes chopped through the attics and with the large red X marking each house—the symbol of the search-and-rescue team—along with the date and the number of bodies found dead on the bottom. I was a bit in shock at the magnitude of loss.

After ten days of collecting samples, I briefly went home to Austin. By then I knew I would be returning.

Solidarity, Not Charity

By mid-October, Common Ground had a number of competent volunteers with a range of useful skills who were committed to staying, many for an indefinite period. We held a meeting at a boarded-up house across the street from Common Ground's first health clinic to discuss plans for the future.[21] Many of us were experienced organizers from the Global Justice movement; we took lessons learned from that arena and applied them to disaster relief.[22] My friend Emily Posner recently shared her memory of my role at this meeting: "You came up, listened, asked some questions, and *bam*, drew a picture of how it might work."[23]

The plan was to respond to the people's needs while creating working groups with pre-designated tasks in each neighborhood we expanded into. Coordinators from each area would meet weekly to share information, tweak operational priorities, and identify volunteer tasks. We began to sort our tasks among short-term versus mid- and long-term volunteers. The latter were assigned as team leaders with clear responsibilities and scopes of authority. As more help arrived, we increasingly put energy into volunteer infrastructure, training, food, and housing. For the short-term volunteers we held daily morning meetings. In the evenings we held periodic trainings, cultural events, race and gender caucuses, and weekly all-volunteer meetings for feedback, questions, and concerns.

Common Ground expanded into the Upper Ninth Ward, opening the Louisa Street house. We had no electricity or water and were surveilled by the police, but we were a beacon of hope for those who had lost their homes. We ran a massive distribution center, a legal clinic, and a mobile health clinic in my friend Elizabeth's van. We removed pumps from abandoned washers for our bioremediation work. We chain-sawed our way through roads to open them up. As we expanded, Malik was still where the buck stopped. He was the primary engine, organizer, visionary, motivator, and inspirer. He was the host, cook, cleaner, and trash man. His home was the heart and soul that infused the work.

As time went on, the needs in the Gulf Coast area remained almost incomprehensible. It was difficult work as we witnessed fresh tragedies play out every day in the lives of the residents. We kept at it, doing everything we could, but we needed more help. With Thanksgiving around the corner, we put out a call for volunteers, calling it Road Trip for Relief, asking people to come for a week in late November with their labor, materials, and tools to donate.

Building infrastructure for the incoming volunteers was a challenge in neighborhoods with no power and few options for safe housing. We lucked out with a connection from people working on a community garden near a two-story warehouse called the Green Project in the Bywater, an area near the Ninth Ward that suffered from wind damage but did not flood. The warehouse had several smaller rooms off to the sides but was mostly a huge room, one on the top floor and one on the bottom. We set up a kitchen, work spaces, sleeping areas, a registration area near the front door, offices, and spaces to store donated goods. The Pagan Cluster set up bioremediation teams and brewed compost tea, which we used to inoculate the ground in the most toxic areas.

The long-term organizers divided into operations teams, including cooking and food, first aid stations, housing coordination, transportation, communications, supplies, and so on. Our work teams included roof tarpers, electricians, housecleaning, house repair, and community gardens. Weeks

Thanksgiving

When Thanksgiving arrived, we were all excited about a meal we planned to serve at the Louisa Street house for residents in the Upper Ninth Ward. We swept the street to clear the dust, mud, and debris that never seemed to go away. Across the street was a big cemetery surrounded by a wall, giving us a bit more protection. We pulled out a bunch of long tables for serving food and put about two dozen round tables, which we borrowed from a hotel, with chairs in the middle of the street. Grumble, our main cook and one of the founders of Seeds of Peace, had been busy preparing turkey, mashed potatoes, sweet potatoes, green beans, collard greens, stuffing, and gravy.[24] It was going to be a feast. The residents started to arrive in the afternoon, and before long there were about fifty people. As platters of food filled the tables, all eyes opened wide, a few with tears. We formed a huge circle to express gratitude before we began to eat. I stood to the side to quietly watch this bittersweet moment. Common Ground was often like that, coming together with joy and community, while pain and suffering were all around.

before, teams had dispatched with trucks of supplies to Houma, a community to the southeast of New Orleans that was the heart of the Houma Nation, an Indigenous people. Now that the Houma operation was more fully established, we spread into the Upper Ninth Ward. Honestly, lots of people were skeptical of us. Our volunteers were predominately white. The Upper Ninth Ward was predominantly Black, and many residents thought we might be taking them for a ride or offering help with strings attached. But as we showed up day after day cleaning, gutting, repairing what we could, and listening, we earned trust in the community. Soon we established a volunteer space at the Mount Carmel Baptist Church on Pauline Street, and eventually we set up a health clinic across the street. As we continued to grow, we expanded into St. Mary's School in the Upper Ninth, furiously dispatching teams to the Upper and Lower Ninth Wards.

Meanwhile, there was a major opening in addressing race relations within Common Ground's work. I was facilitating a morning meeting at the Green Project warehouse when two residents joined in. The woman, Kimberly Richards, lived in Mississippi just over the border and needed help repairing her home. The man, the Reverend Tyrone Edwards, asked if we could provide a team of volunteers to help salvage his church, the Zion Travelers Baptist Church in Plaquemines Parish. We said yes, of course, to both requests.

I had noticed they wore the People's Institute for Survival and Beyond T-shirts. PISAB was the first organization to train me in anti-racism back in 1989, and I headed over to introduce myself as soon as I could, telling them I was forever grateful for their excellent, life-changing work. Then I said, "We need your help." Common Ground consisted mostly of white folks working in a Black city, and many of our volunteers didn't know much about the history of New Orleans or how to navigate the racial dynamics with residents. I asked if PISAB would be interested in a collaboration.

The immediate answer was yes, and in fact we scheduled our first training right then and there. Ms. Richards and the Reverend Edwards integrated material from PISAB's two-and-a-half-day training and condensed this into several hours focused on getting volunteers to understand the history and cultures of the local communities, as well as systemic analyses of how racist institutions affect communities of color.

In New Orleans, the history of race relations is evident at every street and public square. New Orleans was once one of the largest slave ports in the country. Congo Square in the Tremé neighborhood was where slaves were auctioned, and Tremé later became the first free Black neighborhood in the city. The legacy of segregation impacted which neighborhoods flooded when Katrina hit and which were receiving the most assistance from the state—we needed our volunteers to understand this. PISAB trained roughly twelve hundred Common Ground volunteers with their "Undoing Racism" trainings, and I like to think that these young men and women, like me when I first worked with PISAB, started to see the world differently.

Reopening a School in the Lower Ninth Ward

By late December residents of the Lower Ninth were finally allowed back home, and yet it seemed like their efforts to rebuild were being stymied by the state. As it turned out, they were. The powers that be had already decided the Lower Ninth was not worth saving.

From the beginning politicians, developers, and well-intentioned philanthropists wrote off the Lower Ninth Ward by telling themselves and one another that the area was too damaged to save. In the weeks after the hurricane, Alphonso Jackson, the secretary of Housing and Urban Development (HUD) under George W. Bush, informed New Orleans mayor Ray Nagin that "it would be a mistake to rebuild the Lower Ninth Ward."[25] For his part, Nagin said of the Ninth Ward, "I don't think it can ever be what it was, because it's the lowest-lying area."[26] This was, in fact, not true. Other parts of New Orleans—including the wealthy Lakeview neighborhood, which recovered quickly after the hurricane—were lower in elevation. Others argued the Lower Ninth contained fewer homeowners and therefore fewer displaced residents. This was patently false.

Government officials used these specious arguments to justify policies that stymied rebuilding efforts while preventing displaced people from returning. The general willingness to believe the false narratives supporting these policies laid bare the truth: Some people deserved the dignity of returning home, while others did not. This attitude was infamously expressed by US representative Richard Baker, who said shortly after the disaster, "We finally cleaned up public housing in New Orleans. We couldn't do it. But God did."[27]

The Lower Ninth was the last neighborhood to have electricity restored and the last to have drinking water. The National Guard prevented residents from entering for four months after the storm—as compared with one month for most other neighborhoods. Meanwhile Mayor Nagin initiated a project, the ironically named "Bring New Orleans Back" program, that imposed a moratorium on rebuilding in neighborhoods where residents weren't allowed back in. Another of the recovery efforts, "Road Home," was overseen by Governor Blanco. The $10 billion plan's labyrinthine rules made it essentially impossible for poorer homeowners to rebuild.[28] Meanwhile, in early 2006, HUD developed a plan to demolish four of the city's most populous housing complexes and replace them with "mixed-income" rather than "low-income" housing.[29] It was gentrification via disaster.

These and other policies prevented New Orleans's poorest residents from having homes to return to. It is estimated that in 2015, there were still a hundred thousand fewer Black residents in New Orleans than before the hurricane, while the white population had returned to its pre-hurricane numbers.[30] In the years after Katrina, a new era of colonization was under way, and ethnic cleansing was again being deployed.

Despite the scale of what the residents were up against, Common Ground continued to fight evictions and salvage damaged homes. We made a difference in so many ways, and one of our triumphs over the disaster capitalists (as Naomi Klein calls them) still warms my heart to this day.

In January, weeks after the National Guard stood down and residents were allowed back in, the city announced the Lower Ninth Ward would be bulldozed. This prompted a number of lawsuits, and as these snailed their way through the court system, the disaster capitalists in the education industry had a plan—and they moved viciously. Governor Blanco was spearheading efforts to take over the public school system and demolish many of the city's schools. Seventy-five hundred mostly union teachers and employees were fired en masse.[31] The plan was to fold New Orleans's public schools into a public-private charter school system deemed the Recovery School District. This plan was enacted unilaterally by the state legislature.

Before this had begun to unfold, Common Ground secured the "Little Blue House" in the Lower Ninth Ward in late October. This house was a beacon of hope for the residents and a bright light of resistance to the power structures that wanted to drive them out.[32] Over the next few months, the house added a distribution center, a tool library, and a free clothing store. We put cardboard street signs on every block. We gutted many nearby homes, one of which we turned into a kitchen that served a free hot meal every night. We converted two other homes into temporary sleeping spaces so that residents could return for the weekend to work on their homes.

One cold, sunny day in February, during a meeting at the Little Blue House, the residents expressed frustration, outrage, and feelings of despair at being pushed out of their community. I felt powerless. It appeared that Governor Blanco didn't have plans to reopen any of the schools in the Lower Ninth. Vera, one of the mothers at the meeting, said she couldn't move back home if there wasn't a school for her children. She wanted to know why nobody was working on the Martin Luther King Jr. Elementary School.

Several other residents chimed in with the same concern, and eventually we landed on the same question: What can we do to get this school opened? Kendrick, one of the residents, said that with spring break around the corner, we could recruit volunteers to help clean the school. It would be young people from around the country coming to help young people in New Orleans go back to school.

Yes! A sense of power and usefulness returned to us.

We knew this wasn't something we would be given permission to do. But we were not looking for permission. That is the power of direct action: doing what you need to do, when you need to do it, in order to force a change.

We reached out to the school's principal, Doris Hicks, who told us she was working with the state to get MLK included as one of the charter school conversions. She wasn't opposed to what we were doing, but was unable to participate. We received the de facto blessing of several other administrators who supported our plan but could not openly associate with it. Years later, one of these administrators, Hilda Young, told a reporter at *The Nation* about the state's attitude toward reopening MLK: "Their attitude was, 'The mayor is going to green-space the neighborhood anyway.' That's when we realized they didn't want us to open. That's when we realized they didn't want any of the schools in the Lower Ninth to reopen."[33]

In March we made our move. I did a big training with hundreds of volunteers and dozens of residents, and on the morning of the action, we put on our Tyvek suits, grabbed our respirators, loaded up with tools and wheelbarrows, and converged at the school. Residents and parents led the effort, doing a speak-out on the corner first. Then we went in.[34]

The Martin Luther King Elementary School was one of the most successful schools in NOLA, filled with Black history. It was painful to cart out books and photos, putting them into trash piles on the sidewalk and streets for pickup. There were many awards and trophies that we set gently outside the main door to be cleaned up later. We spent the day cleaning and got a lot done, but the next day, Friday, the police were there in force, making it clear we couldn't go back inside.

It took a lot of persistence, but we were able to connect with the School Recovery District's superintendent, Robin Jarvis, and asked for a city council resolution that would grant the residents and Common Ground

Common Ground's logo.

the right to clean the school. Luck be with us, she agreed, the city council passed the resolution, and we were back on track with the cleaning.

Soon more obstacles emerged. The school board told us we had to conduct an inventory of everything we removed, including the pencils. Mind you, this was not the local school board that oversaw MLK pre-Katrina, but the Recovery District's board, which had seized control of local boards all over the city. Ridiculous, but we counted the pencils. Then they claimed the building was unsafe, so Principal Hicks brought in a structural engineer, who verified the building was sound.

For several months the Recovery District did what it could to prevent MLK from reopening, but our community-based efforts deepened. With the beginning of a new school year in September 2006, the children of the Lower

Ninth were to be bused to another school that was still in disrepair. The parents called for a protest, and the Southern Christian Leadership Conference came in to help. We marched to the Recovery District's brand-new building and occupied it as elders conducted a Freedom School for the youth.

These actions and more pressured Ms. Jarvis to commit to reopening the school, and that commitment was realized on June 10, 2007. This was not what the powers that be wanted to happen. Having seen for myself how events unfolded, I am certain the school would be no more were it not for the power of the people. The MLK Charter School for Science and Technology is still going strong today.

The "Power Over" of the Government's Response

Looking back, I'm struck by how the post-Katrina landscape offered a unique perspective on the different forms of power that filled the vacuum of a collapsed infrastructure. Rarely are the contrasts between bottom-up shared-power structures and top-down power-over structures so visible.

My early understanding of power came from Saul Alinsky's landmark book, *Rules for Radicals*. Then I learned about the work of Gene Sharp, the well-known scholar and advocate of nonviolent civil resistance. Sharp described power not as a monolithic, unchanging force held by a select few, but a fluid force that is constantly negotiated between the people who claim to hold power and those who appear to lack it. According to Sharp, power can be taken back. Power is relational. Like energy, it cannot be created or destroyed, only exercised.

Sharp's theories were expanded upon by Robert Helvey, a former US Army officer who argued that the power of the dominant system is embedded within institutions that he called Pillars of Support, including the education system, spiritual systems, economic systems, military systems, and so on. If we chip away at, erode, or remove these pillars, the structure becomes unstable, bordering on chaos or collapse. The pillar model reminds us that while institutions might seem huge and impossible to move, they are in fact vulnerable to collapse if people keep chipping away.[35]

I like to think about *flattening* the pillars rather than toppling them. Yes, we need political, economic, and social systems—but they don't need to function in hierarchies. If we flatten the pillars, we see them as connected within a horizontal network of shared power relationships making up a complex, interconnected web of support. We can see that hierarchical, Power Over systems are not inevitable.

The most difficult part of this work is not flattening or smashing the pillars but changing the foundation that creates the culture in which they operate. The foundations are made of mental models, which I see as the steps. The first step is history, the second is belief systems, the third is values, and the fourth is norms and practices. Combined, these steps form the dominant culture in which we are socialized.

In the US, the dominant culture's history is told as a heroic journey of founding a "new" world. It includes explorers, traders, and pilgrims fleeing persecution and oppression. It's a story of the Doctrine of Discovery and Manifest Destiny declaring that all land not inhabited by White Christians was there for the taking. It is a story that justifies and glorifies violence as patriotic and necessary. It is a story of rapid growth led by rugged individuals who, through hard work and sacrifice, turned a resource-rich land into an agricultural power, then an industrial power, and now a global military superpower. We are not always taught about the genocide waged against Native Americans, the true cost and brutality of the enslavement of African Americans, or the political maneuverings that took place to ensure this new United States was not a real democracy but a plutocracy governed by the white and rich. Nor were we taught the stories of those who resisted this social order, creating pathways to freedom that we still walk today.

Immanent to this version of US history are a specific set of beliefs about the supremacy of whiteness, patriarchy, capitalism, and Christianity, along with cultural values that support individualism, materialism, hate, fear, competition, paternalism, and violence. The dominant culture privileges might over right, white over Black and Brown, men over women, wealth over poverty, individual over collective, and Christianity over all other beliefs.

My dear friend Starhawk, an activist and spiritual leader, gave me a new language to describe and differentiate four types of power as Power Over, Power With, Power Within, and Power Under. I could see all of these playing out in New Orleans.

POWER OVER is the power to impose one's will onto another. It is the power of superiority that permeates our culture and institutions.

Power Over breeds paternalism—the belief that we know what is best for other people. It is the power of external authorities or experts, whether parents, teachers, doctors, politicians, or religious leaders, who tell us what we are supposed to do and how we are supposed to be. It is the power of entitlement that makes us believe we can take what we want, make demands, and impose our will on others. It is the power that breeds arrogance. In a culture of Power Over we are socialized through rewards and punishment to not question authority and to do as we are told, living in fear of what will happen if we don't.

POWER WITH is the power of solidarity. It is the shared understanding that we need one another to survive, that we are not separate but interdependent. Power With is rooted in love, respect, and an understanding that all living things deserve dignity. Power With is about connection, built and practiced through networks and cooperative structures like collectives, cooperatives, assemblies, food co-ops, and councils. There are many examples around the world of larger-scale Power With bodies such as the autonomous communities in Chiapas, the Movimiento Sin Tierra (MST) in Brazil, the Landless Peasant Movement in Bolivia, and the Indignados Movement in Spain. On smaller scales, Power With relationships exist wherever people work together to meet mutual needs with care and compassion, raising the next generation through intersecting networks of family, friends, and community. Power With relationships are compatible with how humans naturally like to relate to one another, but we have lost touch with this—even though it is all around us, every day.

POWER WITHIN is the power we carry inside ourselves. It is the power we create when we assume self-responsibility and take action on our own behalf. Every person can be an agent of change when we open up, trust, and let our creativity, imagination, and generosity shine. When we exercise our Power Within freely, for the greater good, amazing things can happen. Power Within can be found in compassion, conviction, integrity, and courage. Power Within is amplified when we are grounded and connected to those who came before us, those who are with us now, and those who will come after, knowing we all have a place in the magic we call change. Power Within is the spirit at work!

POWER UNDER is when we give up our power to fear, hopelessness, or the belief that we do not matter. Power Under finds its roots in the trauma of internalized oppression and depression, where we believe we are not enough, bad, wrong, inferior, or less-than. Power Under is bred and cultivated through oppressive belief systems and structures that use violence and fear as methods of control. Power Under is a mentality that emerges when you are taught that challenging authority is useless or that things can't change. It erodes self-confidence and authenticity. It encourages us to hide ourselves and follow the rules, even when the rules are inane, illogical, or destructive. Power Under encourages isolation, self-doubt, judgment, criticism, and the belief that our challenges are based on individual weaknesses rather than systemic problems. Power Under is both a result and a tool of the dominant Power Over, white supremacist, hetero-patriarchal culture.

The government's post-Katrina disaster relief, from the city of New Orleans and its police officers all the way to HUD, FEMA, and the National Guard, was implemented with a Power Over mind-set. The government imposed military control when what the people wanted and needed was comfort and support. The state, operating out of a Power Over lens, asserted itself as the authority and arbitrator of who could go where, and when, preventing people from taking action on their own behalf to rescue and bring relief to those who needed it.

Many of the government's actions appear illogical until we remind ourselves they were operating within a hierarchical, bureaucratic system of command and control. The water systems that were working were shut down. The city's only public hospital, Charity, was shut down and never reopened. The public school system was seized by the state and dismantled despite thousands of teachers and administrators who wanted to come home and continue to serve their communities. Volunteers appearing with boats with medical supplies or to assist in the rescue were turned away at gunpoint, told it was too dangerous, while the police and military saw Black and Brown people as criminals, looters, or threats, despite the very obvious extenuating circumstances.[36] There were army vehicles patrolling the streets. In NOLA, the stated purpose was to protect property and keep people safe. Across the river in Algiers, it was to intimidate and force people out, even though Algiers had not flooded.

Meanwhile, residents in the wealthy communities that were underwater were let back in at will. In New Orleans the police opened a makeshift jail because the real jails were flooded. This new jail was a sickening display of priorities, because the vast majority of those arrested were charged with looting. The police were building jails for people who, in some cases, were taking food and water to literally stay alive while hospitals and schools were deserted. Media portrayals deepened the hysteria and fear around the idea of a population gone mad. The press reported on rumors of killings and rapes in the Superdome, which was housing a largely African American population. This misinformation came from Mayor Nagin himself, who claimed there were "hundreds of armed gang members" killing and raping inside the Superdome.[37]

It came out later that there were only a handful of deaths in the Superdome, and these were overdoses or suicides. There was only one documented killing, and it was of a man outside—not inside—the Superdome. His name was Danny Brumfield, and he was a Black man shot in the back by a New Orleans police officer.[38]

The government's response to Hurricane Maria in Puerto Rico had sickening parallels to what we saw after Katrina, but on an island where residents could not easily evacuate. It is now estimated that as many as three thousand people may have perished as a result of Maria. The command-and-control hierarchies of federal relief efforts resulted in food and medical supplies that were never delivered, and skilled personnel like doctors and electricians who never reached the communities that needed them most. The top-down hierarchy was particularly dangerous in this case because the person at the top, President Trump, infamously complained that Puerto Ricans "want everything to be done for them."

It's hard to escape a Power Over mentality, since this is how we're all socialized—so it was not surprising to find it within Common Ground's work as well. In a tense post-disaster environment, it can feel like every person is out for themselves, and the machismo of paternalism, the entitlement of the wealthy, and the superiority of white people come out strong. There was sexism, misogyny, and toxic masculinity on display as the leadership and voices of women were undermined. In some instances, women felt unsafe or harassed. I remember when one of the Black women called out the "racist, sexist bullshit" at Common Ground and left that very day. There were problems with sexual harassment and at least one known report of a rape. In response, we put more work into addressing racism, sexism, and homophobia within the organization and among the volunteers. We published a public letter acknowledging the problem, and there were some creative activities on the part of the site coordinators who posted signs and messages about sexual harassment around the building.

At one point in 2006, a team from Stanford University came to help us assess Common Ground's work. They recommended that I be hired as the overall coordinator, but instead Brandon Darby, an abusive male leader, was put in charge. He began a purge of the organization, starting with the mostly queer volunteer coordinators at St. Mary's Church. It was a time of great pain and harm, creating trauma within Common Ground's ranks. Two years later, in 2008, Brandon was exposed as an FBI informant tasked with infiltrating activist groups. Today he is a columnist at Breitbart, an alt-right online news outlet.

For the most part, I believe that the majority of people were doing the best they could in an extremely traumatizing situation, and Common Ground succeeded in opening the eyes of many people to the harm that can be done through the abuses of a Power Over mind-set. Pain caused growth, but there was still much to be learned about how to confront and heal the differing oppressions we faced.

The "Power With" of Solidarity

Common Ground's motto, "Solidarity, Not Charity," means *with*, not *for*. When the state's infrastructure collapsed after Katrina, the people rose up. When the state responded with military might, we took action with conscience and love. We kept the truth alive when the media moved on. We built another world amid the ruins, giving hope to tens of thousands of people.

In times of disaster, people are moved to help, giving money to big organizations like the Red Cross. But honestly, this can have little real effect. My friend Carolina started as a volunteer with them in Baton Rouge, but seeing how ineffective they were, she loaded a truck with resources and joined Common Ground. As an organizer, she understood that *self-organization* empowers people to take action, and that's what was missing at the Red Cross. At Common Ground our Power With mind-set was one of solidarity, not command and control, and we understood that people need love and support, not orders and directives. Amid everything else, we became grief counselors for the residents. A kind smile, a hot meal, and the willingness to sit and listen can be the difference between the strength to go on versus slipping deeper into depression and despair.

Our values and practices were rooted in self-determination, volunteerism, shared power, mutual aid, and solidarity. We did not try to be saviors. We were not the ones to make decisions about what would happen to these communities. We were, in fact, guests. It was our job to support the people in asserting their interests, needs, and desires in the short- and long-term recovery process. We did not direct or assert outcomes, but were allies and accomplices to those who called New Orleans their home.

With this mind-set we helped people who were abandoned by the leadership of our Power Over institutions. No one was going to help the Vietnamese fishing community in East NOLA, but Common Ground did. No one was going to help the Indigenous fisherpeople in Houma and Dulac, but Common Ground did. No one was going into Plaquemines Parish, but Common Ground did. We brought people, food, cleaning supplies, skills, information, tools, and love. We set up distribution areas and computer centers; we offered to gut homes, trim trees, clean up debris, repair roofs, provide medical and legal assistance, and fight back to protect homes and public housing units. There was little we would not do if asked. It is estimated that we built a network of twelve thousand volunteers and served over a hundred thousand people in seven parishes.

Today the Common Ground health clinic in Algiers is still operating, as is one of our legal clinics, a home-building project, and a wetlands restoration team. You will still find the Rhubarb Bike Shop and the community gardens that we planted all over the city. Our bioremediation project helped to clean up the land. Many churches, schools, and homes still exist today because of the partnership between Common Ground and the blood, sweat, and tears of the residents with whom we worked.[39] This includes the historic St. Augustine Church, which is still open today thanks to a three-week occupation of residents and Common Ground volunteers that took place when the archdiocese threatened to close it.[40]

It was after Katrina that a group of organizers who worked together in the Ninth Ward moved to support the struggle in Appalachia against mountaintop removal, forming a group called RAMPS—Radical Action for Mountains' and People's Survival.[41] Others went on to support the Tar Sands Blockade in Texas, and thousands more returned home, their lives changed forever as they continued to manifest efforts for racial and environmental justice all across the country. Common Ground volunteers became integral to organizations and movements ranging from Occupy Wall Street to the Racial Equity Institute in North Carolina, as well as Occupy Sandy in New York. In 2012 folks who met at Common Ground founded the Mutual Aid Disaster Relief, which has continued the legacy of autonomous, decentralized, anti-racist disaster relief in response to Hurricane Matthew, Hurricane Harvey, and Hurricane Maria, among others.[42]

At its core Common Ground was about people helping people in a time of great need. It was also a traumatic time for many of us as we experienced the inhumanity of the systems that were supposed to help. In today's world of a warming climate and more frequent large-scale disasters, Common Ground offers important lessons about humane organizing, and reminds us that love, solidarity, hard work, and healing are the fuel that sustains and supports us as we reclaim what has been lost and build what is yet to be.

CHAPTER 7

The Gaza Freedom March and the Power of Taking Space

I t was December 31, 2009, and the police in Cairo were on high alert. I got a call from a friend with a warning: The police had locked down the Lotus Hotel, near Tahrir Square, and were not allowing our people to leave. We were a block away, at another hotel. We had to move fast, so we quickly grabbed what we needed . . . food, water, phones, and don't forget the flags! Our little ragtag band of women exited the hotel and hurried down the street, passing the ornate, tannish buildings of downtown Cairo and the many storefront shops and eateries, including a small restaurant I had frequented all week and the newsstand where I purchased my daily paper.

For the past week over thirteen hundred internationals had been showing our opposition to Israel's military actions against the people of Palestine. We were, in fact, supposed to *be* in Palestine—in Gaza—for a Freedom March, but at the last minute the Egyptian government had denied our passage through the Rafah border crossing into Gaza. So instead we stayed in Cairo, demonstrating at the Egyptian Foreign Ministry, holding up signs at the UN offices, camping outside of embassies, and doing whatever disruptive actions we could to be seen and heard.

Egyptian laws under the then president Hosni Mubarak included extreme limits on the rights to protest, speak, and assemble, so our actions had become like a game of cat and mouse, with the police doing everything they could to stop us and keep us invisible to the people of Egypt. Undercover police in street clothes followed us as we traveled from site to site, darting between cars, occupying public spaces, refusing to be cowed. And now, for New Year's Eve, we decided to gather in as visible a place as possible, where the police might feel restrained from brutality. The Egyptian Museum, a block from Tahrir Square, seemed ideal.

We passed the Mogamma, a huge government building across the street from Tahrir Square. The "square" is not really a square, but a giant traffic circle with seven roads leading in and out, ringing a circular park of grass. It was hard for me to imagine people actually using Tahrir's park when you had to cross through traffic to get there, but then again crossing *any* street in Cairo feels like you're taking your life into your hands. As we neared the entrance to the Egyptian Museum, I spotted a group of police, some with gold visors on their hats and shoulder ribbons to denote a high rank, some with berets, some wearing suits, others in street clothes. That was okay—we could improvise. They knew we were here, but not what we intended to do. We held the element of surprise.

I recognized people from our group gathering on both sides of the street, looking, observing, waiting. As our small group made our way toward the museum entrance, the police immediately came toward us—so we quickly bolted into the street, taking our homemade flags and signs out of bags, purses, and backpacks, yelling, "Free, Free Gaza!" Within moments hundreds of us were in the street, veering in unison like a flock of birds. We held our black-and-white signs high. Our message, FREE GAZA, could be seen everywhere in both English and Arabic.

Tahrir was straight ahead. Would we, could we, actually take the square?

I looked back toward the Egyptian Museum and saw the police to our right in hot pursuit. But there were about a thousand of us flooding into the streets now, chanting and surging forward. We veered into oncoming traffic. Up ahead, police in riot gear, with padded vests and helmets, ran toward us, trying to cut us off. To our left was the sidewalk, bordered by the signature green fences of downtown Cairo. We had nowhere to go, so many of us near the front decided to sit down in the street. Farther down the block, a large group of French demonstrators in their bright green shirts were also sitting. One of them was on a bullhorn, leading a chant, "Viva, Viva Palestina!"

The next thing I knew, undercover police were violently grabbing people, pulling them out by the hair, punching them, making arrests. The crowd roared "No!" at every punch. I saw them try to grab the French guy on the bullhorn—and then they came for me. *Shit!* I went limp as they grabbed me and I became the object of a tug-of-war, with the police pulling me in one direction and my friends pulling me in another. Starhawk and others threw their bodies on top of me, a tactic called puppy piling, just a bunch of soft, limp bodies trying to protect me. The police pulled almost everyone off, but Olivia Zemor, a powerful French organizer, was still holding on! It was quite a scene. The police finally succeeded in throwing me over the barricade and into a pen they had constructed on the sidewalk.

I knew that what these officers really feared was not us, but the Egyptians who had gathered on the sidewalks nearby to watch the spectacle. The weeklong effort to keep us invisible to the public was failing, and the day had only just begun.

Locked Out, Locked In:
The Struggle for Palestinian Liberation

I first became conscious of the Palestinian struggle in the 1980s, when I was co-coordinator, along with Mark Anderson, at the Washington Peace Center in DC. When the First Intifada broke out in 1987, a global peace movement rose up, and in DC we organized, protested, and raised our voices.[1] My connection to the Palestinian struggle has continued over the years, one of the many threads in my life. In 2001 my trainers collective helped develop the training protocols for the International Solidarity Movement (ISM), which is a Palestinian-led, internationally supported, nonviolent movement in support of the Palestinian people against the ongoing occupation by the Israeli military.

In July 2002 a group of us from the Pagan Cluster, in coordination with work that ISM was doing in the West Bank, traveled to Palestine. Our trip included an ISM training in Jerusalem; from there we went to Jenin, a northern Palestinian city in the West Bank. As remains true today, the West Bank was divided into areas with different degrees of Palestinian and Israeli control. Life under military occupation was a daily assault, and intermittent skirmishes and battles sometimes became protracted periods of conflict. A few months before our arrival, the Israeli Defense Forces (IDF) (aka the Israeli Occupation Forces, IOF) had attacked six Palestinian cities during Operation Defense Shield, a major military offensive launched after numerous Palestinian suicide bombings in March 2002.

Jenin was a city where the Palestinian resistance was strong. The IDF cut off water and electricity before entering the town, then attacked with infantry, tanks, bulldozers, and helicopters before moving on to the Jenin refugee camp, destroying it with a dozen armored bulldozers, razing 450 homes in the process. When the battle ended, the IDF would not let medical and humanitarian teams in for several days, leading to rumors that bodies were removed to hide the truth of how many Palestinians had been killed. Human Rights Watch eventually estimated that at least fifty-two were killed, and the IDF reported that twenty-three Israeli soldiers had died.[2]

Upon our arrival to the area in July, we were oriented by local Palestinian leaders, who made clear there was a war going on and they didn't want us in the way. They said, "If you see us pulling kids into an alley, go with them. We cannot guarantee your safety if you're out in the streets." Jenin was in a state of partial recovery and being heavily monitored by the IDF. The signs of war were everywhere: half-destroyed buildings riddled with bullet holes, Israeli tanks driving through the streets, and Apache Blackhawk helicopters overhead. Moving outside the town's main drag of concrete beige buildings, you would find sandy dirt roads where dust rose up with the slightest breeze.

The role of ISM volunteers is to witness, accompany, and be a visible presence when the Israelis show up as a way to deter them from attacking. During my time in Jenin, I observed the many ways war is waged, not just with bullets and bombs but with psychological control. If the Israelis said this was a day for stores to be open and the Palestinians left them closed, the IDF would come in, break the locks, and open the doors. When the sounds of approaching tanks got louder, the makeshift tea stands on the streets quickly disappeared, pulled into alleys, only to reappear when the tanks passed. I learned about the humiliating, terrifying checkpoints within the West Bank that take hours of time to get through while standing in the sun, looking at barbed wire–topped fence walls. I learned how war becomes normalized and how to live in 126-degree heat with tanks on the ground just outside the window. I learned what it felt like to travel from an illegal Israeli settlement built on Palestinian land in the West Bank with pristine homes, manicured lawns, and trash cans lining the sidewalks to the bombed-out Palestinian neighborhoods on the other side of the fence.[3]

Life in Palestine is extremely hard and dangerous. I have witnessed the struggle for thirty years, and in that time more Palestinian land has been lost through occupation, illegal Israeli settlements, and apartheid walls erected between Israeli and Palestinian areas on Palestinian land. The children of Palestine don't remember a time of peace—and cannot be told about it by their parents, who don't remember a time of peace, either. Today much of the West Bank is governed by the Palestinian Authority while Gaza has been governed by Hamas since 2007, but both areas remain under IDF control. The Gaza Strip, a twenty-two-mile stretch of land along the Mediterranean Sea with almost two million people, is known as the world's largest prison because the people are not free to come and go, nor to import or export goods. Israel controls the borders to the north and east. The sea serves as the border to the west (though Israel controls the waters), and Egypt controls access to the Rafah border crossing in the south.

Oppressed people find different paths for their resistance—political, legal, nonviolent action, or armed opposition. Gaza has been a home of intense resistance to the Israeli occupation, including a lopsided military battle between small homemade rockets and US-made aircraft missiles, bombs, and concussion grenades.[4] It is always important to make a distinction between the people of any country and the policies of their government. Many Israelis don't support the occupation, and many Palestinians disagree with the violence supported by some of their leaders, instead advocating for nonviolent resistance while trying to live their lives with dignity, freedom, and peace.

In December 2008 the conflict between Israel and Palestine exploded when the Israeli government began a three-week military offensive on Gaza known as Operation Cast Lead. About fourteen hundred Palestinians were killed, many of them civilians. In the months afterward in Gaza, electricity was down, hospitals were destroyed, and fishermen were shot and killed in their own legal waters. With no legal way in or out, tunnels had become a lifeline for desperately needed resources in Gaza, but now those tunnels were under attack and many were destroyed.

In early 2009, at the initiative of the Palestinians, the International Coalition to End the Illegal Siege of Gaza was formed, and Code Pink—a US-based, women-led peace group started in 2002 in response to the war in Iraq—led delegations to Gaza, bringing hundreds of internationals to witness the destruction and commit to organizing when they returned

Ships to Gaza

During the summer of 2010, the first big international Freedom Flotilla sailed to break the siege of Gaza. It was filled with activists and humanitarian aid workers, and the IDF attacked, killing nine people on the Turkish ship the *Mavi Mamara*. This fueled great global outrage, and friends of mine in the US decided it was time to step up our resistance. We organized the first US Boat to Gaza, called the *Audacity of Hope*, which attempted to sail from Greece in the summer of 2011. Our boat was sabotaged and our mission thwarted by the Greek government, which caved to the US and Israeli pressure. (Greece was facing a severe economic crisis at the time, and their own uprising was in progress in the form of a massive popular occupation in Syntagma Square outside the Hellenic Parliament building. I participated in that occupation and was awed by the organization and fierce resistance of the people.) Since that flotilla, I have been the nonviolence trainer and ground crew for the Women's Boat to Gaza in 2016 and the international Freedom Flotilla in 2018.

home. It was during one of those visits that the idea of an international march in Gaza to commemorate the one-year anniversary of Operation Cast Lead took root. Eventually forty-two countries became involved, each organizing local campaigns and preparing people to come to Cairo and then on to Gaza in December 2009.[5]

Cairo and the Power of Being Visible

During the planning phases for the Cairo trip, I was crazy busy as usual with my peace efforts and organizing in the emerging climate movement. I was also working on mobilizations against the big banks that became part of ongoing efforts ultimately leading to Occupy Wall Street—but that is a story for another chapter! Somewhere amid this hectic fall of

2009, I was in touch with friends, including my dear friends Ann Wright, Starhawk, and Laurie Arbeiter, about the Gaza Freedom March.

I had befriended both Ann and Laurie during our time organizing at Camp Casey in Texas in 2005. Ann is a widely respected organizer who in her previous life was a colonel in the US Army and a diplomat with the State Department. She resigned to protest George Bush's Global War on Terror. Laurie is an artist with the We Will Not Be Silent Project, named after the words of a group of student activists called the White Rose during Nazi Germany, all of whom were eventually killed. Laurie's black-and-white signs and T-shirts carrying powerful messages have been seen at protests all over the world, and I was not surprised that she was bringing them to Gaza. I was already planning to be in Europe in December for the Climate Summit in Copenhagen, so I decided to stay on and meet my friends in Cairo.

The original plan was for all 1,350 people to board buses in Cairo on Monday, December 27, travel to Gaza, and meet with Gazan community organizations and leaders before a mass march with Palestinians and international allies on December 31. Despite months of planning and coordination among solidarity organizations, the Egyptian Foreign Ministry, and various ministries in Gaza, ultimately the government of Egypt—which was beholden to US and Israeli interests—understood that a mass march in Gaza might tip international public opinion further in support of the Palestinian cause. They decided to shut the whole thing down.[6]

I flew into Cairo on Sunday, December 26, with my partner, Juniper, and her daughter. During the taxi ride to the hotel, I was amazed at the busyness of Cairo, a massive city of twenty-five million with people and cars going every which way. I saw the minarets of mosques dotting the skyline, almost all of them with dome-shaped roofs. We traveled down huge roads with traffic moving in all directions. The horns were nonstop as people darted between cars. As the taxi came closer to our hotel, the traffic was moving more slowly and I caught glimpses of markets down the smaller side streets. The weather was warm that day, almost seventy degrees, and our windows were wide open. I could not wait to walk around those markets myself.

Our hotel was a small building set back on a side street. The room was simple, with four single beds, a large window with red drapes, and a ceiling fan that creaked as it whirled above. Another hotel, the Lotus, was about fifteen minutes from us, closer to Tahrir Square and where the core march organizers were staying. After exploring our neighborhood, we headed over to the Lotus, where we immediately encountered intense activity and organizing. People were working on small tables at the restaurant, preparing little cards with pink ribbons that we would tie on the busy Kasr al-Nil Bridge, one of the main thoroughfares with eight lanes of traffic over the Nile River, the next day.

We had heard that the Egyptian government revoked their decision to allow us into Gaza, but now my good friend Ann told me they also canceled our large meeting space at the Jesuit College. We were now 1,350 experienced and motivated international activists with nowhere to go. As you might imagine given the members of this particular crowd, this was not the end but rather the beginning of some amazing, creative plans.

The next day, Monday, was the one-year anniversary of the first day of Operation Cast Lead, a reminder to us all about why we were here. That morning, after waking to the sounds of early-morning prayers, I grabbed a quick breakfast of bread, cheese, and fruit, then headed to the Lotus for a meeting. The hotel was packed, every room and hallway full. We committed to keep pressure on the Egyptian government to reverse their decision and discussed plans to organize delegations to our embassies. But first, our street action. We walked together to the Kasr al-Nil Bridge and were silent as we tied the messages in commemoration of the Palestinians who had died in Israel's attack. Before long, police arrived to flush us off the bridge, ripping the cards off as they demanded we leave.

Back at the Lotus we learned that the government had now canceled our reservations to hold a candlelight vigil on the famous felucca sailboats on the Nile. *Damn!* We went to the boat docks anyway with fourteen hundred candles, one for each person killed during Cast Lead. When we arrived at the docks, the police had blockaded the entrance and created a gauntlet on the sidewalk along a busy road. As our numbers grew, they set up barricades across the sidewalk, packing us into a small area, hoping to limit the footprint of our presence. I could hardly move. The crowd erupted, chanting, "Let Us Go to Gaza, Let Us Go!" To the dismay of the police, we were able to pass and light our candles up and down our cramped line on the sidewalk, creating a beautiful glow.

It was dark now, but the city was still teeming. In fact, it never stopped. When you have twenty-five million people, there is always someone on the move! We headed over to the Mogamma and milled about as our people arrived. This was a flash meeting, which meant we first gathered in less conspicuous small groups; when it seemed like a critical mass was achieved, we swarmed together as a big group. This was the perfect tactic for Cairo, with its many laws against public assemblies.

At the meeting we discussed our overall plans for our week in Cairo. It was already clear that the Egyptians had a simple strategy—shut us down and keep us invisible. The Mubarak regime was a police state and there was a law limiting public gatherings of more than five people, as well as a so-called state of emergency that had been ongoing for twenty-nine years. The Egyptian government did not want the desire and passion of the Egyptian people for freedom to ignite the powder keg that indeed exploded two years later.

Under these circumstances we had to be creative. Their strategy was to keep us unseen, and our strategy was to be as visible and disruptive as possible.

Early on Tuesday morning I headed over to the French Embassy, where the French delegation had gone to negotiate with their ambassador, who had promised buses for the trip to Gaza, but then reneged. Being the fierce activists they are, the French did not leave, but lay down in the street in front of the embassy for many hours, blocking traffic, then set up an ongoing occupation on the sidewalk outside their embassy. One side of the street was now lined with green military trucks, the other with a wall of police in riot gear. The police line extended all the way down the block, making it impossible for passersby to see what was going on.

After speaking with someone about an action later that day at the UN offices, I headed back to the Lotus, where I was told that a group was being detained at the US Embassy. I am a fast walker and bolted right over.

I walked by the embassy first to assess. Just inside the gates I saw about thirty people standing in a group with police all around them. I then held back about twenty feet from the entrance to watch. Near me on the sidewalk I recognized a few others who, like me, were trying to figure out what was going on. We were clustered together, talking, when a group of police walked up and asked if we were American. We said yes. They said we had to go inside the embassy with the others. We said no. They surrounded us and started walking us toward the compound. *Damn!* They were using a tactic I knew well—when I want to move someone threatening away from our group, we surround them and walk them out.

I did not want to be inside the compound. It's the same in any country: Law enforcement does their worst deeds outside the public eye. I quickly said to our group, "Are you willing to sit down?" They all said yes. The moment we reached the barricades lining the embassy's drive, we sat down in a circle and linked our arms. The police had no idea what to do—this was not in their playbook. They brought over more police to surround our circle, which frankly was at odds with their overall strategy of keeping us invisible. As we sat we decided to make a few signs that said FREE GAZA in English to hold up to the passing cars. The one man in our group spoke Arabic, so he made a sign that passersby could actually read.

When the police realized what was going on, a couple of cops came over and roughly grabbed the Arabic-speaking man, literally throwing him over the barricade. After things calmed down, we all stood up and held our signs high above the heads of the police, chanting "Free, Free Gaza!" The police tried to use their bodies to block us from view, but otherwise did not get aggressive, I believe because we were all white women, privileged also by our US passports. After another hour or so, they released us, as well as the people inside. We scurried away, knowing we had yet another action within the hour at the United Nations office. Our efforts to negotiate passage to Gaza failed there, as did my attempt to organize a spokes council. While we had a great first meeting, some of the key organizers were not going to relinquish control.

By Wednesday, the tension in Cairo was high. The government was losing ground in its efforts to keep us quiet and unseen. The local papers carried stories about us with big color photos on the front page, including members of our group who scaled the Pyramids, unfurling a giant Palestinian flag three days in a row. The presidential palace was surrounded by military vehicles. Egyptian activists were calling for a protest at the Journalists Syndicate. This is precisely what Mubarak's government wanted to avoid—the inclusion of the Egyptians.

Hedy Epstein and my good friend Jen Hobbs on hunger strike on the steps of the Journalists Syndicate in Cairo. *Courtesy of Angela Sevin.*

That afternoon I was sitting on the steps at the Journalists Syndicate with a group of activists who had begun a hunger strike at the instigation of Hedy Epstein, an eighty-five-year-old Holocaust survivor. Soon the Egyptian activists showed up. While there had been prior communication between us and them, we had been very concerned about putting them at risk. This protest, however, was theirs, and I had the sense we were giving them protection by occupying the public space alongside them. Speaker after speaker got on the bullhorn, some speaking in English, others in Arabic.

Word was spreading through the crowd that Jodie Evans, one of Code Pink's co-founders, had negotiated with Suzanne Mubarak, the president's wife, who then negotiated with President Mubarak to allow two buses into Gaza. Many of the international organizers were shocked to learn this. Code Pink was the primary administrative anchor and initiator of the Gaza Freedom March, but delegations from the participant countries had their own processes within the larger framework and expected to be included in big decisions like this one.

Code Pink is an organization of predominantly white women with a lot of resources and privilege, which is part of why they were so effective in organizing the march. Earlier in the year, they had reached out to Suzanne

OUT OF THE TOOLBOX
Tactics That Take Space

Taking space disrupts business as usual and catches the attention of those nearby. It sends our message powerfully, in words and in actions.

HUMAN BILLBOARDS. I love what I call human billboards! These are big signs that two or more people hold up at intersections or in front of doors. They are incredibly effective at getting people's attention and even motivating them to take action if you amplify the massage by adding a hashtag. They are one of the most effective visibility actions because they pair a human face with the message on the billboard.

DELEGATIONS are a great tactic that allow people to enter the space of power and engage with the actual decision maker or their minions. If the decision maker won't engage, they for sure will know you were there! It's good to have something to leave behind, like a notice, memo, petition, or letter. If they threaten to call the police, you can say, "Please do! There is criminal activity by your office!" You can leave before or when the police arrive. This is a great tactic in banks, politicians' offices, corporate offices, and embassies.

OCCUPATIONS are a very old tactic where people who are fighting for a cause take land or space and occupy it. The tactic itself requires additional layers of planning and preparation: If you want to take something for the long haul, you have to be prepared with food, water, sanitation, and protection from the elements as well as the police.

STRIKES are one of the ultimate direct-action tactics, and you know they are powerful because we see the lengths people in power go to stop them! Strikes are clear acts of non-cooperation as people withdraw participation from the machine that oppresses them. They often use picket lines to block access. General strikes have been extremely effective at creating a crisis, and we could sure use more of them today.

PICKETS are a great tactic for almost any action in front of buildings or entrances. Pickets are very visible and a powerful way to take space near doorways. They can also make it hard to enter the building or establishment. Whether they are silent, chanting, or bursting with song, a strong picket can really shake things up.

TAKING INTERSECTIONS. I have spent a lot of my life in intersections, not just walking through to get here or there, but sitting in, dancing in, and occupying them. At a tactical level, taking intersections can be complex and might involve planning for teams, timing, points of entry, the tactic itself, support with attention to safety, getting your message out, and legal/jail support if there are arrests. It can also be as simple as walking out into the street as a group and blocking traffic by sitting, standing, or holding a banner.

BLOCKING BRIDGES AND HIGHWAYS is a powerful yet dangerous tactic. You need to make sure you have enough people and good signage or flyers to pass out so that people understand the plan. Using props that are hard to move can help, as can designated drivers that stop in front of you. If you don't intend arrest, you need an exit strategy. I've learned that blocking exit ramps can be a safer way to block a freeway with less risk and equal impact.

Mubarak, receiving permission for their earlier delegations to bring humanitarian aid through the Rafah crossing. Now negotiations with her were happening again, but this time none of us knew about it. Some were excited; others were pissed, particularly the South African delegation. Code Pink worked to ensure that each country would have people on the bus, but amid the uproar, many countries refused to send a representative.

The fissures in our coalition deepened when the Egyptian foreign minister—angry at Suzanne Mubarak for undermining his decision to prevent any of us from entering Gaza—began a public propaganda campaign claiming that only the "good" people were being allowed into Gaza, while the hooligans and troublemakers were staying behind. A list was being created by Code Pink and vetted by the government. Ultimately only about 100 people, out of the 1,350 of us, were on the list.[7]

Anger can be destructive, but it can also become a creative force. That night we held a big coalition meeting at the Lotus Hotel to figure out what to do. I'm not sure how I got the facilitation card for this meeting, but it was not pretty. Emotions were high. The buses arranged by Code Pink were not negotiable, and they would leave the next morning. The South Africans reasserted the call for a Boycott, Divestment, and Sanctions (BDS) strategy toward Israel and proposed we create a declaration in support of it.[8] We achieved consensus, and many of us signed a document—still in effect today—that increased international unity and commitment to the BDS strategy.[9]

(Almost) Taking Tahrir Square and the Power of Occupying Space

The next morning I made the rare decision to sleep in. My name was on the list of internationals allowed into Gaza, but I decided not to go. The trip was dividing us, and I didn't want to be a part of that. Still, I was glad that our humanitarian aid would make it in.

I was woken by the phone in my hotel room. It was a friend saying, Lisa, you need to come to the buses, it's getting ugly over here. *Ugh.* I pulled on some clothes and quickly walked over, hoofing past the Journalists Syndicate on the way, where a few Egyptian protestors remained from the action the night before. I turned the corner and saw two buses parked along the curb on 26 of July Street in downtown Cairo. I also saw that the police had placed large barricades on the sidewalk, dividing our group into two sections—those with their luggage waiting to board the buses, and the section of people taunting those waiting to board. The crowd was chanting, "All or None, All or None!" and "Get Off the Bus!" The Egyptian police stood at the perimeters, watching the success of their divide-and-conquer strategy.[10]

It was painful to see members of our group yelling at others not to go. The next thing I knew, about a dozen people got off the bus, and the crowd cheered. One of these people was a Palestinian woman with tears streaming down her face.

Ann asked if I could help bring some calm. I waded into the crowd, feeling uncertain. There were people from all the country delegations— I saw shirts about Gaza in Spanish, Italian, French, German, English, and more, and multilingual banners hanging off the barricades facing the street. I clapped and called out, "Friends, let's come together. Circle up!"

Slowly a circle formed and focus shifted from the buses to our gathered group. The Palestinian woman who got off the bus sat in the center. I asked if she wanted to speak. Through her tears, she told us this was the only way she had to see her family, but she didn't agree with only a select few going. She felt that staying in solidarity with the international coalition was important.

One by one, others spoke out in pain about the devastation in Gaza and their disappointment at not being able to go. We started to sing together, again shifting the energy from anger to love and solidarity. After a while I asked everyone if they were willing to leave and head back to the hotel for a meeting. There was work to be done. Tomorrow was New Year's Eve, and though we had expected to be in Gaza marching fifty thousand strong, instead we would march for Gaza in Cairo.

———

And so it happened that the next day, a thousand of us flooded into the street bordering Tahrir Square, surrounded by police who had spent an exhausting week trying to outmaneuver us. Despite the government's best moves, here we were in a very public, very visible street, the police resorting to outright violence to keep us away.

After the police attacked the crowd and put me and others into a penned-in area on the sidewalk, the scene quieted down. My ribs were hurting and I felt roughed up, but on the whole I thought I would be okay. There were hundreds of us in the sidewalk pen secured at each end by a wall of riot police, who served the dual purpose of keeping us in and hiding us from the eyes of passersby. There was nowhere to go, so just as we had done at the United Nations and Journalists Syndicate, we hung our banners, raised our signs, and began chanting. Some of our people on the outside of the pen were able to hand us food. Later we gathered to talk strategy, deciding to occupy the location until midnight. It was New Year's Eve, and we knew we would get media attention around the world.

But as the hours passed, so did the will to stay. An idea of regrouping at midnight at the Mogamma was taking hold, but I was, like *No*, let's stay here!

I was very upset. Every time we committed to occupy, the political will quickly dissolved. The same thing had happened the day before outside the UN. How could we create a crisis if we kept giving up space? A few others stayed with me, including Ken Mayers, a thoughtful and gentle man from Veterans for Peace who understood my disappointment. But there was nothing we could do. We did not have the numbers to make any real impact, so we left, too, carrying sadness in our hearts.

We went back to our hotel, and after some food we prepared for the New Year's Eve midnight convergence at the Mogamma. We arrived early with candles to spell out FREE GAZA. As we lit the candles, many Egyptians joined in. Once again, the plainclothes police moved in, forcing the Egyptians to leave. It seemed like the police were everywhere in Cairo, following us, talking to us, tracking our every move. It just was what it was.

During the walk back to our hotel, my phone rang. It was a friend from the hotel saying, "Lisa, don't come back, the secret police have been here twice looking for you." I was, like Okay, *shit*. I was exhausted and in pain and wanted nothing but my bed. Instead, we made our way to a different hotel, where I arranged to sleep in a friend's room.

The following evening Juniper packed up all of our stuff, took a cab, got out a few blocks from where I was staying, then walked over to get me. We had tickets for the night train to Luxor. We loaded up our taxi and the driver said, "Twenty geneih." I said, "What? It's usually five." Star turned around from the front seat and said, "Lisa, when fleeing the secret police, do not haggle with the taxi driver."

Right! Twenty geneih it was.

———————

Every uprising has many roots, and I was awed when a little over a year after we took these actions in Cairo, the Egyptian people took Tahrir Square. Many Egyptian activists had been unhappy that the Gaza Freedom March negotiated with Suzanne Mubarak, feeling it gave the Mubaraks legitimacy that countered their campaign to delegitimize them. Many of us understood and agreed. I believe our persistent creative actions provided some inspiration to those Egyptian organizers who had been struggling for years and were now well on their way to changing their world.

From the presidential palace to the United Nations, the US and French embassies, and the jewel of the city, the Egyptian Museum, we took space and took action. The police efforts to stop us failed, for no matter how hard they tried to contain us and keep us invisible, people saw what was happening. Many Egyptian activists supported us and tried to participate in our Week of Actions. Almost every time they did, however, the undercover police forced them to leave, adding fuel to their discontent.

In thinking more generally about the events that led to the Arab Spring, I'm reminded of the lessons from complexity science, which teaches that the process of change and growth is not linear, but cyclical and forward-moving. There is often no clear cause and effect, but small actions, perturbations, and fluctuations that can cause an entire system to change. When the street vendor Mohamed Bouazizi self-immolated in Tunisia, who would have guessed that the monarchy would fall? This is the process of emergence, when something new arises from what once was. These same truths can create negative outcomes as well, as small actions ripple through unstable systems, shifting things in radical, unpredictable ways. From the beauty of the Arab Spring, we also saw atrocities and pain in Egypt and the roots of what became the Syrian Civil War.

As people organizing in this complex world, we can take action and push things in the direction we hope for, while recognizing that we are not in control of the outcomes.

OUT OF THE TOOLBOX
Swarming and Crowd Tactics

Swarming is a natural phenomenon—ants colonize, birds flock, fish school, animals herd, and bees swarm. It is a form of intelligence that emerges from decentralized interactions within a large group.

Swarm tactics are when a dispersed group of people suddenly converge for an action at a specified time and place, like our "ballpark" strategy in Cancún. It can also be more spontaneous or revealed at the last second, like a flash mob or flash meeting.

Similar to the swarm tactic is the *dispersal tactic*, when a crowd suddenly separates and disperses quickly in different directions. This keeps the opposition off guard and unprepared for what you will do next. This is also good for when people get cornered and surrounded by cops. New opportunities are created the second you start moving. With *random crowd tactics*, the general idea is to keep moving, as this creates possibilities you cannot foresee. Never sit still, even when they block your way or when you don't have a plan. The challenge is capitalizing on opportunities once they

As international activists in Cairo, we had many levels of privilege protecting us—yet despite this privilege, the government still tried to repress us. This is why people in authoritarian societies are afraid to confront their governments: The consequences can be brutal. Our privilege allowed us to be less afraid as we demonstrated what was possible. Much of what we did was simply occupying space, being visible to the appear. How do you communicate contingency plans to the larger group: Flags? Texts? SMS? Random tactics can incorporate lots of carnival-like elements.

Tips for Swarm Tactics

Remember that in swarms there is no centralized control, but there is a decentralized process of following and leading.

For swarms to work well, we need to use our judgment and make choices based on the information we have in the moment. We need to avoid fragmentation, where we're not in touch with what others are thinking or doing, and we want to make sure we have built trust so that everyone feels like they're a part of the group.

When beginning a swarm, look at the diversity of options and identify a range of possibilities. From there, narrow the choices and select based on what will work well in that moment in the local conditions.

Stick together, but not too tight. Avoid crowding and collisions.

Go in the same basic direction.

If the swarm is under attack, scatter in a flash in many directions. You might also encircle the attacker or split into multiple groups. Come back together when the threat has passed.

public and uncompromising in our dissent, showing that the people have the power to take, hold, and transform spaces of government control into zones of liberation and resistance.

People's occupations—which essentially just means taking and holding space—are one of the oldest tactics in the book. (Governments can also occupy, and to great harm, which we saw when the colonizers occupied this continent, and see again in Palestine today.) Governments come up with countless laws to prevent the people from fighting for their livelihoods, rights, and needs, but no law can prevent a person from existing in a public space. Sometimes there are severe consequences for doing so, but there is little that can be done to prevent people from showing up and being seen.

Occupations for liberation allow us to hold, reclaim, transform, liberate, move through, and shift space that has been taken by oppressors. Taking space is physical, emotional, mental, and spiritual. Occupations signal that we will hold our ground and that we are prepared to fight for what we love. Resistance can take many forms, but fundamentally it is about exposing and changing those who oppress, refusing to let them fully escape the consequences of their actions—even if the consequence is simply facing the people they are hurting. We may be outnumbered, outspent, and outgunned, but our very presence makes clear that we do not consent.

In Cairo I often felt disappointed at our failure to hold space for longer periods of time—to extend the occupation. But looking back on it, even holding space for a short period had a big effect, because these were spaces the government was accustomed to controlling more fully.

Some occupations are short-lived, but their effects ripple in ways that are never fully quantified or understood. In 2011 the mass occupations of the Arab Spring inspired the occupation at the Wisconsin capital in protest of the then governor Scott Walker's anti-union legislation and pro-corporate budget. That occupation sent waves of joy across the US, and even though that particular battle was lost, our imaginations had been ignited, making the idea of Occupy Wall Street more possible. Occupy Wall Street, in turn, helped inspire the occupation of Gezi Park in Turkey in 2013 and the Umbrella Revolution in Hong Kong in 2014.

Longer-term occupations, like the one in Tahrir Square, can succeed in permanently displacing the people in power. Downtown Cairo became a place and space of liberation, and though the government retaliated, it ultimately had to flee.

Thinking about the Global Justice movement as a whole, the ongoing protests of the G8, the WTO, the FTAA, and others caused the people in power to erect fences around entire portions of cities because the people occupied the streets. In this case it wasn't a particular government, but rather capitalism, neoliberalism, and intergovernmental trade deals that the people were protesting. By occupying literal physical spaces, we also occupied and eroded the psychological spaces where world leaders allowed themselves to believe that their polices were inevitable.

When the powers that be need to hide away behind fences or in hard-to-get places, it has a psychic effect. It erodes them at some energetic level. They might feel anger, humiliation, or just inconvenience—whatever they're feeling, they are forced to think about their actions. Their conviction that what they're doing is just certainly diminishes, if only in a small way.

When we choose the ground on which we will fight, our opponent cannot ignore us, at least not for long. Great examples of this were the protests surrounding the G8 summit in Heiligendamm, a small city on the northern coast of Germany.

Germany 2007: Taking Space in Heiligendamm

The global protests against the G8 summit in Heiligendamm, Germany, showed a resurgence of energy not seen since Seattle. It somehow made sense that the anger in Germany in 2007 matched how people felt in Seattle in 1999. The neoliberal policies that we in the US had been living with since the late '70s were really beginning to peak in Western Europe, where contracts and legal obligations among labor, the employers, and the government have always been stronger, with better employee benefits and a more reliable safety net. Europeans were beginning to suffer from the corporate practices that had long been a mainstay in the US, such as dodging employee benefits via part-time, contract, and temp arrangements. They called it precarity.

Major global summits like the G8 had historically met in large cities, but the Global Justice movement had the capitalists on the run, forcing them to choose secluded, rural locations where they hid from the people they claimed to represent. For the 2007 G8 summit, the administration of Chancellor Angela Merkel chose Heiligendamm, an isolated resort town on the northern coast of Germany. The summit itself took place at the Grand Hotel Heiligendamm, an exclusive luxury hotel on an isolated compound surrounded by a dense border of forests and the open fields and bogs of the countryside.

A $17 million fence was erected around that hotel.[11] The government thought the location would be easy to secure, but they underestimated the power and creativity of the people.

There was a tremendous infrastructure set up to support the anti-G8 mobilization. With the summit in the middle of nowhere, convergence centers were established in multiple cities, including Rostock (twenty-five miles from the Grand Hotel), Hamburg, and Berlin. Informational booths about the mobilization were set up in parks and on street corners.

Two main camps were erected closer to the summit. One, Camp Rostock, was organized by mainstream NGOs and the Block G8 effort. The other, Camp Reddelich, was only five kilometers from the Grand Hotel and housed the more militant direct-action-oriented folks. This was where I stayed. Camp Reddelich was stunning, perhaps the best infrastructure of any camp I have participated in thanks to the Wandergesellen, the German craftspeople who built bathrooms, showers, a stage, a bar, a playground, and a watch tower. Tents were set up neatly in rows, and a massive central tent had geometrically arranged hay bales for seats. An Indy Media Center, a pirate radio station, and a group of videographers calling themselves G8TV not only documented everything that happened, but also projected each day's events in the evenings for people to watch.

On June 2, several days before the summit began on June 8, over a hundred thousand people converged in Rostock for the Make Capitalism History march to protest the G8's lack of action on critical issues like poverty, war, and the climate.[12] The march was festive, but the tension between police and demonstrators was hard to miss. The German police had waged a crackdown, raiding homes, offices, and convergence spaces in Hamburg and Berlin. The media was amplifying the politicians' unfounded accusations of terrorists among the demonstrators. Nothing was found to prove these accusations, but the police used these public scare tactics to legitimize illegal actions like no-go zones, canceling permits, and instituting travel bans to prevent international protestors from joining.

As we got closer to the summit's opening, thousands of us hunkered down in the two camps, Rostock and Reddelich. Our goal was to somehow block access to the hotel on the two primary roads leading to it. Both were rural roads. One was to the west of the municipality of Reddelich, the other was to the east, coming from Rostock and the town of Bad Doberan. Between the hotel and both of these roads were open fields and woods.

At Camp Reddelich, I offered some direct-action prep sessions and attended those held by others. As the opening day of the summit neared, these trainings shifted toward a plan put forth by some of the German anti-nuclear activists called the Block G8 initiative: Together they were advocating for mass civil disobedience and something called the five-finger strategy. This turned out to be one of the most brilliant space-occupying tactics I have seen.

The goal of the five-finger strategy in Heiligendamm was to block the roads leading to the Grand Hotel. On both sides of these isolated roads were wet, boggy open fields. We knew the roads would be protected by hundreds, if not thousands, of riot police.

During the training I watched in amazement as the Germans demonstrated how to approach the police not in row formation, but in column formation, with multiple columns approaching a line of police. As the columns get closer to the police lines, they begin to spread out, like the fingers on a hand separating slowly then straining wide apart. These separate fingers, or streams, divide into yet smaller streams, and when they reach the row of police, the person at the front of each stream tries to jump between two officers. When those two officers reach for that person, the next person in the column jumps through the space opening up in the police line, and this process continues one person after another.

The Germans believed that by using this strategy, we could flow between the police lines and successfully achieve a peaceful occupation of the road.

A group of us from the US had formed an affinity group, and as the first Day of Action began, we were undecided about which action to join.[13] Ultimately our group decided to split up and participate in different actions, with myself and three others taking off to catch up with the five-finger march. We made our way up a dirt road and came out into a field bordered by giant evergreen trees, where about a hundred yards to our right, along the tree line, we saw a massive human river of parallel marching columns flow over a rise in the hill. It was thrilling.

We ran to catch up and joined one of the columns. Our backpacks were filled with food, extra layers of clothes, and a space blanket that the organizers distributed to everyone. We held yellow net bags filled with hay, which the organizers had also distributed. I didn't really get why we had those bags until we came over a rise and had to cross a shallow creek. The bags were piled together to create a little bridge to step across without soaking your feet. Brilliant!

Over the next rise, our mass march began to divide into columns of five, each streaming forward but with increasing space in between. Before long, we could see the road ahead. Sure enough, there were police all along it, facing the fields. As we got closer to the road, each human river continued to separate into smaller streams, each running parallel to the next. The time was upon us to take the space. The first person in each line jumped between two police, and as the officers leaned in the grab them, the next person jumped through.

We were determined and we moved quickly. Jump here, jump there, jump through. Thousands of us did this, one after the other. We were like water flowing through every possible opening, flooding past the police and onto the road. It was working! We completely overwhelmed them, and before I knew it we had taken the road.

The police gave up and retreated to the security fence, now the only thing standing between us and the hotel. It was not necessary for us to take down the fence, as we had already shut down access to the hotel by occupying the road.

It was a gorgeous, sunny day. Our occupation became like a festival as our joy in success was abundant. We shared food, conversations, and fun. A group in superhero costumes moved through, stopping here and again to do a piece of street theater demonstrating their superpowers. The clowns had moved to the security fence and were blowing bubbles through it. Some cut down the green net fencing on the side of the road and made hammocks in the woods on the road's perimeter. Soon enough mobile kitchen trucks from our nearby camp appeared and began distributing food. All those wonderful hay-filled bags made great seats, from which we ate and watched as the police landed helicopters in the surrounding fields. Out of them came more riot police.

When night approached and the cool air settled around us, the hay bags became pillows while the space blankets kept us warm. I walked among the crowd, the space blankets reflecting the moonlight like a shim-mering sea. This calm sea rocked us deep into sleep as we rested, preparing for potential rough waters ahead.

The next morning we learned that those blocking the other road, the one leading from the town of Bad Doberan, had been hit hard by the police, who emerged from helicopters in the fields and started just beating people. We also learned that a small road to the southwest near the town of Wittenbeck was being used by G8 attendees to get in, so we made a new plan. Some of us would stay, while others would try to get to the other road. I had a rental car and we decided to go. Once there, I saw that the police had created a checkpoint. Pretending to be a tourist, I asked a cop what was going on. He said there were protestors everywhere and nowhere. At that exact moment hundreds of people bolted out of the woods, crossed the road, and headed into the woods on the other side. We joined in.

The woods opened into a field, and on the other side of the field was the back road we sought, now lined with a fence and water cannons. The day became a dance of people challenging the fence, using tarp banners for protection from the water cannons. A group of drag queens showed up with giant multicolored beach umbrellas. There were clowns every-where and a naked bloc that marched in formation toward the police only to be pepper-sprayed in their most vulnerable places, and oh that did not look fun.

In the end, the roads leading to the Grand Hotel were blockaded or occupied during the three-day summit. Leaders of the G8 had to arrive and leave via helicopter or boat. No matter how hard they tried, they could not hide as we exposed the unpopularity of their policies and undemocratic processes.

Some occupations last for years, while others last for hours or days. In either case they create space to practice self-organization, as well as time for infrastructure building, strategic action planning, and care for one another. From these spaces, we can launch myriad actions that both disrupt and liberate. In my experience, occupations can be successful in less tangible ways because they are so visible. They ignite imaginations; they build community and can change the narrative put forth by the state.

We see occupations happening all the time. In February 2018 teachers in West Virginia occupied the state capitol during a teachers' strike, which led to a 5 percent pay increase. These courageous actions inspired similar teachers' strikes in Oklahoma, Arizona, Colorado, and Los Angeles. Groups around the country have attempted to occupy ICE facilities, and while there has been limited ongoing success, there were days when the facilities or courts had to close. These actions speak for themselves and keep the resistance alive. Increasingly we are seeing occupations by students, by immigrants, and by climate activists. The occupation outside the Tornillo child detention camp in December 2018 inspired people across the country to step up their creative resistance to immigrant detentions.

With every election cycle, a lot of people become focused on voting, believing that it's the best way to change things. But occupations and other space-taking tactics remind us this isn't true. It's an insidious argument. Democracy is not just pushing a button every two years; it's how we live our lives and shape our future every day. It requires participation, effort, commitment, and risk. We are all agents of change, whether we see it or not. But change requires action, creativity, and, at times, sacrifice—a willingness to risk what you have for something greater. We all make choices every day that can either oppress or liberate. We can keep perpetuating the negativity of the status quo, or we can choose life—engagement, community, self-organization, and action. Which do you choose?

CHAPTER 8

On May 12th, Occupy Wall Street, and the Power of Multiplying Our Strategies and Tactics

O n the morning of September 17, 2011, I hopped on the subway at 33rd Street in Manhattan, disembarked at Wall Street, and entered street level on Broadway. It was a lovely autumn day. This was the first morning of Occupy Wall Street, a movement that would sweep the country and then the globe—but I wouldn't have guessed it then. Our initial group numbered in the dozens. By afternoon hundreds were gathered, and by nightfall, thousands of us filled Zuccotti Park. We had become the 99 percent.

I had flown into New York several days prior to help train a gathering of about fifty people who were organizing in response to an advertisement printed in July by the Canadian anti-consumerist group Adbusters. The call to action featured a striking image of a ballerina standing atop the iconic Wall Street bull, and the accompanying caption stated, #OCCUPYWALLSTREET. SEPTEMBER 17TH. BRING TENT.

This public call for occupation is often credited as the origin of Occupy Wall Street, but I hope to show that OWS was the beautiful, organic, unpredictable fruition of organizing that had been ongoing for several years. The truth is, OWS did not begin with the occupation of Zuccotti Park, and it did not end when the NYPD shut that park down. The seeds of the Occupy movement were planted during the financial crisis of 2008 and in 2009, when organizers around the country coalesced around the idea that big banks were robbing the people. And the spirit of Occupy continues today as politicians proudly call themselves socialists, as the call for free college and child care has become mainstream, and as the fight for a $15 minimum wage has made inroads in state after state.

When I look back on the Occupy Wall Street time period, I don't see a protest at a single park in New York City. I see deeply and inextricably linked people-powered movements, campaigns, and protests unfolding all over the country and all over the world.

One such campaign occurred four months before Occupy began. In some ways it made Occupy more possible. In early 2011 I worked with a consortium of labor, grassroots, and community groups on a Week of Action called On May 12th that culminated in a march on Wall Street that was twenty thousand strong. The model used for On May 12th was soon replicated by a campaign called the New Bottom Line, which carried out similar efforts in ten cities rolling out over the fall of 2011—the same time period that Occupy encampments popped up all over the country.

To my delight, folks with the New Bottom Line began working with the Occupiers: Occupy Oakland, Occupy Los Angeles, Occupy Chicago, Occupy Boston, and more. This was a moment when mainstream initiatives like the New Bottom Line leveraged the grassroots, direct-action efforts of Occupy, and vice versa. It was a fascinating time to watch the dance between the mainstream and the margins.

When it comes to tactics, I have always advocated an "all of the above" approach. Multiplying our strategies and tactics means multiplying our power. We don't need to choose between civil disobedience and so-called mainstream tactics like permitted marches. We can weave all of these together, making the fabric of our resistance stronger and more beautiful.

Movements are not just about winning policy victories; they are about inspiring a sense of power in the people. Movements create an embodied experience of a new paradigm. They are a place of intersection between diverse forces with similar agendas. The autumn of 2011 was a time when movements converged, putting out a clarion call about the importance of getting corporations out of politics and putting democracy back into our daily practice. Nearly a decade later, that mission is more urgent than ever, and the creativity, compassion, and commitment of this amazing time offers needed lessons for today's political realities.

All Roads Lead to Wall Street

In the winter of 2011, I got a call from my friend Stephen Lerner, the long-time labor organizer I worked with on the Justice for Janitors campaign in the mid-'90s. Whenever Stephen calls and asks for help, I show up! Like me, he is an in-betweener, working with people and groups from varied backgrounds, trying to ensure everyone is at the table—unions, policy researchers, community-based groups, nonprofits, attorneys, artists, and of course direct actionists.

Stephen asked if I was available to help create some disruption around the budget crisis in New York, where billionaire mayor Michael Bloomberg had proposed cutting $91 million from essential programs like teachers' salaries, early childhood education, libraries, senior centers, programs for the homeless, and firehouses.[1] Meanwhile, Bloomberg's real estate development policies had caused New York rents to rise by 10 percent between 2005 and 2011, the same years that median household incomes fell.[2] Stephen described an emerging coalition between the United Teachers Federation—a mainstream labor group—and a number of community groups aiming to intervene in the budget process.

Fortunately, I was planning to be in NYC anyway working on the US Boat to Gaza, so I was, like, Sure, tell me more!

New York, like other cities across the US, struggled with budget shortfalls as the devastation from the subprime mortgage crisis was still playing out. Deregulation, lax regulations, predatory lending, and quasi-government cover through Fannie Mae and Freddie Mac had enabled tens of thousands of low- and moderate-income families to buy homes they couldn't afford. The sham mortgages were bundled and resold as good investments. This large-scale scam was exposed when people were unable to make payments on their mortgages, and the US housing bubble burst in 2008.

There was a brief moment when it seemed possible that those who had orchestrated the disaster would pay the price. Instead, the banks got bailed out and the people got sold out! The US government bailed the banks out to the tune of $700 billion, all while working people were evicted and foreclosed on. By 2010 unemployment had skyrocketed to 10 percent as homelessness, suicide, and bankruptcy rates increased. The pain was great; the anger was greater.

During the first years of the recession, national community-based networks like National People's Action, Alliance for a Just Society, the PICO National Network, and Right to the City, among others, advocated for policies and regulations to hold the banks accountable. These folks rose up together with the common goals of holding banks accountable, winning policy changes, and mitigating damage to homeowners through new policies like principal reduction on loans. They were taking action, targeting JPMorgan Chase, Bank of America, and Wells Fargo, as well as key industry groups like the American Bankers Association and the Mortgage Bankers Association. By 2011 these groups decided on an alignment, calling themselves the New Bottom Line.[3]

There was a general feeling in the air that all of these activities would result in something important. I remember sending an email to my network of direct action friends saying that this movement was building and could benefit from more of us getting involved.

Little did we know that the struggle for economic justice and democracy was about to dominate the global scene. On December 17, 2010, a struggling Tunisian street vendor, Mohamed Bouazizi, self-immolated as a drastic form of protest against the economic conditions and police harassment that were devastating his business. His act inspired a revolution that ousted the Tunisian president and spread hope to other Arab nations. In January 2011, the Egyptians rose up, occupying Tahrir Square, instigating the fall of the dictator Hosni Mubarak. Closer to home, students in Wisconsin occupied their state capitol. When Egyptian activists ordered pizza for these students all the way from Tahrir Square, you could feel the love and solidarity. We were witnessing the emergence of a global community connected by social media and bound across languages and oceans by the belief that another world was possible.

On May 12th was born in the midst of all this. Stephen was working with three others—Jon Kest of New York Communities for Change, Michael Kink of Strong Economy for All, and Michael Mulgrew of the United Federation of Teachers—to build a coalition with the capability to roll out a full Week of Action in Manhattan.[4] An overarching goal was to change the narrative about wealth inequality in New York from a story about poverty to a story about a revenue crisis. The people weren't the problem; the billionaires and the banks were the problem as they drained the city coffers through fees, interest rates, and tax breaks, forcing politicians to cut basic public services like education and health care. Politicians needed to recoup our stolen money rather than continue to cut programs.

Michael Mulgrew, the president of the United Federation of Teachers (UFT), was heading a huge union representing most of NYC's public school teachers. The union was concerned because six thousand teachers' jobs were on the chopping block, not to mention educational and child welfare programs. The union had the political and financial backing needed to create a true crisis for the city. We put a proposal together for a Week of Actions involving collaboration among over a hundred NYC organizations—education advocacy groups, community-based groups, religious groups, anti-poverty organizations.[5] You name it, we all had a reason to fight this battle. We worked for several months at the office of Strong Economy for All in the UFT building on Broadway, in the heart of Wall Street. But Mulgrew wasn't ready to commit the funding for such a large, risky mobilization.

A meeting was planned for early April, and I wanted to attend. I hadn't been invited to previous meetings—maybe because I'm a woman, maybe because I'm a scrappy street girl. Whatever it was, I needed to be at the table. I got off at the Wall Street stop that morning and walked to the office slowly, trying to breathe deeply and calm myself. I have a tendency to get frustrated when I'm being excluded from the table with people in power. But I also knew that if I practiced patience and calm, I could be a steady force to open things up between the players.

I rode the elevator up to our offices and headed to the conference room, where Michael Kink, Jon, Stephen, and I discussed strategy. I said, "Listen, I need to be there. I think I can help."

They all agreed. *Well, that was easier than I thought!*

We headed over to the meeting space, where Jon introduced me as the action coordinator to Michael Mulgrew, who asked right away if I could lay out the plan. I responded the same way I do when training activists: I created a simple vision of a complex mass action.

Our goal, I explained, was to make it impossible for the mayor to ignore us. We wanted to reframe the narrative: The city wasn't out of money. The big banks had stolen money from the city and needed to pay it back through increased taxes and decreased loopholes. Our policy experts had prepared a report showing how the city could reclaim up to $1.5 billion simply by changing the contracts they had with the banks.[6]

Meanwhile, we would put public pressure on the banks. We had identified dozens of players in Wall Street, Midtown, and the Upper East Side, including the headquarters of the big banks, the law firms representing them, companies like the American Insurance Group that worked with the banks, private equity firms, and of course the New York Stock Exchange. We would engage all of these players with office delegations, public leaflets, protests, and more in a week of actions that would build excitement for a big rally, march, and possible civil disobedience on May 12.

I asked Mulgrew to imagine thousands of people pouring into Wall Street from every direction. May 12 would begin with a number of separate rallies gathered around core issues—public education, housing, transportation, immigration, health care, the peace movement. These separate gatherings would peel off at a predetermined time and simultaneously march toward Wall Street. Once we flooded the area, teach-ins all over Wall Street would educate the public about the same topics highlighted in our marches—the banks' impact on education, health care, and so on. Tourist groups do this all the time while gathering on city streets. Instead of an architectural tour, these would be educational tours about the budget crisis.

Dozens of organizations had already committed to provide leadership to helm the actions. On May 12th would therefore provide excellent training for leaders in unions and nonprofits across New York—including, of course, Mulgrew's own union, the teachers. *So . . . what do you think?*

There was a pause and some silence. Finally, Mulgrew said he liked what he heard, but he wanted the teachers' march—by far the largest—to be permitted. He liked the teach-in idea and imagined there would be many volunteers for it. He wasn't sold on acts of civil disobedience, but he was open to it. He supported our plan and prepared to commit the funding we needed to make it all happen.

Multiplying Our Tactics and Mapping Each One

During the next month we worked furiously to coordinate a week of actions involving over a hundred participant organizations. I was staying in Midtown at 34th and Lexington, a straight shot north on the green line from Wall Street. The apartment belonged to Johanna Lawrenson, Abbie Hoffman's partner in both life and activism. The two of them had no kids together, but there are about six of us who consider ourselves their kids.[7] Staying at their home reminded me every day that we walk on the ground laid by others. In 1967 Abbie and other anarchist protestors threw dollar bills on the floor of the New York Stock Exchange, causing the men in suits to scramble after the crumpled bills. Here I was almost fifty years later creating a different kind of scramble on Wall Street . . . I hoped, anyway.

We were determined to make the mobilization fun, energetic, and impactful. To this end, we incorporated a wide range of strategies. Foremost was our openness to the mix of groups involved. There were unions, community-based organizations, social service agencies (these agencies rarely participate in large mobilizations, but it's awesome when they do!), nonprofits, student groups, grassroots groups, and artists.

Artwork is too often seen as a frill or an "extra," but really, artwork is fundamental. Can you imagine a large-scale mobilization without colorful signs, posters, banners, puppets, and music? Not to mention, these works of art are useful in taking up and holding space. I asked my friend David Solnit, a master of art and revolution, to come help us anchor the artwork . . . and he did! Little by little, I was pulling in my direct-action friends. The strategic incorporation of artwork requires resources and preparation. You need lots of materials, tools, large spaces, artists, and imagination

We secured a huge indoor area at the Coalition for the Homeless as an art space and asked local artists to contribute posters, signs, stickers, flyers, and more. The release of our street art began weeks in advance, including promotional materials and images for media outreach. Closer to the Week of Action, we wheat-pasted posters, put up stickers, and kicked off a social media campaign to create visibility and a sense of momentum.

Our strategy was similar to what Stephen and I worked on nearly twenty years prior in the Justice for Janitors campaign—a model that has proved successful again and again. The idea is to escalate our actions over time and place, creating a sense of crisis for the power brokers, as discussed in chapter 2 on Weeks of Action, including the importance of research, targeting deep and broad, media strategies, and building it up with multiday actions!

We were planning ten marches organized around topic areas, and we needed to recruit and train the leadership for each. One of the most important decisions was whether the marches would be permitted. When a march is permitted, the city and police essentially barricade you in, dictating where the march can go and what you're allowed to do, curtailing your ability to create a sense of unpredictability and limiting acts of civil disobedience.[8] We decided that with the exception of the teachers' union

Mobilization poster for On May 12th actions on Wall Street.
Courtesy of Seth Tobocman.

march, all marches would be unpermitted. This decision alone created a sense of real excitement.

We planned to use public parks in the Wall Street area as assembly sites. In New York it's legal to assemble and march on sidewalks without permits, so we planned to depart from our assembly sites and march along the sidewalks, and from there take the streets. Without the permits, where we got squeezed was the use of bullhorns. In the early 2000s the police started requiring permits for bullhorns, which are extremely useful when trying to direct the flow of thousands of protestors. We were able to adapt by using the "people's microphone," whereby the crowd repeats the words of each speaker, amplifying their statements. This became famous just a few months later at OWS.

Essential to our planning was the use of maps, calendars, and action grids. The following pages outline how we did it.

Mapping Your Targets

It's impossible to exaggerate the importance of mapping in both planning and executing strategic actions. I have always loved maps. The map isn't just a tool or guide, but a key picture of the terrain on which we operate. Maps allow large groups of people to have a common image in their minds about the area and the plan of action. Maps illuminate ingress, egress, flow, one ways, exit ramps, and allies. They are safety tools in unfamiliar areas, illuminating hospitals, churches, and other safe spaces. They help us decide where to concentrate our resources.

During the planning phase, it's all about visualizing where your action targets are located and planning actions around multiple locations. The first step is researching and listing the potential targets—something that is discussed in detail in chapter 2. The basic idea is to compile databases with the corporations, businesspeople, and politicians who have the power to make the changes you're hoping for, along with power-mapping the various organizations (industry groups, religious groups, sports clubs) with whom they're affiliated. We had about thirty targets for On May 12.

Once you've figured out who and what the possible action targets are, upload your spreadsheet into a mapping program and shazam! I've worked on multiple campaigns in which the central strategy aligned only *after* we analyzed the maps; this was the case with On May 12th. Our zones of concentration became clear—we had more targets in Midtown than on Wall Street! This resulted in a decision to focus our morning activities in Midtown, shifting to Wall Street during the shorter afternoon hours. Concentrating in geographic zones also magnifies the impact on the people in that area.

We used Google Maps to visualize the layouts of our action targets, placing "pins" on their relative locations. Some of these were larger, well-known locations like the JPMorgan Chase headquarters, while others were smaller targets, such as hedge funds, where we might stage a smaller action like an office delegation. We also mapped high-end restaurants, private clubs, and the political and cultural gems that support or entertain powerful people.

We used such maps to strategize our schedule, allowing for big impact in short periods of time. One of our morning delegations chose the cluster of targets on Park Avenue, while another delegation organized actions at the Fifth Avenue and 51st Street cluster. We were able to roll out more actions in a compressed time period because each cluster had only a few blocks to walk from site to site.

Maps can be used to plan and organize all sorts of actions, not just delegations. Today's online maps are extremely useful at understanding traffic flows and points of constriction where traffic backs up. Whether you're planning a banner drop, a marching route, or a blockade, maps can help everyone understand where they need to go. Action leaders might have separate, more detailed maps for single actions, including where all the other groups are located at any given time. I have learned that when everyone has a common vision and understanding of what's happening, where, and why, our chances of success are greater.

Calendaring

Using internet research, newspapers, or handouts at tourist centers, you can build a calendar of meetings and events for the city council, industry group, private clubs, corporations, cultural centers, hotels, and the public. Each event can add a piece to the puzzle of how to escalate action when we're trying to create social disruption. We may want to go to the public to educate and garner attention, or we may want to go to the symphony, opera, museums, or theater productions where our targets are on the board, or are donors. We may want to go into hotels for conventions, and so on. Once you have a good calendar, you can decide which events make the most strategic sense.

Action Grids

Once you have your targets, your maps, and your calendar, you can start organizing it all into an action grid. This will allow you to plan your tactics. It helps you see which targets will be engaged, where, and what resources you will need for each activity. Weekly and daily action grids can be planned weeks in advance, with adjustments made along the way. Ideally you're doing dozens of actions every day, with mealtimes, training, and debriefs built in.

Our actions for On May 12th escalated over a course of four days, culminating with the On May 12th rally and marches. Each day brigade—carrying out smaller actions involving only five to fifteen people—needs a leader, a plan, materials for visibility and noise, and tools like letters or petitions to engage your targets. We then organized one public action each day that involved more supporters and included announcements to the press. These public actions helped to build momentum and get media and created a sense that something big was going down.

Table 8.1 replicates the weekly action grid that provided everyone a holistic understanding of the four-day campaign. Each day began with coordination meetings for the folks leading the actions, followed by registration and an action and legal orientation for the participants. By 8 AM the day brigade or action teams headed out just in time for morning rush hour.

In addition to this weekly schedule, each individual action had its own more detailed action plan. In both the mornings and the afternoons, our delegations fanned out at locations in Wall Street and Midtown, including corporate offices, bank lobbies, private clubs, restaurants, and politicians' offices. The delegations were made up of staff, members, or volunteers from the organizations that were a part of our effort, alongside grassroots activists and students.

On Monday, our first Day of Action, we had ten teams leafleting subways and then hitting five locations each. Those teams then converged to do bigger actions outside of key offices—that's over fifty hits going down within the first couple hours of a weeklong campaign! We then rolled out another twenty or so actions in the afternoon.

It's good to start the week with "introductory" activities that engage the public in as many places as possible, like leafleting at subway stations or noise actions on street corners. We needed the public to feel like something different was going on. We then followed the public actions with

Table 8.1. Action Grid

MAY 9–13: WEEK OF ACTIONS SCHEDULE, NEW YORK		
Time	Monday, May 9	Tuesday, May 10
7:00	Coordination Meetings	Coordination Meetings
7:30	Registration/Coffee	Registration/Coffee
7:45	Orientation	Orientation
8:15	10 Teams Head Out	
8:30	Building and Subway Leaflets	Tax Event for Private Equity and Hedge Funds, Princeton Club (15 West 43rd St)
9:00		
9:30	Delegations Midtown (10 Teams) Deliver Letter	Midtown Intersections, Carnegie Hall (881 7th Ave)
11:00	Break	Travel
11:30	Bank Conference, DoubleTree (569 Lexington Ave)	World Financial Center
12:00	Real Estate Board of NY, REBNY (570 Lexington Ave)	Goldman Sachs (85 Broad St)
1:00	Lunch	Lunch
1:30	Debrief	Debrief
2:00	Orientation	
3:00	ATM Actions Wall Street Delegations (6 Teams)	Marches Through Wall Street, Flash Mobs at Targets
4:00	Human Billboards / Leaflets	
5:00	Travel	Debrief
5:30	Boehner Speech at Economic Club Forum, Hilton Hotel (1335 Ave of Americas)	
6:00		
6:30	Teacher Training	
7:00		Action / Legal Trainings
8:00		KOCH Brothers Action

Wednesday, May 11	Thursday, May 12	Friday, May 13
Coordination Meetings	Coordination Meetings	
Registration/Coffee	Registration/Coffee	
Orientation	Orientation	
Teams Head Out	Teams Head Out / CCA Action	
Building and Subway Leaflets		
	Corrections Corporation of America Action	Debrief Week of Action
Midtown Lobbies (2 Teams)	JPMorgan European Midcap Conference (383 Madison Ave)	
	Living Wage Rally, City Hall	
Break		
Bank of America (115 West 42nd St)	Special Actions Prep	
Lunch		
Debrief		
	Pre-Action Meeting	
Downtown Lobbies (2 Teams)	Prop Distribution	
	Assemblies Begin	
Debrief	Wall Street Marches Begin	
Volunteer Training	Street Teach-Ins Begin	
Action Coordination Meetings	Public Assembly and Dinner	
	Close	

delegations to offices. These tactics might then escalate to picket lines, human billboards, lobby actions, office occupations, and street protests, which build hype and tension for the culminating events on Thursday.

All told, there were about seventy-five actions on corporate America going down on Monday alone, which certainly started the buzz going.

On May 12th: Taking the Streets

The first day of On May 12th was a beautiful, sunny Monday, with the air that nice mild temperature between spring and summer. Our ten teams fanned out all over Midtown, handing out flyers and sending delegations to targets in the finance industries. Five teams convened to picket at JPMorgan Chase, while another five picketed at Bank of America. All ten then converged at another Bank of America, one of the most corrupt entities in American banking, and together headed up the block to a nearby hotel.

We had recently learned about a conference at the DoubleTree with many of the biggest players in banking attending. We entered through a side door, made our way up the back elevators, and walked right into the conference room, where we saw the podium and microphone unoccupied.[9] This seemed like a lovely opportunity to educate bankers about how their greed resulted in cuts to education and health care programs, so we walked up, took the mike, and explained how we were sick and tired of the banks taking our money and our homes. We appealed to them for support, but instead they came at us with security. We took our exit, chanting as we went.

We then crossed the street to REBNY—the Real Estate Board of New York, which had fought so hard to take away renters' rights and affordable housing in New York. We set up a picket line and used the people's mike to tell the story of what REBNY was doing. At this point, the police grabbed our first arrestee—a young, queer, African American man, proving once again that racism is alive and well in the NYPD. We dispatched our legal team to the police station, finished up our REBNY action, then headed back to our convergence space for lunch and a debrief.

Another last-minute action was added to the schedule when we learned that House Speaker John Boehner would be addressing the Economic Club at the Hilton Hotel on Sixth Avenue. We decided to crash the event while throwing a party for the rich in the hotel lobby.

OUT OF THE TOOLBOX
Materials for a Week of Action

This list of material considerations is only partial, but it gives you a taste of the ingredients for success!

PROMOTIONAL MATERIALS. Public flyers, email blasts, social media campaigns, posters, stickers, online ads, newspaper ads, calendar listings, materials for your political and media strategies like reports, informational flyers, delegation letters, teach-in handouts, PSAs, press releases, op-eds, and letters to the editor.

ART SPACE MATERIALS. Big sheets of cardboard, rolls of cloth and bedsheets, paint, masking tape, duct tape, wire, bamboo poles for flags, assorted lumber, markers, zip ties, rope, glue, paintbrushes, cans and cups for paint and brushes, rags, utility knives, hammers, screwdrivers, staple guns, drills, glue guns, drop cloths, LCD projectors, worktables . . . and more! Common art projects include placards, flags, banners, puppets, action props, light signs, and more.

MATERIALS FOR MARCHES. Route maps, flags, banners, noise-makers like whistles, drums (five-gallon buckets; sticks and rope), or popcorn kernels inside soda cans, cameras, chant sheets, bullhorns, chalk to leave messages, identification for roles (vests, armbands, sashes, patches).

FOOD AND BEVERAGE NEEDS. Supplies for meetings, trainings, and day-of. Considerations include who is in charge of food, how many to expect each day, restaurants that might donate meals, and bulk buying for high-volume needs like water, cups, and granola bars.

TACTICAL COMMUNICATIONS MATERIALS. Bikes, runners, phones, radios, sound systems (stationary and mobile), text loops, conference call numbers, bullhorns, social media, flags, and whistles.

To that end, we pulled together helium balloons, party hats, horns, and suit jackets to dress ourselves up a bit. Upon arrival, half of us went to the second floor to crash Boehner's speech, while another group headed to the lobby with the balloons, horns, and party hats. We threw quite a party, marching around in a circle under a big crystal chandelier, chanting, "Banks Got Bailed Out, We Got Rich." The hotel security was on us fast. I peeled off to warn the folks on the second floor, but they didn't need a warning; security was already on them and the police were on the scene. I was almost out the front door when a cop grabbed me. *Shit!*

I hadn't planned to be arrested that evening and expected to get out fairly quick, but the cops told me their captain had instructed them to put me through the system instead of the typical citation release. I watched them try to decide what to charge me with, since really it was a bogus arrest. Before long I was moved to a small cell upstairs and locked up for the night. Later they brought me cold McDonald's. It turns out McDonald's has a contract to provide food in the NYC jails. Now, imagine that . . .

By the time Thursday rolled around, I was exhausted but happy at how well everything came together. Our culminating event—marches, rallies, and teach-ins—would start at 4 PM, allowing teachers time to get off work and travel to their assembly site near City Hall.

There were eight assembly sites for marches all over southern Manhattan. I headed over to the art space around two o'clock to make sure our distribution operation was under way. Folks were busy loading vans with banners, flags, posters, and noisemakers. Meanwhile our leadership arrived at each assembly site to greet and organize their teams.

I got on a bike and rode from site to site. The advocacy groups at the South Street Ferry had about a thousand people so far. Over at the Wall Street Plaza, unions had gathered for a march and rally focusing on jobs. At the Vietnam Veterans Memorial, the peace assembly had gathered. Over at the Staten Island Ferry, the group marching for housing rights was also packed with almost two thousand people. I hopped back on my bike and headed to Battery Park to check on the immigration march. There, too, everything seemed to be in place. Nearby, the Transport Workers Union, TWU, was holding down Bowling Green across from the MTA office. And finally I headed over to the youth group, who were drumming and dancing around the Wall Street Bull.

All the march coordinators were on a conference call together, so they knew when each site was ready to roll.[10] I marched out with the youth group, then jumped back on my bike. Through the narrow, winding roads of the Wall Street area, I saw people marching, then I made my way to where the narrow roads flowed on to Wall Street and down to Water Street, the site of our teach-ins. I saw the marchers pouring in from both sides. It was already packed, and the ten thousand teachers were still on their way!

I remember seeing Ken Srdjak, an artist from DC who came in to help, up on his stilts in the middle of Wall Street with one of our massive bright yellow flags, MAKE BANKS PAY, flying high. In every direction, the bright yellow banners and flags lit up the financial heart of the economic superpowers. Soon the Rude Mechanical Orchestra marched into Wall Street, and the crowd boomed with delight. We were one big family, taking the streets, chanting and singing, feeling connected as together we demanded economic justice for the people.

The On May 12th Week of Action was ultimately successful in pressuring lawmakers to make concessions on the New York City budget. The mobilization and ongoing work prevented the layoffs of forty-two hundred teachers and pressured the city council to restore over $100 million in funds for schools, childcare, libraries, and firehouses.[11] The governor of New York reversed his stance on taxing the wealthy, instead choosing to *increase* the millionaire's tax.

The longer-term impact of On May 12th was that it fueled ongoing resistance, as many of the people became organizers and participants in Occupy Wall Street.

Occupy Wall Street: Taking the Bull by the Horns

The first round of resistance after May 12th was a three-week encampment outside City Hall called Bloombergville. This was put together on a somewhat ad hoc basis by an anarchist-leaning group called Organization for a Free Society and a socialist-leaning group called New Yorkers Against Budget Cuts, both of whom had been key participants in On May 12th. Bloombergville included daily teach-ins and nightly assemblies, structures that were replicated during OWS.

In July, when Adbusters put out a public call to Occupy Wall Street just two weeks after Bloombergville disbanded, the folks in New Yorkers Against Budget Cuts were continuing to organize, using traditional tactics like marches and rallies. Meanwhile another group of people, mostly anarchists inspired by the Arab Spring and uprisings in Greece and Spain, started to discuss the idea of General Assemblies (being used in Europe) as a democratic process and space that could allow large numbers of people to get involved.[12] Hoping to advance this strategy, they worked with New Yorkers Against Budget Cuts, calling a gathering for August 2 that was dubbed a "people's general assembly." But in fact this proved to be nothing more than a typical rally, which frustrated the anarchists who had a different vision of what could be possible. Georgia Sagri, an artist who had participated in the recent street protests in Greece, shouted, "This is not the way a General Assembly happens! This is a rally!"[13]

With that Sagri and others, including David Graeber, the well-known anthropologist and activist, formed a new group, the New York City General Assembly, NYCGA. Leading up to September 17, they organized numerous activities on Wall Street to create momentum. Lo and behold, an organizing vision and process for OWS were under way.

During this time, I was working with the New Bottom Line to replicate the On May 12th model in ten cities around the country, dubbing it the Fall Offensive. I was fired up and elated that the Week of Action model would be used to continue our offense against the big banks.[14]

While I was furiously preparing for these mobilizations, I received updates from my friend Marisa Holmes about the New York City General Assembly's organizing around S17.[15] Marisa is an organizer, filmmaker, and media worker who got involved early with the NYCGA process. The folks I was working with in the New Bottom Line—mostly union and nonprofit people—were curious but doubtful about these plans to occupy Wall Street, but I kept telling them it felt real. Oh, the irony, because by the time we rolled out our New Bottom Line Week of Action in Oakland, Occupy Wall Street was on fire, and they supported our work!

In the days before September 17, I took a week off from my organizing with the New Bottom Line to fly to New York and train folks in the

Lisa at the OWS Action Against Police Brutality on
March 17, 2012. *Courtesy of Erik McGregor.*

New York City General Assembly. There were about fifty people in attendance—smaller than I expected, but it was a devoted group. The training,
like many of my others, focused on building relationships, exploring our
emotions, practicing our reactions to police violence, and engaging in
role-plays of our tactics. I formed the group into a circle and asked a
series of questions. Is this your first time at an action? Has your family
been impacted by the financial crisis? Who has been to jail for justice? We
were not planning for civil disobedience, but we provided everyone with
legal information and gave out the legal hotline number.

Our favored location for the occupation was Chase Plaza off Pine
Street, a block away from the Stock Exchange. But law enforcement got
wind of these plans and by September 17, Chase Plaza was barricaded.
Zuccotti Park then became the favorite because it was a big space and
open to the public twenty-four hours a day.

OUT OF THE TOOLBOX
Scouting and Reconnaissance

Mapping is important if you want to understand the opportunities for action, but mapping alone isn't enough. There is also tactical reconnaissance, which is a fancy way to say, go scouting! Buildings and streets will tell you what you need to know if you take the time to look. Google Maps is pretty awesome, but nothing can replace your own two eyes, live, in real time.

Before you set out, look for online maps with floor plans or tenant lists in target buildings, and draw a map if you need to of your action area. Visit the site several times, especially during the time of day you expect to take action. Once you have observed and understand a space, action ideas often emerge. Taking photos can be useful when your memory fails!

Things to Look for When Scouting Buildings

Security: desks, cameras, personnel

Entrances, exits, loading areas, fire escapes

Sidewalk space, landscaping, trees, benches

Windows: Think about the visibility in and out

We had no idea what would happen next, but we were ready.

On the morning of the seventeenth, I walked down Broadway, feeling right at home, having taken this route so many times during preparations for On May 12th. As I approached the Wall Street Bull, I spotted my friend Mike McGuire, my buddy for the day. We commiserated over the

Places for possible
  banner drops
Parking and parking garages
Retail outlets/eateries

Janitor/staff schedule
Bathrooms
Wi-Fi access

Things to Look for When Mapping a City

Highways (entrance and exit
  ramps), roads, and streets,
  noting lanes and traffic flow
Bridges for banner drops
One-way streets: great to
  go against the flow and
  harder for police to follow
Police stations, jails, and
  courthouses where your
  people will be brought
Meeting spaces and commu-
  nity centers for trainings
  and support
Parks to assemble and create
  safe space; hearts of the city
  where people can gather

Construction sites that will
  have materials
Parking garages: to park,
  to film from, or for
  banner drops
Tourist sites and cultural
  centers like museums,
  theaters, operas
Public transportation for
  getting to and from actions
Hospitals in case people
  are hurt
Public buildings, bus
  stations, and libraries:
  places to escape to if the
  police attack

small numbers. I looked around and saw people of all ages, including a group of youth doing yoga.

Little by little, the group grew from a couple dozen to a few hundred. Some folks started to march, circling the Bull. We had a couple of people on the media team filming; the legal team, with their green hats, stood by in case they were needed. We were a scrappy lot surrounded by the businesspeople of Wall Street hurrying by in their suits and shiny leather shoes.

Finally we started to march, heading toward the Stock Exchange, chanting, "Banks Got Bailed Out, We Got Sold Out!" The Exchange was barricaded, so we changed course and headed to Zuccotti. We flowed into the park, down the stairs, passing a giant red sculpture of arches. We spread out, filling the space. The crowd was chanting, "Whose Streets? Our Streets!" Before long, some of the organizers told the crowd that dinner—peanut butter sandwiches and fruit—would be served around six, followed by a General Assembly.

The crowd was growing, so the organizers huddled to talk about conducting an assembly with so many people. We decided to stand on the marble benches in the northeast area of the park. We had bullhorns, but the sound didn't travel far enough, so again we used the people's mike, a process where the crowd repeats back what the speaker said. It worked! The main item of business was at hand: Would we stay and occupy the park?[16] We broke off into small groups to discuss. There were probably two thousand people in the park by now, and many intended to stay!

Working groups were in place to provide food, legal support, media outreach, and more. We reconvened into the General Assembly, and I addressed the crowd about the process of self-organizing. As I stood on the bench, all I could see was a sea of people in all directions. That's when I realized the gravity of what was happening. It was getting dark and starting to cool off, but the energy all around was like a fire warming my soul. I urged the crowd to self-organize. Just like our brothers and sisters in Egypt, Spain, Greece, and Wisconsin, it was our time! I reiterated that infrastructure was in place, but we needed to organize ourselves to make this work. At the simplest level, we needed cardboard—lots and lots of cardboard! It was going to be a cold night, and this would provide needed insulation to sleep on, not to mention great sign-making material.

At some point during that first evening, the park was renamed Liberty Plaza.

We began the next morning with a protest on Wall Street. The media was not interested, but there were plenty of police. Chants of "We Are the 99 Percent" echoed everywhere. This was the beginning of daily marches to Wall Street to protest and ring in the People's Bell at the same time the

Stock Exchange rang in their opening bell. The media was still ignoring us, but the people were paying attention, and they were joyously traveling to New York to join us.

Two Movements Converge

Several days after OWS began, I took my leave, needing to continue my organizing with the New Bottom Line in Oakland, then Los Angeles and Chicago. Little did I know that Occupy would soon sprout up in all of those cities. It was inspirational and awe inspiring to witness the synergy that developed between these two movements—divergent in philosophy and tactics, yet united by a common belief that we needed to hold the capitalists and the big banks accountable for the economic recession and all of its miseries.

The New Bottom Line had coalesced in 2011, becoming a highly organized collaboration using strategic policy research to expose how the banks and mortgage lenders caused the foreclosure crisis, and how city budget shortages weren't about scarcity ("there's not enough money") but rather the exorbitant fees our cities pay the banks. Corporations were bankrupting our cities, and we aimed to get that money back.

The New Bottom Line's fall offensive began with a Week of Action in Denver, then Oakland, Boston, Los Angeles, and Chicago. In California the foreclosure crisis was hitting hard. ACCE, the Alliance of Californians for Community Empowerment, was working statewide to win legislative reforms to support working people across the state. Their campaign, Re-Fund California, targeted the billionaires and banks that were draining state coffers and displacing thousands of homeowners.

During the planning stages for our Week of Actions in Los Angeles, I became acquainted with Rose Gudiel, a member of ACCE and also the Service Employees International Union (SEIU), one of the country's largest unions. In 2009 Rose missed a single mortgage payment on her home after she suffered two simultaneous setbacks, one of them a tragedy: Her brother, Michael, was killed, and around the same time her job with the California Economic Development Department was temporarily furloughed as part of the state's budget crisis.

When Rose started to repay the next month, her bank, OneWest, refused her payment and said she needed to go through a loan modification process, which ultimately had to be approved by Fannie Mae, which owned the mortgage. This process was lengthy, labyrinthine, and opaque, and the bank eventually rejected Rose's loan modification without explanation.[17]

In September 2011 Rose received an eviction notice. She decided right then and there to stand up to the lenders. Fannie Mae and Freddie Mac had received a $187 billion bailout from the federal government while working people like Rose were losing their homes.

Meanwhile, Occupy LA was kicking off its occupation of City Hall on October 1. I decided to attend that evening's General Assembly and asked Rose if she wanted to come along and share her experiences. We made our way down to City Hall, where everyone was milling about or spread out on the lawn. I ran into a few people I knew from when I lived in Los Angeles, and they helped me navigate how to get Rose up to the podium as a speaker.

Rose was nervous. It was a big crowd, and this wasn't her usual community. I said, "Rose, these people are going to love you and support you. They might even get involved and help you occupy your home."

When Rose's turn to speak came, her voice was strong. She told the gathering about the death of her brother as tears rolled down her face. She said she was not going to let them take her home! The crowd roared. In this moment the connection between two disparate forces—Occupy Wall Street and the New Bottom Line—was cemented. Our Week of Action was set to begin in two days, and now the Occupy organizers were fired up to help us out.

———————

One of our most creative actions that week in LA was an encampment outside the $26 million Beverly Hills home of Steve Mnuchin, then the head of OneWest Bank.[18] (Today Mnuchin is secretary of the Treasury in Donald Trump's cabinet.) We pulled our cars off to the side of the road and walked single-file up the steep hills of Bel Air toward the mansion with our props—a mattress, blanket, pillows, a side table, a lamp, a rug, and a few signs. From these hills we had a beautiful, panoramic view of the city. When we reached Mnuchin's gated home, we set up our "bedroom" in his driveway and held up our signs, the largest of which read, YOU TAKE ROSE'S HOUSE, WE'RE TAKING YOURS!

The media arrived quickly, followed by the police. Our police liaison talked with the officers, negotiating for more time while Rose spoke out. We then gathered our props and started back down the hill, enjoying our view every step of the way.

Wednesday brought another creative action as we converged in a Pasadena parking lot near Fannie Mae's offices. With a little rope-a-dope distraction at the security desk near the side door, we whisked in through the front door and quickly set up our props in the lobby: a table, chairs, and a sign that read NEGOTIATION TABLE. Our intention was to negotiate with a Fannie Mae representative regarding their unethical foreclosures. We were, after all, their customers. If this was a legitimate business, shouldn't they want to speak with us?

Rose, her eighty-year-old disabled mother, and their parish priest sat down at the table. We asked if we could please speak with a Fannie Mae representative regarding Rose's mortgage . . . but instead, they sent the police, who arrived along with the media. The folks in the lobby were on the phone with people up in the offices, and for a moment we thought they might actually send someone down. They did not. Instead, the police arrested Rose, her mom, the priest, and two allies. Along with these arrests came more media exposure for our campaign.

The next day was our big march in downtown LA, which was now co-sponsored by SEIU . . . and Occupy LA! Within just a week Occupy had become an important ally. The Occupiers were pretty green when it came to marches and street actions, while ACCE and SEIU had lots of experience. This was a great opportunity for the union folks to teach the Occupiers a thing or two about taking the streets.

It was a beautiful, sunny day in LA, and the streets were our domain. Working in teams, our two marches flowed out in different directions, each part of the march with its own tactical team and list of targets to visit along the way. As we neared the intersection of Seventh Street and Figueroa, a third team took over a Bank of America lobby, holding up a giant banner calling for repayment of the billions of dollars that BOA owed the American people.

As the BOA actions caused chaos on the corner, I called our sound truck guy—who was waiting down the block—and said, "Now!" He slowly moved the truck into the intersection as we began to fill it, blocking off all

Logistics for a Week of Action

During a Week of Action, there are a lot of balls in the air at once. One of the ways to deal with all the tasks is to form *working groups*, which are typically needed for bigger actions. Working groups include logistics, research, action, media, publicity, training, art, and more. By allocating responsibilities among working groups, the breadth of logistical considerations becomes more manageable. Here's a partial list of what our On May 12th working group coordinators were dealing with:

SPACES. Finding spaces for trainings and meetings; phone banking spaces; week-of organizing spaces that can hold large numbers; spaces for housing people, et cetera.

PUBLICITY AND RECRUITMENT. Getting as many groups and people involved as possible through phone banks, flyers, email blasts, social media campaigns, and street posters.

CREATING HYPE. This can be done by preparing well-researched reports that expose the problems and the people who are creating them. Visability actions also help.

incoming traffic. A group of union activists and Occupiers began a sit-in, blocking the intersection. And just like that, we had occupied both the intersection and the bank.

Right then Jono Shaffer, a brilliant strategist and a good friend from my Justice for Janitors days, called down to me from the back of the sound

ACTION. Action planning includes site scouting, developing a scenerio or action framework, and creating roles for people to fill when planning and executing the actions, including tactical people, traffic pacers, leafleters, police liaisons, banner holders, chant leaders, legal observers, videographers, tweeters (somebody in charge of Twitter and other social media), media liaisons, and more.

TRAINING. This team makes sure that everyone is oriented to the plans, has the information they need, and has practiced the tactics in advance. Training builds confidence, discipline, and cohesion.

ART SPACES. These need to be large and ideally accessible 24/7. They each need tables, walls, floor space, and big doors to get giant props in and out.

FOOD. For meetings, trainings, volunteers, and actions!

LEGAL. Recruiting lawyers and legal observers, setting up legal hotlines and people to staff them, establishing a system for tracking arrestees. Also, lining up drivers for jail support, lining up food and water for jail support, raising bail money, and organizing a legal defense fund.

MEDICAL. Contacting medical collectives, organizing street medic trainings, compiling and disseminating information including a list of nearby hospitals and recommended materials for first aid kits.

truck: "The bank called Rose and they're going to renegotiate her loan. The eviction and foreclosure are off!"

Holy shit! We did it! We hugged one another just as the riot police mobilized. We quickly got Rose up on the truck to tell everyone the good news. The crowd exploded with cheers and a dance party broke out right there in the intersection. The police backed off and let us have our celebration, and after about ten minutes, we wrapped up our street blockade and called for others to stay in the fight. We had only just begun.

Collaboration, Not Competition

Rose's fight for her home ignited a movement of labor unions, community-based organizations, and Occupiers. It was called Occupy Homes, and it spread across the country, adding to the work of other groups working with people to protect their homes, like the Home Defenders League and Take Back the Land. Occupy Homes and Take Back the Land took militant action, occupying homes and land, while the Home Defenders League kept the legislative pressure on, leading to successes like the California Homeowner Bill of Rights, which passed in 2013.

Occupy Homes wasn't the only effective collaboration that emerged between preexisting organizations and Occupy activists.[19] Collaborations included Occupy Student Debt, ongoing work around the Robin Hood Tax (which continues today), and multiple climate actions, including the People's Climate March and Flood Wall Street.

In retrospect, these collaborations seem inevitable—as desperation from the economic crisis spread, the existing mainstream organizations needed a boost, and Occupy provided that and more. These groups were all concerned about the economic crisis, but their approaches were different. Occupy believed the system needed to be radically reimagined. It embraced self-organized networks, direct action, and people's assemblies as spaces for self-governance, whereas many of the mainstream organizations believed that policy reform would solve the system's problems.

When OWS was in its planning stages during the summer of 2011, some of the folks I worked with in the New Bottom Line had a sense of disdain. These were national organizers from labor and community-based groups, and more than once, when I shared news about the momentum building around S17, I heard things like "But do they have any resources?" or "We're not sure it makes sense to align with them."

I have found that large organizations often underestimate the power of the grassroots. They mirror the dominant culture, embodying traits of hierarchy and Power Over found in white superiority, patriarchy, and capitalism. There tend to be decision makers who hold a lot of power at the top, then managers, staff, and members at the bottom. Even groups that talk about being member-led can suffer from the many ills of hierarchical-based organization, including a lack of transparency, unhealthy working conditions, competition for resources, fear of challenging power, and the desire to control in order to protect the brand. Within this mind-set, only groups that are *already* organized, or that *already* have resources, are seen as having power and worth.

What we experienced during Occupy was mainstream organizations supporting, then sometimes co-opting Occupy's energy and language. This is a historical phenomenon that repeats, with the mainstream either excluding the margins or pulling them inward, trying to assimilate us into their strategies. This could be seen in the 99% Spring trainings in 2012, which were led by national groups that started off embracing civil disobedience before tamping it down, excluding all talk of civil disobedience in the trainings.

I have worked in both worlds and recognize and respect both. Organized people within structured organizations can be very powerful. But they're wrong to dismiss the potential of unorganized people to self-organize in times of crisis. Self-organized movements are dynamic, creative, and flexible. They don't always last long, but they can create rapid, radical change. I believe that movements are strong when people with different perspectives can work together, adding value to one another. This is something that requires respect and mutual support.

One of the beautiful things about Occupy Wall Street was its people didn't come into it carrying their organizational affiliations, even if they had them. This allowed OWS the flexibility to join forces with organizations like the New Bottom Line who already had plans and campaigns under way.

About a month into Occupy, the New Bottom Line abandoned its uncertainty about the Occupy movement and wrote an open letter to encourage ongoing collaboration. The letter read, in part:

Dear Friends:

The New Bottom Line expresses support for the Occupy actions initiated on Wall Street that is now spreading to hundreds of cities across the nation. . . . We admire and are inspired by your energy, creativity, and commitment. . . . The New Bottom Line has worked together with Occupy groups in Boston, Los Angeles, Chicago, Iowa City, St. Louis, Seattle, and other cities and looks forward to continued collaborations toward our shared goals of holding Wall Street accountable.

Campaigns like On May 12th, the New Bottom Line, and Occupy Wall Street were born from different strategic orientations, but were woven together into the fabric of resistance against the banks and impacts of global capitalism. On May 12th benefited from paid staff, a large budget, a tactical understanding of the reforms and policies needed to create change, and grassroots direct actionists whose creativity and courage made all the difference.[20] Occupy benefited from creative, youthful energy and courage, anarchist principles, and a nation full of angry people who were hurting. It understood the power of self-organizing and direct action to make change. Occupy, without the confines of by-laws or boards, was flexible and continuously evolved the infrastructure needed to meet our growing community's needs as they arose.[21]

Both types of organizing are replicable; we saw this in real time as hundreds of OWS encampments emerged all over the world, and as the On May 12th model was replicated by the New Bottom Line in ten cities around the country. One model is not "better" than the other, and both delivered victories for the people. In fact, I don't believe you can see these as two separate movements, as I personally witnessed and participated in the many collaborations that took root and spread. The initiatives supported and reinforced each other. During Occupy, for example, I trained the action working group on many of the same strategies and tactics we used in On May 12th, including mapping targets, scouting action zones, and developing leadership.[22]

In our political work, we tend to act out of white culture by competing, comparing, judging, and acting as if there is only one way—but in truth we need a diversity of strategies and tactics. We are all called to different approaches and risks. That is why I'm always looking for that sweet spot where these various forces come into relationship with one another, each doing what they do best as they support, not co-opt, other parts of the movement. For this to work we need respect and openness.

Looking back, I see more clearly that the collaborative spirit of OWS explains why its cultural, political, and policy effects have been far reaching. The Occupation ended on November 15, 2011, thanks to a massive police action coordinated by the Department of Homeland Security. But the work continued. For over a year, Occupiers continued to meet and organize actions targeting banks, hedge funds, and million-aires. We organized a huge Day of Action for the one-year anniversary, shutting down the Wall Street area with creative mobile actions. We all felt like OWS was taking root in a new way, but a few weeks later, Hurricane Sandy hit, and Occupy Wall Street morphed into Occupy Sandy. The strong networks, technological acumen, and creative orga-nizing power of OWS rose up in a people's response to hurricane relief that was more effective and efficient than the Red Cross or Homeland Security combined.

Occupy Wall Street put the discussion of wealth inequality front and center. Student debt became a national issue, and President Obama enacted a student loan forgiveness program. Strike Debt, whose slogan was "You Are Not A Loan," raised money through their Rolling Jubilee Fund to buy personal debts at a fraction of the loan and then forgive them. In this way, millions of dollars in debt were forgiven for working people. Labor unions in particular benefited from the OWS movement, with huge successes seen in the Verizon workers' strike, the Southbury strike, and workers' strikes at Hot and Crusty. Huge energy went into the Fight for $15, with great successes in many states.[23]

Occupy Wall Street fueled the climate movement, adding energy to the successful fight against the Keystone XL Pipeline (KXL). When I traveled to Standing Rock in 2016, former Occupiers were there. Relationships made during Occupy created the grassroots swell around the Bernie Sand-ers campaign in 2015 and 2016—and in turn, those who organized around Bernie were some of the same folks who organized around the 2018 midterms and now around numerous candidates in the 2020 elections.

When white supremacists and neo-Nazis have taken the streets, many former Occupiers made up the Antifa forces using their bodies to stop them. During the protests against Trump's family separation poli-cies, Occupiers set up occupations at ICE offices and deportation courts. During the hearings for the appointment of Brett Kavanaugh, Occupiers were there as well, taking action to protest the railroading of an accused sexual predator onto the Supreme Court.

When Trump and his corporate, corrupt, crony-filled administration came in, policies put in place to protect the environment, reproductive rights, immigrants' rights, and so much more were taken away, leaving many more vulnerable. Yet the resistance has spread. Millions of new people have joined the movement. Occupy continues to inspire us, and the story of Occupy Wall Street reminds us that our resistance is what changes culture and creates social justice warriors for life. The organizing we do today will help create the yet-unknown victories of tomorrow, and it all starts by believing that unimaginable things are possible when we take action together.

CHAPTER 9

Ferguson and the Power of Liberation

If you have come here to help me, you are wasting your time. But if you have come because your liberation is bound up with mine, then let us work together.

—LILLA WATSON

When the people of Ferguson rose up in August of 2014, years of pent-up anger poured into the streets, fully righteous against police violence and murder. Michael Brown, an unarmed teenager, was shot in a street near his home and left to die, lying out in the sun for four hours and twenty-five minutes. The anger of the protestors combined with the militarism of the police created a dance of power that went on for weeks, months, and then years as people all over the country woke up to the reality of a country fractured by racism.

The struggle in Ferguson was waged by poor Black people who'd had enough. Day after day, night after night, hundreds gathered in vigils, marches, and lines with their hands in the air chanting, "Hands Up, Don't Shoot." They laid bare their pain and vulnerable bodies to tear gas, stun grenades, rubber bullets, live bullets, police clubs, and arrests. The people refused to back down, and in doing so, birthed a new era of the Black liberation movement, which had been seeded two years earlier, in February 2012, when Trayvon Martin, another unarmed Black teen, was killed by George Zimmerman, who was acquitted under Florida's Stand Your Ground law. Then in July 2014 Eric Garner was killed by New York police for selling cigarettes. They kneeled on his neck as he yelled "I can't breathe," but they did not let up, murdering another Black man and father.

When Michael Brown was killed, the movement exploded. It was out of the box, and it was not going back.

Ferguson was not about size, but heart. The resistance was both structured and organic. There was a willingness to be visible and raw in pain, sorrow, and anger, demanding that the world know Black Lives Matter. Police murders of Black and Brown people matter, and real accountability for those responsible matters—not just in Ferguson, but in every community across this country.

Ferguson was about action. It brought together many sectors, including youth, faith, labor, and peace and justice groups. Some people of faith initially held back in condescension, but with the fierce leadership of Reverend Traci Blackmon and Reverend Osagyefo Sekou, they rose up in the spirit of Moral Monday to face the police. Reverend Sekou, a religious leader who grew up in St. Louis, moved them by calling for a willingness to take militant, nonviolent direct action from a place of deep abiding love against the system.

Deep abiding love against the system. The people in Ferguson did not want to play by the rules because the rules did not serve them. Social change requires a real challenge to state power and the institutions that hold up racism and supremacy. In my life as an organizer, I have often spoken about dismantling structures of oppression while building structures of liberation. We can't do one without the other.

In Ferguson local organizers were wary of outside groups and demanded that white allies recognize their privilege. My experiences in Ferguson caused me to reflect on how much I still must learn about building an anti-racist world. These changes will not come easy. Centuries of structural and systemic oppression are so deeply embedded that neither white folks nor many people of color truly understand all the ways in which racism and capitalism have made us sick. Dismantling the unjust structures that keep huge numbers of our population in trauma, impoverished, and uneducated will take intention, resources, and healing work.

The questions we must ask ourselves are: What am I waiting for, and how can I contribute? Or better yet, thinking again about the words of Reverend Sekou, who counseled clergy on how to respond to Black youth who are angry or upset—simply tell them, "I'm sorry it has taken me so long to show up."

Ferguson October and Moral Monday

On August 9, the day Michael Brown was killed by officer Darren Wilson, community members gathered around the eighteen-year-old's body, which lay for over four hours where he fell on Canfield Drive in Ferguson, a predominantly African American suburb northwest of St. Louis. The people were distraught; another young Black man was dead. The following evening there was a peaceful candlelight vigil and scattered incidents of property damage. In response the police sent 150 officers in riot gear, and thirty-two were arrested.[1] This was enough fodder for the national media to start broadcasting images of civil unrest with story after story about looting, not the peaceful protests.

By the third night officers wearing fatigues and riot gear tear-gassed a peaceful demonstration and fired stun grenades into a crowd. Reporters were arrested along with protestors, and the community's calls for accountability were not answered as the militarized presence increased. By August 17 the National Guard was called in, and even before then, Mine-Resistant Ambush Protected vehicles—MRAPs—were rolling through the streets. These huge tanks were developed during the Iraq War to withstand land mine detonations and IEDs. Police officers were carrying both shotguns and rifles, prompting servicemen and -women watching this unfold on TV to observe that they packed less heat while at war.[2]

Elected officials got involved, speaking out, but their stature did not always protect them. When St. Louis alderman Antonio French tried to document the protests, he was dragged from his car, thrown to the ground, and arrested for unlawful assembly.

Throughout August and September the protests continued, sometimes sporadic and sometimes sustained, while a series of political events unfolded, including a visit by Attorney General Eric Holder, fact-finding delegations from Amnesty International, and statements by President Obama. New grassroots organizations emerged while long-standing ones solidified their support for the movement.

One thing that made Ferguson special is that grassroots groups maintained the bulk of the power even when the movement became sophisticated and spread across the nation. Two of the long-term organizations in the St. Louis area became anchors for much of the work. The Organization for Black Struggle, or OBS, had been in St. Louis for over forty years, with a rich history of political and cultural action.[3] OBS was the hub for art making, cultural work, and strategizing among the Black organizers. The other local group, Missourians Organizing for Reform and Empowerment, or MORE, founded in 2010, was a community-based organization working in the legacy of ACORN that focused on economic justice issues like housing and foreclosures. New local groups emerged as well, many of them Black- and youth-led, including Hands Up United, Millennial Activists United, and lesser-known groups like Lost Voices, Black Souljahs, Freedom Fighters, and Tribe X.[4]

When historic people-powered movements like this one rise up, there are patterns that tend to repeat. You'll often see a grassroots ground-swell from the margins that is ignored, shunned, or criminalized; then grassroots organizers with skills to offer start hitting the ground. As time goes on, national groups send people in, generating action alerts, starting publicity and fund-raising campaigns while more established local groups translate the resistance into political reforms. During this process, money became a big issue in Ferguson, a community that had none. While there were attempts to redistribute resources locally, it proved difficult to create a structure to do this well.

When everyone gets involved like this, it's clear that a real movement is under way. In September plans were being made for a national convergence called Ferguson October, a four-day mobilization with marches, speeches, and direct actions that would culminate on Monday, October 13.

———————

I was at home in Austin, Texas, on the day Michael Brown was murdered, and like many others I watched in horror at the militarized response to a community's outcry for justice. I checked in with a friend in St. Louis, Jeff Ordower, the executive director of MORE, who felt it was not the time for white organizers to come in yet. I understood.

When the public call for Ferguson October was issued, I knew I would be going. I contacted my friend, the artist Laurie Arbeiter, and we agreed to meet in St. Louis.[5]

After landing at the airport, I picked up some flowers for the Mike Brown memorial. Driving into Ferguson, I made my way up West Florissant Road, where much of the protesting had occurred, and saw the

QuikTrip store that burned on August 10. I turned onto Canfield Drive and silently got out. I was struck by the tranquility of the neighborhood, with small houses, apartment complexes, and green spaces. The memorial was in the middle of the street, stretched out along the double yellow line. It was made up of candles, flowers, stuffed animals, a basketball, and some signs. One of them said, BUT WHERE IS JUSTICE? Over on the sidewalk there was a huge pile of stuffed animals around a light pole with a picture of Mike Brown wearing mortarboard from high school graduation. He was supposed to start college a few weeks after his death.

I didn't stay long. I placed my flowers on the memorial and took a few moments to honor the life of Michael Brown, whose death had changed our world.

I headed over to MORE's offices in the World Community Center in St. Louis, where some of the organizational efforts were being housed, and was impressed to see that the building held offices for many social justice groups including Show Me $15, the Women's International League for Peace and Freedom, and the St. Louis Palestine Solidarity Committee. These offices had become a major infrastructure hub, including legal and jail support, material resources, food, training, and meeting space for the growing resistance. The place was buzzing, with people everywhere.[6]

Ferguson October was a collaboration among OBS, MORE, and Hands Up United, a new group funded by outside forces, creating some complicated dynamics. A gift to the movement arrived as Maurice Mitchell and Mervyn Marcano, two organizers from out of town, provided a vision for the weekend and skillfully bridged the divide between local and national organizers. As the challenges with Hands Up United continued, the Don't Shoot Coalition was formed, growing to over 150 local organizations working for political reforms, including a proposed set of "rules for engagement" for the police.

Three days before Ferguson October began, I attended my first meeting, with Celeste Faison, a young Black woman from Ruckus, facilitating. We discussed the planned direct actions for Monday, and I was asked to be an action coordinator. I was hesitant, unsure about taking the lead as a white woman who had just arrived and didn't know the turf. I asked if I could support the trainings and actions without being a coordinator, which everyone was okay with.

Emotions were high that evening after an off-duty police officer shot and killed VonDerrit Myers Jr., an eighteen-year-old Black teen, in the Shaw neighborhood just south of downtown. Vigils and marches were being organized and would continue each night.

On Saturday we trained hundreds of people in nonviolent action. As with all my trainings, I urged as many white people to risk arrest as possible, knowing it helps them grapple with their privilege. On Sunday we marched and rallied in downtown St. Louis. Speakers addressed the crowds with incredible passion about the need for justice in a city of injustices. The Ferguson police had been harassing, arresting, and financially sapping Black folks for years. It was a lived experience that was affirmed by the Justice Department's investigation, released eight months after Brown's death, which the *New York Times* characterized as so scathing, and delineating so many constitutional violations, that the city was being asked to "abandon its entire approach to policing." Amid other findings, the investigation "described a city that used its police and courts as moneymaking ventures, a place where officers stopped and handcuffed people without probable cause, hurled racial slurs, used stun guns without provocation, and treated anyone as suspicious merely for questioning police tactics."[7]

On Sunday evening there was a mass meeting at the Chaifetz Arena with over a thousand people attending. The speech given by the president of the NAACP was interrupted by some youth in the audience who demanded to take the stage. Many in the crowd roared "Let them speak!" as others tried to shut them down. Within minutes Tef Poe and Ashley Yates had the stage. Poe was a local rapper who became a key person in Hands Up United, while Yates was one of the founders of Millennial Activists United. They talked about anger, pain, and the impact that police violence had on them personally and on the community. They then declared, "This ain't your daddy's Civil Rights Movement. We're doing this one our way."

To me this moment said everything about the organizing in Ferguson. It was grassroots, Black-led, youth-led, and fierce. They were not taking no for an answer.

The young folks announced there would be a march that night launching from the VonDerrit Myers memorial. By 11 PM close to a thousand were gathered there. The march led to St. Louis University, where we poured into the Clock Tower Plaza, a big circular area around a fountain.[8]

This was the beginning of a sit-in that lasted about a week and ended with an agreement by the administration to improve its African American studies programs and increase financial aid.[9]

That early-morning sit-in was the beginning of the Moral Monday Day of Action, named in solidarity with the movement founded by the Reverend Dr. William Barber in North Carolina. At least nine actions rolled out that day. I was supporting the plan for civil disobedience at the Ferguson Police Station, led by Reverend Sekou, whom I had worked with at United for Peace and Justice. He had been living in Boston, but the uprising convinced him to move back home, and it was good he did. Sekou is a small man but a huge force. He is not afraid to speak his mind and call out the clergy for their inaction. At heart he is a revolutionary who knows the system is as guilty as hell!

I arrived at the church and sat quietly in a back pew as he prepared the church leaders to depart for the police station. His call for nonviolent, respectful, righteous action was strong. His words reminded me of my early days of civil disobedience, when the calls against the US's dirty wars in Central America were led by religious leaders and strongly rooted in spirit. I was feeling at home and glad for the opportunity to support this strong leader. For his part, Reverend Sekou was equally glad that I was there; he liked to call me the Jedi Master. I knew he was not being flippant, because it so happens that on the airport shuttle after arriving in St. Louis, I ran into Bishop John Sellers and his wife, Pamela, friends of the reverend. As I was telling them about my work, they said, "We know you! You're the Jedi Master that Sekou was telling us about." Needless to say, I was both embarrassed and honored.

The time to march had come. It was a gray, rainy day, but we were not deterred. On the way to the police station we passed a few commercial strip malls with locally owned stores and corporate chains like Subway, which made a hell of a lot of money off the protests. Over a hundred religious leaders in their robes and brightly colored adornments flowed into the streets. The police station was barricaded off, including the door we wanted to get to. As we assembled out front, a man lay down and we drew chalk lines around his body. We all chimed in to sing "Ella's Song" inspired by the civil rights leader Ella Josephine Baker, written by Bernice Johnson Reagon, and recorded by Sweet Honey in the Rock. Ella Josephine Baker was one of the most influential organizers of that era. She worked with Dr. Martin Luther King at the Southern Christian Leadership Conference and was a founder of the Student Nonviolent Coordinating Committee. Baker is an unsung shero and role model for all who want to better this world. The words of the song reminded us that we cannot rest until the lives of all children of color are as important as the lives of white children.

The clergy linked up their arms and moved forward toward the line of police—many of whom were dressed in riot gear—offering to take confessions and demanding to meet with the police chief. Among them was Cornel West, who had asserted the night before at the town hall meeting that he did not come to talk, but to get arrested. The first wave of clergy was indeed arrested, and another wave stepped right in to replace them. This was a powerful moment, because it was some of these same clergy who had aligned with the conservative establishment early on after Brown's death, creating lots of conflict. But now they were putting their bodies on the line.

I supported multiple other actions throughout the day, and all told, sixty-four people were arrested on Moral Monday. The uprising in Ferguson had become an organized, effective movement, and the world was watching.

The Power of Learning Strategies for Dealing with the Police

I was grateful for the young men and women in Ferguson. They were fearless, from the leaders and organizers down to the kids who just showed up. They took whatever space they could and moved skillfully, emboldening those who might follow. They chanted, "We're Young, We're Strong, We're Marching All Night Long," and they meant it. Simply put, the youth of Ferguson did not back down when they faced police or politicians. I watched people kneel in the street, laying their bodies bare to whatever the police might choose to do. They did not care about the media. They did not care about messaging. They did not care about making friends with politicians or bankers. They had one another, and that was enough.

And of course, they were not rising up against police violence alone. In the words of one of their chants, "The Whole Damn System Is Guilty as Hell." They were rising up against the school-to-prison pipeline and the institutions that criminalize and cage. They were calling for an end to laws and policies that keep communities in the cycle of poverty. They were calling for an end to police abuse and racial profiling. They were demanding accountability for police violence and community-based alternatives to incarceration.

The youth were fighting for their lives. According to a 2017 report, in 2016 young Black males were at least nine times more likely to be killed by police than other Americans.[10] African Americans are four times as likely to experience the use of force during encounters with the police, and one in three African American men will go to jail at some point in their lifetime.[11] The criminalization begins at a young age. In many of the nation's largest school districts, including New York and Chicago, there are more police officers per school than counselors, and students are arrested—*arrested!*— for offenses like talking back to their teachers and "disorderly conduct."[12]

As someone who has spent decades interacting with the police, I have a deep understanding of the fear of law enforcement, yet cannot imagine what it is like to be targeted by the police just for being Black, knowing that the badge is a license to kill.

Despite being white and privileged, I have felt vulnerable to state terror and violence, from being labeled a terrorist by the media, to being targeted by the police, FBI, and Homeland Security, to the times I have feared for my life. Once such frightening incident occurred in New Orleans a few months after Katrina. A bunch of us were cleaning up after a memorial service for Meg Perry, a young volunteer at Common Ground Relief who was killed in a tragic bus accident. We held a beautiful service and tree planting with Meg's family in the garden she had worked so hard on. Afterward I left to give people a ride home and got a call that the police were at the garden.

I raced back to see everyone lined up with their hands on the police car. I walked up slowly, asking respectfully for whoever was in charge. I was answered with, "Shut the fuck up, get your hands up!" This cop was screaming and pointing his gun at me.

As asked, I slowly walked toward his car. He pushed me up against it and put the gun to my head. I breathed as deep as I could. I noticed that Josh, an eleven-year-old kid, had a red dot on his head, the laser marker for a gun. The cop stepped back as more squad cars rolled up, and as they approached I called out, "Is there a reasonable cop among you? Please

OUT OF THE TOOLBOX

Tips for Dealing with Police

In the context of protests, mobilizations, and uprisings, we are often confronted with the police or National Guard. There are many different strategies for dealing with law enforcement, but I prefer the ones that focus on mitigating harm.

When police are on the scene, pay attention to their body postures and movements. Learn to read their energy. Are they chill and standing down, or agitated and poised for attack? Do they have horses or dogs on the scene?

Pay attention to their gear. Do they have batons or handcuffs at the ready? Do they have tear gas masks? Are there horses or dogs? What other weapons or vehicles have they brought onto the scene?

You may want to bring protective gear of your own—goggles, masks, and earplugs.

Make sure you have scouts who are looking around to see where the police are staging in locations that are out of view.

Know your exit strategy from the area. Look around to find places to take cover to protect yourself or nearby stores you can duck into.

Pre-designate people to document with cameras, and organize legal observers who will be a public presence to document the events.

Remember that police work with command-and-control strategies. They expect people to do what they say, and can get agitated and escalate the situation when we don't.

Police typically follow a chain of command, so learn what their uniforms and ranks mean, and observe when the superiors start issuing directions to the troops.

In some contexts you may choose to empower someone to be a *police liaison*. This person keeps the channels of communication open and buys time. When I have taken the role of police liaison, here are strategies that have helped:

I access the part of myself that is authoritative and confident. It might seem counterintuitive to act authoritatively toward officers, but they are used to following orders and clear communication and direction. It's possible that this strategy works for me largely because I'm a white woman.

I rarely approach the police alone. It is always good to have a team, with one person speaking and the others witnessing.

I approach them with respect, while also asserting our right to do what we are doing. Always assert your rights.

If they say you are violating a code, ask them to show you the code.

Each situation is different. If the officers are stationary and calm, it might not be necessary to speak with them. If the action is more intense and it seems like the officers might come charging in, I try to speak with them and attempt to de-escalate their response.

If the officers begin to escalate, I try to speak with them and point out that they're making the situation unsafe. Safety is a key talking point. If one cop is escalating, it has worked for me in the past to ask a superior to remove them.

I sometimes tell the officers about the reason we're taking action and ask if they know anyone who is affected by this issue to assess if they're sympathetic to the cause.

Remember that officers expect people to do what they're told, even if it violates their rights. Many cities now take out insurance policies for major political events. This shows that they plan to violate people's rights and ensures they'll have money to pay off lawsuits.

come talk to us!" Finally, one did. I asked if he remembered the recent bus accident and explained this was the memorial service for the woman who was killed. The other officer was defending himself now, saying he thought we were looters. Maybe one could make that mistake, but all it takes is asking what we're doing, not running in pointing guns. You can see how easily people get killed by cops.

Learning how to deal with police is not a joke or a game, but something that can save your life. The movements against police brutality and mass incarceration continue to grow, but until the system changes, the police will do what they want. They expect the blue code of silence and worry about repercussions or lawsuits later.

I have dealt with officers who are brutal and vicious, those who are respectful, and everything in between. My approach to cops is not so much about *Fuck the Police*, but appealing to them to put their guns down and join the people. Until then, they are complicit, no matter how decent a person they might be.

Facing the police has become an inevitable part of protests and mobilizations. Plans are necessary, but you must also plan for unpredictability. And if your plan from the beginning is to non-cooperate with the police, unpredictability is inevitable. Non-cooperative acts require courage and bravery, which is what I saw every single day in Ferguson.

The Non-Indictment

In the days after Brown was killed, the action in the streets was a raw uprising of the people. By the time of the non-indictment on November 25, the people were organized and powerful, and the movement was national, with almost a hundred actions taking place across the country.

In early November I was back at home in Austin but still inspired by the actions in Ferguson. I reached out to my dear friend Michael McPhearson, the executive director of Veterans for Peace.[13] We had served together as national co-coordinators of United for Peace and Justice, and now he was one of the cofounders of the Don't Shoot Coalition. I let him know I was interested in coming back to St. Louis to provide more training and support. He brought my request to the Don't Shoot Coalition, which extended an invitation to come.

I made my arrangements to arrive on November 6 and immediately connected with Julia Ho, one of the organizers at MORE who was working to train and develop young organizers from Tribe X, Freedom Fighters, and Black Souljahs. All of these were locally led youth organizations formed after the uprising.[14]

Many of these young people were living together in an apartment with limited resources. We went over for a visit and were greeted warmly. We hung out for a while as I asked questions about how they were doing. I could feel the edges of trauma all around. These kids had been living their lives disempowered and pissed, and now everything had changed. They were passionate, if exhausted. I shared with them how much respect I had for their street skills. They were the ones who led a lot of the marches during Ferguson October, including the one that converged at St. Louis University for the sit-in.

The following day I arrived at the training space early to set up. As streams of people began to file in, it was clear I couldn't do the training as planned for so many. This is the kind of problem that's good to have. Michael and Montague Simmons from OBS opened up, and then I shared the history and power of direct action. We used Q&As to address issues around the police, health, trauma, and how to stay safe. I spoke about self-organizing and the importance of working in small groups. We began to lay out a vision of geographically based organizing and how to plan actions around specific locales. We talked about the importance of being prepared for any scenario, including police violence and arrest, by packing a go-bag that had water, a bandanna, a map, an energy bar, protective gear for your eyes, a battery charger for your phone, and so on. Before we closed, we suggested that people get their friends together to circle up and form affinity groups.

The meeting was a hit. Afterward Michael, Montague, and I talked about developing a series of mass meetings, mass trainings, and an action council as we prepared for the grand jury verdict. Our intent was to have spaces where both unorganized individuals and new groups could come together. Over a thousand people were trained over the course of those meetings, which created an open container for people who had not yet been in the streets. We developed a common framework for mass direct action that was principled, militant, and practical, emboldening people to take to the streets in organized groups that could also create their own actions. This effort also sent a strong message to the local power structure, including the politicians and police, that the movement was getting increasingly organized.

This organizing was similar to the affinity group model I learned in the 1980s during the Central America antiwar movements, and it has also been used in the anti-nuclear movement, the Global Justice movement, Occupy Wall Street, and others. These models embrace the principles of direct democracy, self-organization, shared power, and mutual aid. In the US the model has been used predominantly by white folks—though its core principles really trace back to Indigenous ways that have been used all over the world. It seemed clear to us that the emerging action council would need to be an explicitly anti-racist space convened and facilitated by people of color.

Once we got started, we learned that the people were hungry to be organized. We were able to cement a number of affinity groups while also teaching young leaders how to facilitate consensus meetings. Two young Black women, Kayla Reed and Brianna Richardson, became excellent facilitators. Both were new to the movement, politicized by the uprising—Kayla had been a pharmacy technician and Bri had worked in corporate America. The nights in the streets changed their lives. Kayla facilitated the first big meeting, and I was thrilled to see that sixteen newly formed affinity groups representing hundreds of people showed up. We called this emerging structure the Ferguson Action Council, and a version of it, now called Action St. Louis, is still around today.[15]

One of the unforgettable actions prior to the non-indictment was a die-in outside the Tivoli Theatre, on a popular strip of Delmar Boulevard near Washington University. The plan was for us to play the roles of the cops shooting, people dying, and people chalking the bodies and laying down flowers. We divided into two marches, each with a set of props for the funeral procession.

It was a cold, wet, and lightly snowy day. We carried the coffins, which were donned with bright, vibrant flowers.[16] My group had to walk on a sidewalk where construction was under way, and one in our crew, a larger man named HJ, pulled up a wooden construction stake and started marching with it. The stake was supposed to be a "sword" to match the

Action Council

- GROUPS ACTIVE IN THE STREETS can participate
- ONE SPOKEPERSON represents each group
- THE COORDINATION TEAM moves the process forward
- PARTICIPANTS AGREE to points of unity

YOUTH ORGANIZATIONS

LIVESTREAMERS

JAIL SUPPORT

MEDICS

FAITH GROUPS

ALLIES

ACTION COUNCIL
COORDINATION TEAM
smaller group for action council
planning, logistics and facilitation

PROTEST ARTISTS

LABOR UNIONS

SELF-ORGANIZED ACTION GROUPS

COMMUNITY ORGANIZATIONS

LEGAL OBSERVERS

The Action Council is a space for groups in the movement to coordinate and support each other. The Action Council can be used to plan one major event or can be a longer-term space to coordinate within and across movements. One of its defining features is that it allows relationships and coordination to be fostered between formal organizations with less formalized clusters of activists.

Illustration courtesy of Emily Simons.

large wooden shield he and others carried to protect themselves from police batons. I was, like, *Oh shit*—being a large Black man with a pointed stick was the kind of thing that could make you a target. I sidled up to HJ and said, "Do as you wish, just know you could become a target." He did not give a fuck at all.

Our two groups convened at intersections a few blocks from the theater. As we arrived, we deployed our traffic blockers and poured into the street. Those of us playing the cops shouted and threatened as the people put their hands in the air. As we "shot" them, bodies fell onto the street. The snow was coming down softly around us as dozens of onlookers stopped to watch. We carried in the coffins and flowers and mournfully chalked the bodies. Dhoruba was on the bullhorn, telling onlookers his story about what it was like to be a Black man in this world, the sorrow, anger, and pain. At one point I looked over and saw HJ just standing there, the shield and sword lowered at each side, a tear coming down his cheek. Gazing into the street at our dramatic scene, he said, "I didn't know it would be so beautiful." I, too, felt the tears in my eyes.

Die-in action outside the Tivoli Theatre on Delmar Boulevard in St. Louis,
November 2014.

This is the power of direct action. When we create acts of beautiful,
meaningful resistance, something inside us changes. It is that bittersweet
knowing that we can create beautiful worlds, and that we can make it so,
every day, using conscious choices.

The sweet moment was broken as the amplified voice of the police
blared, "This is an illegal demonstration. You must leave now, or you will
be arrested!"

We prepared to complete our action, chanting, "Stand Up, Sit Down,
We Do This for Mike Brown!" As planned, these words prompted the
dead people to rise up and join the chant. We formed back into one big
march and headed right toward the police, flowing around and through
the spaces in between their cars. We knew the best way to confront the
fear and potential danger was to move right toward it with our love and
light. That is just what we did, and the police could do nothing about it.

We didn't know when the verdict would be announced, but as November passed, you could feel it coming. There was tension all around. Businesses were boarding up, schools prepared to close, barricades appeared around the Justice Center in Clayton as well as City Hall. There were rumors of gang violence. Protests continued every day and night at the Ferguson police station as helicopters flew overhead, shining bright lights down on us. We produced an online map pinpointing fifty possible action targets including police stations, political offices, and businesses. The map also included safe spaces and hospitals. My own plan was to be at the Ferguson Police Department whenever the news came in.

Finally we got word from the Brown family that a verdict would be announced the next night, November 25. When I arrived at the police station, it was already a crazy scene with hundreds of people and dozens of media outlets with their tents and trucks. It was cold and dark; you could cut the tension with a knife. The crowd was in constant motion, people moving here and there, pacing back and forth. When the announcement came, I was standing next to Mama Cat, a local woman who had been in the streets since August, cooking for and feeding the people. She was listening on her phone, repeating back what was said: There would be no indictment. Darren Wilson would walk away free.

The crowd roared, "NO. NO. NO."

Lezley McSpadden, Mike Brown's mom, was standing on the back of a truck amid the crowd. She broke down. Mike Brown's father held her as they both cried. The crowd was stunned and slowly woke with anger. Things started to fly—bottles, signs—toward the line of riot police. In a surreal moment I looked at a red-lighted sign over the road that said SEASON'S GREETINGS with the large line of riot police below. This was certainly no holiday season.

The crowd spread and scattered. A grouping of giant military tanklike vehicles moved north on South Florissant toward the crowd. Tear gas was flying. Shots were fired—from where, no one knew. People were yelling and screaming. Within moments you could see a fire burning down the road: A police car was ablaze.

I was with Julia and Derrick Laney from MORE. Derrick needed to get a ride to his car. We got to my car and drove toward Derrick's, but as we turned onto that street, it was lined with cops, their guns raised. I backed up. Once the police were redeployed to another street, Derrick got to his car, and now I needed to drive my friend Julia to *her* car. This was another fool's errand. As we drove through an alley, a line of cops raised their guns at us. The red dot of a sniper laser was on my dashboard. I was, like, Julia, we're getting your car tomorrow. We got the hell out of there and made our way to a church, one of the pre-designated safe spaces. We caught our breath and then headed back out, trying to make our way down West Florissant. Horns blared; people were running everywhere. Many buildings were on fire; smoke and tear gas filled the sky. We headed in a different direction but shots rang out in the intersection we were trying to move through. We got low in the car and safely made our way out of the area.

We drove to MoKaBe's, one of the movement hangouts in the Shaw neighborhood. It was crazy there as well. The police had tear-gassed the café and people were walking around with the milky white residue of Maalox on their faces—Maalox, when mixed half and half with water, is the favored treatment for tear gas and pepper spray on the skin.

Folks were worn out from the emotional pain and relentless actions. I knew that Ferguson would be burning all night long. I also knew we had a plan to shut down intersections in Clayton first thing in the morning. I dropped Julia off at her home, headed back to where I was staying, set my alarm for 5 AM, and collapsed into bed.

The Power of Facing Racism

On the one-year anniversary of Michael Brown's death, one of the groups founded in Ferguson, the Deep Abiding Love Project, distributed a manual called *Coming to Ferguson* to activists arriving in St. Louis.[17] The goal was to communicate that Ferguson wasn't a movement to tap into once, feel good about yourself, then go home with a badge of honor. It was a movement dedicated to the hard, lifelong work of undoing racism and white supremacy. The manual encouraged newcomers to "show up and shut up":

> **SHOW UP AND SHUT UP:** Understand that your role in Ferguson
> is different than your role in your own community. Here, the only
> credential that matters is how many times you have shown up.

Your role as an outsider is to be present, to really listen. Be flexible and learn to recognize the new forms leadership has taken in this movement, figure out how to listen to new voices without putting that burden on local organizers or giving unasked for counsel.[18]

The activists in Ferguson were super conscious of supremacy—race, gender, and class—snaking their way into grassroots groups. The privileging of the voices and ideas of white people and white men can be insidious and difficult to recognize, which is why it's so important to be explicit and specific about how privilege shows itself. Personally, I've learned that I'm acting out of white superiority when I work with urgency or demand perfection, if I am patronizing, when I believe there's only one right way to do something, or when I act or feel like a savior.

Without having done the hard work of learning, white folks are mostly unaware when they're acting from a place of internalized superiority, and tend to deny it when it's pointed out. This denial causes people to hide behind other common behaviors of internalized supremacy, like distancing, fragility, and arrogance.

The privileges and rewards of being white, male, straight, able-bodied, and Christian have been woven into the fabrics of our cultures and institutions since the country's founding. The Naturalization Act written by the very first Congress in 1790 defined US citizenship as being available only to "free white people," making the United States of America the first country on Earth to put the concept of "white" into law. For centuries, white men carried the privilege of laws that allowed them, and only them, to own property and land, while all men were socialized and given the power to subjugate women.

As such, white people and men became invested in the process of keeping things the way they are—but the way things are creates irrational fears about "others" and justifies complacency to injustice and the use of violence and oppression. These acts and traits of internalized superiority sap energy, create trauma, and deny the humanity of others as well as ourselves. The values of supremacy breed competition, control, individualism, greed, and the use and acceptance of brutality and force.

As taught by the People's Institute for Survival and Beyond, the flip side of this internalized superiority is the internalized inferiority experienced by people of color, which has created generations of traumatized people who pass that trauma to their children. Superiority and inferiority make us all sick. It's just that white people, men, and rich people are comfortably sick.

Liberation is not a word I typically associate with white people, but undoing racism and superiority is liberating for people of all backgrounds. Funny enough, even the dictionary definitions of *liberation*, written by white people, carry hierarchy and white supremacy within them. One example is: "the act of setting someone free from imprisonment, slavery, or oppression; release." We speak of "setting someone free" as if people cannot free themselves. We see liberation as the forceful undoing of some external imposition—and it can be, but true liberation comes from within, because it is our minds, as well as our bodies, that have been colonized and bound.

In the book *My Grandmother's Hands*, therapist Resmaa Menakem writes about how the culture of white supremacy is so endemic to our environment that we're all walking around traumatized because of it. This book was eye opening for me. Menakem proposes that white Americans suffer from the "secondary trauma" of having witnessed or been complicit in racial violence, going back generations to white Europeans who witnessed or inflicted unspeakable brutality on other white people.[19] The colonists who came to this continent brought this violence with them as they waged a campaign of genocide against Indigenous peoples, then captured and enslaved Black and Brown people as well as poor white people, though the latter were freed of their indentured servitude. Menakem's premise is that the racial tensions in our culture are literally hardwired into our bodies, creating symptoms of chronic fear and hypervigilance.

Racism infects every aspect of our society, and anti-racist work must be explicitly practiced within and between movements, as well as within ourselves, our families, and our communities. The work of undoing racism and all forms of supremacy is lifelong work, it is difficult work, and it is essential to creating the world we hope for. As the civil rights leader Bayard Rustin once wrote,

> If we desire a society of peace, then we cannot achieve such a society through violence. If we desire a society without discrimination, then we must not discriminate against anyone in the process of

building this society. If we desire a society that is democratic, then democracy must become a means as well as an end.[20]

Undoing these oppressive and violent belief systems requires consciousness and strategy that move beyond "issue work" and into the daily practices of noticing and changing beliefs and behaviors.

In the 1980s I was a co-coordinator at the Washington Peace Center in Washington, DC, an organization that had been composed primarily of white folks since its founding in the '60s. In 1988 a new co-coordinator came on board, Mark Anderson, a smart, skilled organizer who called upon us to step out of our unconscious white privilege and address head-on the racial divides in Washington, DC. We participated in the People's Institute for Survival and Beyond's Undoing Racism training, which forever changed my life. This was the beginning of a process in which we addressed racism personally and in the organization, leading to many changes, including the leadership of the board, the programs we organized, and how our services were offered. At one point six people of color joined the board at the same time, unlike the many organizations that bring in one person of color, which is both untenable and tokenizing.

Years later, in the fall of 2002, I was involved in organizing a new antiwar group initially called United for Peace. The older peace movement in the US espouses concepts of "peace" that often lack racial analysis and make invisible the inherent racism in US wars. Myself and others advocated to change the name to United for Peace and Justice—there is no peace without justice. Believe it or not, there was resistance, but we held firm.

As part of the anti-racist process at UFPJ, we included racism in our analysis of war, acknowledging that people of color must serve in disproportionate numbers as a way out of poverty and that most of the wars being waged are against brown-skinned people. We also made a conscious, deliberate effort to center the voices and leadership of people of color. Our steering committee was majority women, majority people of color, with 15 to 20 percent queer and youth representation. We got very explicit about the numbers, which can be extremely helpful. We also agreed that the leadership body had to have equal representation, fifty-fifty between local groups and national organizations. This intentional building of a diverse leadership body is a must if we are to undo racism.

Healing Racial Divides

Being compassionate and seeing ourselves in others is an important step toward liberation. In 1995, when I was working on the Justice for Janitors labor campaign in DC, racial tensions surfaced between the Latinx and African American workers, undermining our cohesion in the streets. We brought folks together to talk it all out. One of the African American janitors, Glenda, talked about being raised by a single mom in Anacostia, a poor Black area in DC. She talked about how there wasn't enough food on the table, how there was no playground, how the police hassled folks in the streets. As she spoke, a Latinx woman, Maria, was crying. She told her story of growing up in San Salvador, the capital of El Salvador. She, too, was raised by a single mom because her father, a union leader, had been disappeared by the death squads. There was always a shortage of food, and the kids were afraid to go outside. Listening to this, Glenda was in tears as well, and the two women came together in a tender embrace. The solidarity and love between them pulled everyone else together, and that was the end of the racial tensions.

One of our co-chairs, George Friday, grounded our mass assemblies in anti-racism work. She introduced me to the concept of *strategic use of privilege*, describing how the heavy lifting of reform must not be left to the peoples or communities most affected by injustice. So if homophobia is in the room, straight people must speak to the importance of LGBTQ rights; if there are young people in the room, elders must step back and make room for young voices; if sexism is playing out, the men must acknowledge and combat it; if folks with disabilities don't have access, able-bodied people must fight for it; and if racism is alive, white folks must interrupt it and hold other white people accountable. I learned that the people with the most power and privilege have the greatest obligation to undo the injustice. George also teaches about the importance of working in community and building relationships as integral factors in combating racism and patriarchy, all of which requires work, time, and integrity. Strong relationships allow us to talk about the elephant in the room—oppression.

The monumental task of undoing white supremacy can feel daunting, with undefined goals and parameters. Like all oppressions, it is working at individual, institutional, and cultural levels. Yet there are very tangible injustices that can be fought against every day as members of our communities are taken to jail for petty crimes, evicted from their homes, or torn from their families by ICE. In response to the recent escalated threats to immigrant communities, Muslims, and Jewish people, folks are providing support along the border walls, showing up at airports, and building human perimeters of protection at spaces and events. Communities have formed rapid response networks to thwart and minimize harm by the Trump administration's disturbing executive orders.

No matter who is in power, we need to develop an offensive political strategy that creates and tightens a web of restraint around the activities of the police and agencies like ICE that play out daily in many communities. We also need an offensive strategy to protect ourselves, our neighbors, and our communities from the growing white supremacist movement. Some ideas to protect ourselves and our communities include:

Educate yourself about systems of oppression, as well as about what's
    happening in your own community. What is its history of race
    relations? What are the patterns and practices of local police?
    Which communities are being targeted? Who is already organizing
    for racial justice?
Develop authentic relationships and have real conversations with
    people who are different from you about the elephant in the room—
    systemic oppression.
Become mindful of your language. Use people-centered language. For
    example, instead of saying *slave*, say *enslaved person*, or instead of
    illegal alien, you could say *undocumented immigrant*.
Get together with your family, friends, neighbors, or co-workers to raise
    money for an Undoing Racism Training with the People's Institute
    for Survival and Beyond.

Show up at (or organize) local protests against police brutality, acts of
    oppressive violence, gun violence, and the mistreatment of immi-
    grants or marginalized communities.
Support local organizations that provide legal defense work. Raise
    money for groups that are most affected by oppression. Start a
    community bail fund. Bail people of color out of jail.
Speak out when you hear or see racial bias in action, and share your
    strategies with your friends, on social media, or in a letter to the
    editor of your local paper.
Talk about your values and beliefs with friends, family, and neighbors. Be
    an antidote to the relentless right-wing propaganda campaigns that
    dehumanize people of color and "the left."
Get groups of friends and family together and tap into community-
    wide rapid response networks that respond when activated by groups
    of color.
Set up safe houses.
Organize campaigns that disrupt business as usual for public officials;
    call for accountability for acts of violence, hate speech, and
    unjust ordinances.
Provide food, child care, or transportation to people of color who
    are organizing.

The uprising in Ferguson is a model for how community-based activism can lead to real changes and inspire community-led efforts elsewhere.
The groundwork built in 2014 has given rise to movement forces and
infrastructure, including the tactical use of social media platforms. I
remember as recently as 2006 when the immigrants' rights movement
used the radio to organize that year's Day Without Immigrants. Black
Lives Matter was one of the first to use Twitter as an effective organizing
tool to not only raise awareness but also let people know where protests
are and what's happening, with live updates, and DeRay Mckesson and
Johnetta "Netta" Elzie developed a huge Twitter following about the
uprising.[21] Social media cannot replace on-the-ground relationships,
but when used strategically, it can rapidly expand your base and advance
your message. This is the sweet spot where social media enhances on-the-
ground organizing—and vice versa—in a true synergy.

The Ferguson uprisings led to the emergence of the BlackOUT Collective, a Black-led direct-action trainers network led by Celeste Faison and Chinyere Tutashiada. Local organizers have elected progressive Black officials who will represent their interests. Multimedia artist and organizer Damon Davis, with Sabaah Folayan, went on to make an award-winning film, *Whose Streets,* and Taylor Payne went on to form The Yarn Mission, knitters for justice.[22] Ferguson also led to The Artivists, a group created by my friend Elizabeth Vega, who saw the power of creative direct action and has not stopped since.[23]

And it was in Ferguson that Black Lives Matter, a movement that began online in 2013, really put boots on the ground. Patrisse Cullors, one of the three queer women who founded BLM, mobilized a group of six hundred to travel to Ferguson over Labor Day 2014. Soon local BLM chapters sprouted in communities all over the country. Over these years BLM has grown into a powerful network that continues to take action for transformative change. In 2015 the Movement for Black Lives emerged and became a political force developing a policy platform for the movement that is being used in communities across the country to bring about systemic change. This platform was backed by Showing Up for Racial Justice (SURJ), a white solidarity organization that grew fast after the murder of Michael Brown.

The Ferguson uprising crystalized the call and uplifted the tactic of shutting things down. Their chant—"If We Don't Get It, Shut It Down"—was repeated in hundreds of cities across this country. The tactics we used included shutting down highways, shutting down streets and intersections, shutting down offices, and even shutting down the police station. People were fed up and were not going to take it anymore, instead taking action to creatively disrupt business as usual using their bodies, hearts, and minds, each time repeating the powerful words of Assata Shakur: "We have a duty to fight for our freedom. We have a duty to win. We must love and support one another. We have nothing to lose but our chains." One cannot underestimate the power of such actions. When we lay down our fears and act from our hearts, there is really nothing that can be done to stop us.

The uprising in Ferguson was loving and fierce. Building on the bravery of the youth and the wisdom of the elders, a new path was laid forward.

We have not overcome or undone racism, but Michael Brown's death made it a national discussion. Mass incarceration is being challenged; police violence is being challenged. We have finally seen convictions of police who have murdered. More people are recognizing white supremacy and are joining the fight against it by taking action. We have not reached the promised land, but this new generation is teaching us that we must take a stand, we must shut things down, we must rise up, and we must fight and heal together.

CHAPTER 10

Standing Rock and the Power of Stories and Spirit

My time at Standing Rock in 2016 was filled with deep learning as I was offered lessons and gifts that I hold dear to this day. The Great Sioux Nation rose up with the call that Water Is Life to stop the construction of the Black Snake, the Dakota Access Pipeline, which threatened the water source for eighteen million people downstream and cut through treaty lands established in 1851. The Standing Rock uprising was a beacon of hope and prayer for all that is good and just amid the ongoing legacies and realities of violence and generational trauma.

The convergence in North Dakota was a mix of love and pain. Of hope and dejection. It is a story of spirit rising against the brutality and hate of a white supremacist state. In the face of this violence, ordinary and humble people from all walks of life gathered to put their bodies on the front lines without backing down. Children, grandmothers, healers, horse people, storytellers, workers, veterans, people of faith, mothers, fathers, cooks, boat people, organizers, and activists offered their resources and love to keep us whole. The strategy had many facets, from prayer to political work, from direct action and storytelling to resource gathering and support from big-name stars. It was to become the largest gathering of Indigenous people in a very long time, fulfilling an ancient prophecy about the reunion of the Eagle and the Condor, people from the Global North and South.[1]

Never in my lifetime have I experienced such resiliency of the human spirit against all odds. In the roller coasters of victory and defeat, we held one another, prayed, imagined, and manifested another world in the moment and for the future. Meanwhile the politicians and police spent millions in taxpayer money to inflict harm. The people stood bravely in the face of bulldozers, guns, water cannons, barrier walls, surveillance planes, snipers, concussion grenades, tear gas, rubber bullets, Tasers, checkpoints, anti-drone missiles, and the capture, starving, and murder of the buffalo. We stood strong against each escalation in the heat, rain, and snow of North Dakota blizzards.

The anti-DAPL protests were hard, as the generational trauma of settler colonialism permeated everything. Those of us who were white brought with us unexamined, unconscious privileges and entitlement, acting with misplaced certainty without feeling any need to ask consent, repeating the oppression set down over seven hundred years ago. I witnessed struggles around power, land, strategies, tactics, warrior culture, and the role of elders. There were such tremendous psychological and physical stresses that people sometimes turned on one another, eroding trust within and among the communities.

Despite these challenges, the people at Standing Rock didn't merely imagine a better world; they actively succeeded in creating one. Social change work is too often just about the dismantling of structures of oppression—always fighting against, against, against—and less about building our imagined better worlds. At Standing Rock, we lived together in camps, shared meals, laughed, danced, cried, and walked in the mud and on the ice. Everyone had access to medical care, a place to sleep, and meaningful work to sustain the community—cooking, chopping wood, tending fires, cleaning up trash. While we failed to prevent the construction of the DAPL Black Snake, together we created new communities and inspired generations of young people not only dream to about walking a different path but truly begin walking it.

Arriving at Oceti Sakowin

Over the summer of 2016 I, like many others, was tracking activity at Standing Rock. The struggle began around April 2016 when construction for the Dakota Access Pipeline—to be built by Energy Transfer Partners, a Fortune 500 company—was approved. It was the Indigenous youth who first rose up in opposition, started a social media campaign, ran 2,000 miles to Washington DC to deliver their message, and built an encampment that came to be known as the Sacred Stone Camp on the land of LaDonna Brave Bull Allard, an elder of the Standing Rock Sioux Tribe.[2] Sacred Stone was located where the Cannonball and Missouri Rivers meet and overlooked the area where drilling to put the pipeline under the river was to begin. As the struggle grew over the summer of 2016, Rosebud Camp formed down the hill on the same side of the river, along Highway 1806. This became the ongoing home of what would become the International Indigenous Youth Council.

Just across the river to the north of Rosebud was the Oceti Sakowin Camp, which was set up in August. Oceti Sakowin means "Seven Council Fires," a reference to the political structure that made up the Great Sioux Nation, a union of the Lakota, Dakota, and Nakota peoples who live in what is now known as North and South Dakota, Montana, Nebraska, and Wyoming. The camp was on treaty land and legally belonged to the Sioux, yet the empire believes that the Army Corps of Engineers controls that land with the power to grant permits for the construction of DAPL.

In October I got a call from my friend Colonel Ann Wright, who was joining the Veterans for Peace camp at Standing Rock and asked if I wanted to go. Mark Tilsen, a young Oglala Lakota poet and organizer at Standing Rock, had recently put out a call for people with direct-action experience to come, so I felt comfortable going with that open invitation. We stayed at a hotel in Bismarck, North Dakota, our first night, and the next morning we drove south through the city of Mandan, just west of Bismarck.

As we started down Highway 1806, it was a clear and sunny day. I had spent little time in this part of the country, and it was beautiful. This was big sky country, with vast, gently rolling plains. Not too far out of town we came upon a military checkpoint that was stopping all cars. We explained we were headed to visit the Sitting Bull Monument and they waved us through. Our understanding was that Highway 1806 was the site of clashes between the water protectors and police.

The battle over DAPL was being fought on the land and in the courts, with many twists and turns. The Standing Rock Sioux Tribe was exploring every available option for legally stopping Energy Transfer Partners from continuing its violation of treaty lands—not to mention its destruction of sacred artifacts and burial grounds—including a July 2016 lawsuit against the Army Corps of Engineers for violating the Clean Water Act and the Historical Preservation Act. In August the tribe asked for a preliminary injunction to stop the pipeline. That lawsuit was denied in early September; an appeal was filed, and ultimately the US Department of Justice (DOJ) asked for drilling and construction to be halted twenty miles east and west of Lake Oahe while the appeal moved forward. Energy Transfer, in defiance of the DOJ, ignored the request. In November President Obama stepped in, saying he was working with the Army Corps to hold off on granting the easement for construction on 1851 treaty land until the corps could review the National Environmental Policy Action, NEPA, for violations.

Amid this legal uncertainty, Energy Transfer Partners hired private security companies like G4S and Tiger Swan to surveil, disrupt, and intimidate.[3] These paid mercenaries were aided by the Mandan and Bismarck police and North Dakota governor Jack Dalrymple, who in September declared a state of emergency, allowing the activation of the National Guard. The Guard immediately established a checkpoint just south of Mandan on Highway 1806. This was the situation we literally drove right into that morning, and it's wild how quickly we got caught up in the action.

Not long after we crossed the checkpoint, I got a call from my friend Carolina about an action caravan that was coming our way. Ann and I, being the action people we are, were now focused on finding the caravan. Goddess was with us as we slowly got the information we needed to take County Road 136 West. The sun was now toward our backs as we headed through the vast rocky hills scattered across the plains. Soon we saw the helicopters—always an indicator of where the shit is going down. As we came over a rise in the road we saw dozens of cars pulled off to the side. We pulled over and joined the crowd gathered on a patch of grass by a four-way intersection. We found our friends Carolina, Laurie, and Jen in a large group carrying colorful banners—the message WATER IS LIFE surrounded us.

I could see there was a smaller group of Indigenous people with a banner, sage, and drums up at the intersections. They were offering prayers to the police who had blocked our way on the road. Before long the police withdrew and we all joined together, walking over a quiet and vast terrain. Miles onward we came upon another police line, and once again there was a ceremony at the line. But this time the police did not withdraw. We held the space for some time. Various people offered words and more prayers as we waited for what was next. We learned that a small group of protectors had locked down to construction equipment over the hill behind the police, and that people had been arrested. Our work was done and it was time to leave.

During the long walk back to our car, support vehicles came along with water. They also gathered up other drivers, who then could get their cars and give others a ride back to the starting point or back to camp. Before long a string of vehicles came along to pick everybody up—elderly first, then kids and mothers or whoever felt they could not walk. This was my first taste of the community experience that was immanent to Standing Rock as we all got into, on top of, or in the back of trucks and vehicles. It was a beautiful thing.

Once back at our car, Ann and I gave a young Indigenous man a ride, and we headed south down Highway 1806. He pointed things out along the way: the pipeline, and then the small Scout Camp that had been set up along the road, directly in the pipeline's path. Soon after, we reached a line of flags over a rise in the hill marking the entrance to the Oceti Sakowin Camp. What I saw took my breath away.

The camp sat down in a lowland surrounded by water on three sides, and scattered on the grasses were collections of tipis, big tents, little tents, yurts, and wooden structures. Smoke from fires scattered throughout. The Sioux Nation is a horse nation, and there were many horses free roaming around the camp. Oceti Sakowin was the name for the camp as a whole, but there were many smaller camps within it, including the Oglala, Two-Spirit, Dine (also known as Navajo), the Haudenosaunee Six Nations, California, and the Red Warrior camp. At that point, Oceti Sakowin had been sanctioned by the Standing Rock Reservation Council and its chairperson, David Archambault II, but it grew bigger, beyond what any one person or group could imagine or govern.[4]

When we reached the entrance driveway, we were stopped and questioned by the Akicita, the "warriors" who were security for the camp. They made sure all who passed were welcomed home and asked to respect and

Oceti Sakowin camp at Standing Rock. *Courtesy of Desiree Kane.*

OUT OF THE TOOLBOX
Settler Colonialism

At Standing Rock a group called the Solidariteam compiled awesome resources about settler colonialism. Their definition was:

> Settler colonialism is a process of "destroying to replace." A colonizing power exports resources and people, and seizes and settles on land, exercising violent control over the original inhabitants. Indigenous versions of governance, land management, cultural practices, etc. are destroyed through conquest, disease, land theft, and cultural genocide, and are replaced with the settler versions of those things. Settler colonialism is not an event that we can neatly box into the past, but rather a persistent form of violence that impacts every aspect of life in settler states. Settler colonialism is still happening.[5]

Like everything, understanding settler colonialism is life work because the legacy and current-day practices of colonization run deep and are often unconscious or unrecognized. Some of the things I am learning about include:

We must start with ourselves, working with forgiveness for what we have done and how we've been taught.

We can educate ourselves by reading books like *An Indigenous Peoples' History of the United States* by Roxanne Dunbar-Ortiz or *Our History Is the Future* by Nick Estes. The Indigenous people on this continent had advanced societies, stewarding the land for thousands of years before the Europeans came, and they have resisted colonization ever since.

We must own up to the fact that we live on stolen land and that millions of people were murdered so that what we call the United States could come into being.

We can learn the history of the Indigenous peoples and nations whose territory we live upon. Were the Indigenous people displaced? What treaties did the US sign or break? Where are they now, and what efforts for land return, land protection, sovereignty, or federal recognition are they engaged in?

We can recognize that an understanding of settler colonialism has been left out of much of the anti-racist teaching offered today. It was the Europeans who brought white, male, Christian, and capitalist superiority to this land.

We can become an ally by earning it. Better yet, we can become accomplices, as called for by Indigenous Action Media, by truly putting our skin in the game.

We can learn to show up in any space in a good way, in right relation. This means listening more than speaking, honoring elders, being humble, and recognizing that each of us is sacred and worthy of humane treatment.

If we're working with Indigenous people, we must come with respect, be open to ceremony and prayer, and observe and follow the leadership offered.

We can learn to live more simply, throwing off the culture of consumerism and the myth of materialism as a path to happiness. We can conserve and protect natural resources, knowing that our insatiable desire/greed for more and more is killing us all. We live in a world of abundance, not scarcity, and must use our resources wisely and with respect.

We can educate others about the struggle and stories of Indigenous peoples, raising money, or returning land like the Jesuits did by giving back 525 acres to the Rosebud Sioux Tribe. We can demand that universities and cultural institutions return

Native artifacts kept in museums or storage, and that burial grounds are recognized and honored.

We can take direct action with consent to stop industries from violating Earth and her peoples, whether it be building dams, imposing pipelines, or culturally appropriating Indigenous wisdom, art, or practices.

We can learn that there is so much more to learn! Those of us of European descent know very little about our own people. We can learn our own histories and cultures and call on our ancestors for support and guidance in this work.

We can take the time we need by connecting with the natural world, being still, sitting on the earth, listening to the wind, putting your skin in the water, observing the flames, and feeling the passion in our hearts. We can practice the Lakota values, which help us reclaim our humanity: prayer, respect, compassion, honesty, generosity, humility, and wisdom.

abide by the agreements that had been set forth. The Lakota elders had offered the community a set of values and agreements—they were not trying to control, but to align people with healthy practices and right relations. Faith Spotted Eagle, a Yankton Sioux matriarch, was an important elder in the camp and a leader against the KXL pipeline. In 2016 she was the first Native American to receive a vote in the Electoral College. Faith Spotted Eagle said many times that when you go into another person's home, you ask before entering or doing. It is as simple as that. The camp guidelines included no drugs, alcohol, or weapons. Everyone was asked to contribute their labor whether it was cooking, cutting wood, tending the sick, picking up trash, or participating in ceremony or actions. This was not a vacation but a place to learn to walk in a good way as we struggled to stop the Black Snake and protect the water. I developed a deep appreciation for the Lakota values offered at Standing Rock: prayer, respect, generosity, honesty, compassion, humility, and wisdom.

At the gate we explained that we were headed to the medics' area to connect with our friend Carolina, a midwife. The gatekeepers told us how to get there, and into the camp we went. Humbly and quietly. We knew we had just entered sacred ground.

A Container for Direct Actions: The Emergence of the Action Gaggle

During my two-month stay at Standing Rock, I moved among three homes. One was the Prairie Knights Casino, the only hotel within sixty miles, which became essentially an annex to the camps. As the camp grew, it was harder to get a room, but those with rooms offered hot showers, a bed, or floor space to those in need. When I walked in on my first night, there were people everywhere in the lobby—on computers, in chairs, on the floor—who had arrived from all over the country and world. When all the people's movements come together like this, you know you are in the sweet spot of change.

In Oceti Sakowin, my first home was in the midwives' yurt, hosted by Carolina Reyes and Melissa Rose from the Haudenosaunee Six Nations. As the midwives' yurt became fully functional, I was super grateful to be invited into Remy's yurt up on the hill.[6] Remy, from Black Mesa, Arizona, and I had connected over the years at various mobilizations. He is an Indigenous activist and artist from the Navajo Reservation in Arizona, with special forces military training as a navy rescue diver. At past mobilizations, he was easily found working in the art spaces producing banners, posters, or props. Here his role was much greater.

Remy had organized an affinity group that carried out strategic nonviolent actions, and he welcomed me, introduced me around, and created space for me to contribute what I could offer. I am honored that he calls me a general in the People's Army. I sought out his wisdom and direction, and we became partners in action and close friends.

Life at Standing Rock was full of ceremony. In the mornings at sunrise, I woke to the sounds of elders on the microphone calling out: "The Black

Snake is not sleeping, wake up!" It would be quiet and still dark as we gathered at the sacred fire for the daily water ceremony, the fire's flames radiating light and warmth. The Indigenous women, wearing skirts as was tradition, moved clockwise around the circle with bundles of burning sage, stopping in front of each one of us, offering the gift of cleansing whatever negativity we carried. This ceremony ended with a procession to the river, which was done every morning by a dedicated group of water protectors whose job it was to carry the water, the tobacco, and the prayer. At night we were lulled to sleep by the voices of the elders expressing gratitude for the day.

There were morning meetings in the green army tent up on a hill led by a man named Johnnie Aseron, a Haudenosaunee/Lakota artist and storyteller who served as the Wellness and Interfaith Coordinator at Standing Rock. As more people arrived, some white folks came to the meetings with constant questions about their needs, like how to get a ride into town, which kitchen to eat at, or the best way to get firewood. It was exhausting, an insulting expression of settler colonial privilege that was derailing the important work of organizing the camp. Artist and writer Aurora Levins Morales, an Indigenous Caribbean woman, was at Standing Rock observing these dynamics. She initiated conversations with Mark Tilsen (Oglala Lakota from Porcupine, South Dakota), Susan Raffo (mixed white and Anishinaabe), Becka Tilsen, and Berkley Carnine from Black Mesa Indigenous Support to develop materials and organize the Solidariteam.[7] The Solidariteam Collective, working with Johnnie, asked newcomers to participate in their orientation before attending the morning meetings. The group estimates that close to nine thousand people attended these orientations.

During my initial days at Standing Rock, I observed and listened, giving particular attention to how actions and trainings were carried out. By the time I got there, one of the practices for action mobilization was for trucks to drive around in the morning with a bullhorn, calling for people to line their cars up at the South Gate, forming a caravan to begin the day's action. There had been many prayer actions and work-stoppage actions, with people going onto worksites, placing their bodies in front of the bulldozers. One day, these water protectors were viciously attacked by security dogs. This was caught on film by Amy Goodman of *Democracy Now!*, and the disturbing images galvanized support for the struggle. Lockdown actions were also continuing. These were carried out by small groups of people working secretly to get onto worksites, using lockboxes to attach their bodies to the machines. These actions were highly effective but also risky. The risks were accepted; some people had come to Standing Rock prepared to risk their lives.

I slowly realized that for some of the Indigenous leaders and groups, nonviolent direct action wasn't part of their culture—though there were some Indigenous-led groups, like IEN (Indigenous Environmental Network), a long-standing nonprofit, and IP3 (Indigenous Peoples Power Project), that advocated this approach. I came to learn that what white communities call "nonviolent protest," Indigenous groups might call spirit-led prayer or ceremony. I also learned that actions began and ended with saging those included, prayers, and that spiritual leadership from the tribal elders was essential, but difficult, as it was often unclear who the elders were. Another challenge was that with no collective decision-making process in place, some of the actions were putting people in dangerous situations without their consent. The absence of a collective action strategy was one of the greatest challenges the camp faced.

On November 1 some of the folks in the Solidariteam Collective pulled me into a big interfaith gathering in Cannonball Gymnasium. It was an amazing gathering, with hundreds of people who came in solidarity to denounce the Doctrine of Discovery. This was a church-backed doctrine established in the 1500s declaring that any land not already inhabited by Christians was there for the taking, thus justifying the massive theft of land from the Indigenous people on this continent. During the colonization of Native lands, 130 million Indigenous people were killed by massacre, displacement, and smallpox, all so that the descendants of the Europeans could claim the land as their own. *Take that in for a moment.* The magnitude of violence and suffering caused by the colonizers is almost unimaginable.

A group of us met at the end of that meeting and crafted a plan for a direct action to engage the governor the day after a massive religious procession from camp to the Backwater Bridge.[8] This action went forth as planned. We succeeded in shutting the capitol down, then walked over to the governor's mansion, where several religious leaders were arrested as they kneeled and prayed on his lawn.

This was a powerful action that inspired us to discuss how to create a solid container for action planning and coordination within the camp. I was becoming demoralized by how difficult it was to solidify peoples' involvement in direct actions. Led by IP3, action trainings occurred every day at camp, but there weren't strategies for follow-up, organizing into action teams, or systems to support newer people before, during, and after actions. People rarely knew details about the actions in advance.[9] A few of us connected with the IP3 trainers about creating action terms, and they consented to affinity group–formation sessions after the daily trainings. This did not stick, however, so we decided to switch strategies.

I talked with Dallas Goldtooth, an organizer from the Indigenous Environmental Network, about the idea of creating a space to gather allies into daily action assemblies to get people better plugged in. Goldtooth was strongly in support and said he would ride his bike all over camp, spreading the word.

To our delight, hundreds of people came to the first assembly. We burned sage before we began, opened with a prayer from an Indigenous elder, then introduced ourselves as the Action Gaggle.[10] We were a multiracial, multi-gendered group of Indigenous, Black, Brown, and white organizers. We announced that there would be action council meetings every morning at seven for representatives from the different camps or groups to discuss action proposals, and after the council, there would be a larger action assembly, open to all, every morning at eight. After the assembly, we would deploy for the day's action.

That meeting was the beginning of some amazing work, and together the Action Gaggle organized a hell of a lot of actions. But before getting into that, I want to explore how the Gaggle was guided by principles of organizing that have been evolving, especially as groups from different cultural backgrounds are coming together to work with and learn from one another.

The How-To of Conscious, Transformative, Anti-Oppressive Organizing

Many of us in the Action Gaggle drew from years of grassroots organizing experience, including a model of horizontal networking. In more recent years, with the rise of the nonprofit model, it has been difficult to get people to understand the power of small self-organized groups as an ongoing structure for our movements—yet this model has been a vital part of some of the most successful people-powered movements in recent years, including the climate justice movement, Occupy, and Black Lives Matter. The model the Action Gaggle used at Standing Rock was similar to how some of us organized in Ferguson in advance of the non-indictment of Michael Brown's murderer. It was a combination of mass meetings/assemblies and mass trainings to gather folks together, build affinity groups, and share a common language, analysis, and organizing strategies.

As a white person participating in these movements, it has been helpful for me to think of this type of organizing as both conscious and transformative. By *conscious organizing* I refer to the intentional, day-to-day work of building a culture that restores our humanity. Our movements can't only be about the practical outcomes. If we don't succeed in stopping the Black Snake (the desired practical outcome), the movement is still important because we have organized ourselves according to a different vision of how the world can be.

To be conscious, organizing needs to understand the roots of the Power Over mentality of the empire we are living in. We have been colonized, colorized, capitalized, and gendered, and those same dynamics continue today in all sorts of groups, including groups within our social justice movements. Conscious organizing acknowledges these realities and is deliberate in practices of decolonization, undoing white supremacy and patriarchy, healing trauma, and redistributing resources. All of this creates the patterns for healthier relations and living conditions.

Conscious organizing addresses the most fundamental need we have as humans to belong to a community. We need to be wanted, accepted, nourished, included, loved, and secure in knowing that we belong and that we are good enough. When we have these things, we can feel fully present, curious, and engaged. Our connection and love for one another give us the courage to take incredible risks. We have all been raised in a culture of violence and hate, propagated by a country that values guns over people, that has the highest incarceration rate in the world, that invades, bombs, and spreads war, death, and destruction. Conscious organizing is how we fight and transform this oppression and trauma into life-feeding energy.

To accomplish this, we must understand that we have differences, and that this is a strength. We are not all starting in the same place, and we cannot all take the same risks. We need to shift the dynamics of power and space to prioritize the leadership, vision, and voices of those who have been most impacted, ensuring that their agency is paramount. We must also understand that within our difference we are all the same—we are human.

Organizing that is *transformative* allows people to experience their power, Power Within. Once they embrace their power, it's so much easier to imagine different realities. We first imagine, and then actively transform ourselves and the world as we know it by manifesting our dreams.

These truths about conscious, transformative organizing aren't just abstractions; they guide my strategies as a horizontal direct-action organizer and help me understand how to welcome people into our movements. Organizing is all about relationships, and building relationships builds trust. Conscious organizing allows people to experience and express their anger, pain, and fears, as well as love, compassion, and courage, as we create new patterns and practices. Our fears, rooted in separation, lead to judgement. Fear is a powerful obstacle to overcome. Organizing starts with simply having a conversation, listening, asking questions, and then agitating or guiding into commitment and action. When we cross lines of divide, whether it is race, gender, sexual preference, class, age, or ability, there is enormous power. This is how we heal separation and fragmentation.

Ron Chisom, co-founder of the People's Institute for Survival and Beyond, says that an organizer is simply anyone who brings together two or more people for a collective purpose. An anti-racist organizer knows it's not just about how many people you're organizing, but the *way* you're organizing—uprooting and undoing the inequities and injustices as we work.

White people are not taught about colonization or racism, what they are, how they work, or how you can undo them. Nobody is taught this in school, really. We can bridge this divide, and it starts with learning our history, then developing a shared analysis and a common language. Chisom says that "issues are tissues," meaning that people with privilege can choose their issues, but front-line communities often don't have a choice because for them fighting for "issues" is literally a matter of saving their lives. In either case, if we don't have a humane organizing process that builds power and community instead of fear and dependence, we are missing the boat.

Conscious, transformative organizing requires courage because it means going against the grain of how things are typically done. For a white organizer, this means understanding our unearned power and privilege and the way we have been indoctrinated into believing we're superior and therefore entitled—the legacy of settler colonialism, which taught that Indigenous land was for the taking. For people of color, this means transforming the generational trauma of violence and of being taught you are inferior. Becoming conscious means keeping the dynamics of internalized oppression transparent and having relationships that are healing and can hold you accountable in a loving way.

Most people see accountability as a negative thing, like you have done something wrong. I see it as a gift and a process of sharing what we're doing and learning, especially from our mistakes, for the benefit of the whole group.

In our Power Over society, people believe democracy is about representation. We think that somebody else is in power, and therefore our problems are somebody else's responsibility. If something is wrong, we feel powerless to fix it, always waiting for someone else to solve the problem, leading to resentment, weakness, apathy, or anger. Organizing is the process of inspiring people to look within and find the power they need to take action and make decisions about their lives. The ongoing process of conscious, transformative organizing typically includes:

Moving people from indifference, powerlessness, rage, or victimization
    into a clear identification of the problems and solutions.
Asking people questions and listening. This often leads people to the
    information they need to know.
Getting people to identify their vision for the future and then developing a
    realistic and collective plan to get there using simple, achievable steps.
Remembering that organizing is not about "helping" people, it's about
    laying down the challenges and making the choices clear. It is work-
    ing *with*, not for.   •
Organizers can create situations, or "containers" (such as participation
    in direct actions), that allow people to experience their power and
    to take action despite their fears. Anger directed is a key to change;
    it arises out of what we care for, what we love, and what has hurt us.
    Unconscious fear can stop all action.

In her talks about revolutionary love, the civil rights activist Valarie Kaur
says that joy is the gift of love, grief is the price of love, and anger is
the force that protects love.

In my experience, conscious organizing can happen only within a
nurturing community structure with authentic relationships. The Pledge
of Resistance taught me the importance of relationship building in organizing, and everything I have experienced has only deepened my belief
that organizing is only as powerful as the relationships in the network. This
is where the affinity group model comes in—small groups of individuals
making a commitment to one another for emotional support, exploring
our hopes and fears, strategizing, and making plans and decisions together.
All of this requires intentionality and a shared understanding that staying
connected as humans is how we transform the empire.

I've always loved the simple framework of the United Farm Workers
(the labor union for farmworkers in the US) whose acronym about the
basics of organizing is AHUY! I think about it often because these four
words really capture the spirit of conscious organizing:

ANGER. Righteous anger that exposes injustice and propels action.
HOPE that another world is possible and that together we can make
    things better.
URGENCY. Knowing that injustice has existed for hundreds of years,
    yet we still need to act in the *now*, continuously, to mitigate damage
    while creating alternatives.
YOU can make a difference. Not tomorrow, not when you are braver, but
    today. You already have everything you need! You have gifts; you are a gift.

Organizing is a process of emergence where things percolate from the
bottom up. The more interactions we get going, the greater the potential for change. Organizers power-map communities, meet new people,
connect others, and identify and recruit people who are willing to become
more active. Organizers must be inclusive, welcoming, and purposeful.
Organizing provides the glue that moves us from individual agents to
collective actors working together as a potent force for change. People
Power is what it is called, and this is sacred work.

Table 10.1. How Organizing Transforms

UNORGANIZED PEOPLE MAY FEEL . . .	ORGANIZERS CAN. . .	ORGANIZED PEOPLE FEEL . . .
Confused	Interpret	Understood
Apathetic	Motivate	Active
Scared	Challenge	Confident
Divided	Unify	Unified
Unmotivated	Plan	Purposeful

The DAPL Stockyard Action

In early November, Remy asked me to join an organizing committee for a strategic action that included the American Indian Movement, Black Lives Matter, the Brown Berets, the PICO Network, and the Indian Problem. That initiative turned into an amazing action.

Our hope was to stop the drill from getting to the DAPL worksite, but the drill could not be found. We figured it was being stored at the DAPL stockyard, but when I scoped out the stockyard in Mandan, I couldn't find it. Still, it was an important site to shut down. Workers gathered and dispatched from there every morning, and the yard had a lot of heavy equipment being used to impose the pipeline. I came back with a report about what I thought was possible.

As I participated with this group, I held in my mind everything I knew about conscious, transformative, anti-racist organizing. I wanted to move with care and intention, knowing that I was a guest on Indigenous land and the only white person in this group. Together we created an action where all were welcome, from all camps and all groups, staying in alignment with what the elders had asked for—keeping it sacred.

Hundreds of people came to the prep. There was hardly room to sit down. Chris from Black Lives Matter and I led the prep, reviewing how to stay in alignment with the direct-action principles and requests from the tribal elders, how people could form protective lines, and how to protect yourself from police violence. Our legal and medical teams provided needed information to the group and asked anyone who might risk arrest to fill out legal forms. We closed in prayer led by Ray Kingfisher, a Northern Cheyenne elder from the Pacific Northwest who was supporting the action.

Our vision was to create a spiritual ceremony at the stockyard working with the medicine wheel, which represents Indigenous beliefs about the circular nature of life, including beliefs about the connections between the health of peoples and the health of the earth. We created four large circles from cardboard and painted them according to the traditional color scheme—red for the north, yellow for the east, white for the south, and black for the west. These colors represent different races.

As with most of our actions, we didn't announce where we were going, knowing there were infiltrators in the group. We decided in advance that during the ceremony, the white allies would form a human perimeter to block the stockyard workers or police from interrupting. We knew we needed an advance car to wait at the intersection of Highway 6 and the main road in Mandan to make sure the caravan could get through all together. Fortunately, a group of four young people volunteered for the job.

Over 150 cars mobilized for the caravan. As with every action, we saged everyone as we circled for prayer before we left. An eagle circled overhead. This was a powerful sign.

As we rolled out of camp heading south on Highway 1806, horses galloped to the fence to greet us. Chills went through my body as the power of the Horse Nation blessed our work. As we turned north onto Highway 6, we saw a helicopter overhead. Our anxiety grew as they started flying low in front of our caravan. We saw police cars ahead at a DAPL worksite, then more police at the junction of Route 135, then again at Route 136. As we came to the main intersection in Mandan, the four young people held

Medicine Wheel action at the DAPL stockyard. *Courtesy of Desiree Kane.*

the intersection, as planned. The police intervened and arrested one young man who bravely held the intersection open until we got through.

Once at the stockyard, we had a team directing everyone to pull in, swing around, and park close to the car in front of them, facing the road. We had planned this positioning in advance so we could get out quickly if needed. We carried the medicine wheels out as sage burned all around. The white people divided into three groups—one to surround the ceremony, another to block the driveway into the work site, and a third to stay back several hundred feet on the road to ensure no cars drove in.

After the ceremony began, I could hear something happening down the road, and the next thing I knew, shots were being fired. I ran over to the first blockade to find our first line in distress. A subcontractor working at the stockyard had tried to drive straight through the people blocking the road, including an elder man who couldn't move quickly to get out of the way. One of our people had their foot run over. At this point the driver pulled out a gun and pointed at our group; a young woman leapt forward, trying to stop him. He pistol-whipped her hand, breaking her finger, before he pointed the gun at her head. This is when my dear friend Carolina dove forward, knocking the woman away. The man accelerated and floored his way through, heading straight toward the ceremony. Lucky for us, he cut off onto a dirt road, firing several shots in the air as he took off.

It was terrifying—but our first line regrouped and reestablished our blockade. The ceremony never stopped, and our perimeter there had held strong. It was not long after that we saw the police amassing in the stockyard. I saw SWAT police, armored vehicles, LRAD sound cannons, and guns. They had come in through a back gate. We reinforced our lines, making it clear they would have to go through the lines of white people in order to attack the ceremony.

The police stood where they were, making no move to advance as we completed the ceremony. Our group began to process back to the cars, but some of the young Indigenous people did not want to leave. An elder carrying a staff stood with them, facing the police. I spoke to the group of youth, urging them to go. It was in that moment that the elder began walking toward the police. We stood silent, frozen, watching. As he got closer, several of the police came forward. The elder reached out his hand to shake theirs, which they accepted. He burned some sage and appeared to offer

Human perimeter to protect the ceremony during the DAPL stockyard action. *Courtesy of Desiree Kane.*

a prayer. When he was done, he walked back to our group and together we all walked down the road to join the others as the cars were departing.

This was the first action we had done where the police did not advance, showing that utilizing our white bodies to block the forces of empire can be strategic. There were over six hundred of us there that day.

After we all made it safely back to camp, we were called to the sacred fire. We were apprehensive at first, not sure if we would be scolded for our action, but we learned it was to honor our work. A thank-you song was sung by a Standing Rock matriarch, and the Honor circle began. It started with us, and we turned one at a time to face the next person in line, connecting our eyes and our hands. Everyone in the line followed us, one at a time, wrapping around and creating a circle within a circle. It was not completed until everyone shook the hand of everyone else in the circle.

Police Violence at the Mall in Bismarck

After the DAPL stockyard action, we continued to organize. Our action council and action assembly met in the mornings at seven and eight, respectively, and we held action preps to train for specific actions. Hundreds of people continued to come. These assemblies became instrumental in helping people feel informed, connected, and prepared. We promoted the meetings by word of mouth, and by posting signs along the road, at the kitchens, and on the Porta-Potties.

As the days and actions went on, more people got involved, some taking on responsibility for publicity, others joining the caravan prep team, others taking up art or making the props. Our work included civil disobedience actions that shut down the capitol, the Federal Building, the Bank of North Dakota, and the Mandan police station, where a dozen were arrested protesting the police attack on the night of November 20, which had left hundreds wounded, including Vanessa who lost an eye and Sophia who lost part of her arm.[11] We offered prayers outside of the National Guard and marched on NBC and Wells Fargo to confront their lies and immoral investments. We organized to support the massive women's action at the Backwater Bridge, another action at the stockyard, and several actions at Turtle Island.

The Gaggle's actions created opportunities to involve more people and develop more accountable leadership in the actions. That is part of the model—creating opportunities for people to step into their power in accountable ways. This included the use of multiple teams, just like flying squads. These collaborations seem especially important when you're working with a multicultural group because the model allows people from different backgrounds and camps to team up together. The assemblies became a space to help facilitate discussion and where elders like Faith Spotted Eagle could address the group and see the work that was being done.

At times I felt anxious that the Action Gaggle wasn't in alignment with the desires of the Sioux elders. One day at the end of our action council, I approached one of the elders with tobacco and asked if we could speak. I explained that we had not received permission for all of the actions, yet we were doing the best we could to be in alignment with what the elders had asked. I was seeking his guidance on how to proceed. He looked at me and said, "You are all doing good work here, we want it to continue." *Whew!* I felt relieved, feeling able to release the anxiety. I have learned that when I'm uncertain, working in a sacred way with humility and care is what is required.

The last major action by the Gaggle was on the day after Thanksgiving. The plan was to converge inside the Kirkwood Mall in Bismarck at exactly 11 AM to say a prayer outside the Target store. This was the first action where we announced our location in advance, because we needed people to enter the mall in what I call civilian style—alone or in small groups that converge

OUT OF THE TOOLBOX
Assemblies

Across the world, social movements are experimenting with assemblies as a form of self-governance and direct democracy. At Standing Rock we had an Action Assembly that was dedicated to meeting every day. Occupy Wall Street called it a General Assembly. Others call it a People's Assembly. Whatever the particular form these assemblies take, there is a growing awareness that our elected officials are not accountable to the people most affected by their policies. Assemblies are a political space where many voices can contribute and create, collectively informing a course of action. At the most basic level, people want the power to determine their own lives, and assemblies are a space and process that allow people to get a sense of their own power.

Convening an assembly is not rocket science, but it requires planning and intention. Here are the basics:

Find a large space
Invite people to join

at a predetermined place and time. As eleven o'clock was approaching, I moved into the mall and recognized a number of our people as well as a lot of police on high alert. It was obvious that somebody had tipped them off.

Right at eleven, around thirty or forty of us circled up, but the police were on us instantly.[12] They brought in the mall's manager, who announced that we had to leave. A moment or two passed, and then the police grabbed two people. We began to move as a group toward the exit, chanting softly, but as we approached the door, the police tore at us, throwing people to the ground.

Form a big circle where people fill the whole space
Get a good sound system or use a people's mike
Begin with time for people to express problems, concerns, or fears
Develop a shared analysis of why these problems are happening
Seek out ideas on what people want
Synthesize the ideas
Have an open discussion on what we can and are going to do to
     get what we want
Make a collective decision about a few key action steps
Create ad hoc working groups if needed
Close with a clap, song, whoop, or prayer!
Reconvene the assembly at a regular time and place to update,
     reflect, and plan more action

The process of working together builds power and hope. We develop new relationships with people who have a common cause. Assemblies create momentum and a sense that we are part of something much bigger than ourselves. We are exercising our power in the moment and practicing direct democracy, the very act of which inspires and ignites the changes we seek.

They tackled Noah, a member of the action group, who was differently abled and used crutches. At least four cops took him down. The police threw me to the ground hard, and the next thing I knew they were cuffing my wrists with zip-tie plastic cuffs. It was done with vengeance and anger. I knew immediately that I was in trouble as the cuffs were extremely tight. A young woman who they had arrested was sobbing against the wall. Most of the standers-by in the mall had a look of shock on their faces.

I finally convinced a cop to get some clippers to change my cuffs, but they were on so tight, he couldn't get the clippers under them. I was lucky that they finally got them off, and when they cuffed me again it was still tight but at least I had circulation.

They moved us outside the mall and started to take and bag our property; we saw them steal phones and money. As we were placed in vans, I was so grateful to see our legal observers on the scene, taking notes, trying to get information. We were brought to the Mandan jail and put in chain-link pens. After a while it became clear they were going to ship us four hours away to Fargo. Hours passed before they boarded us on the bus with a policewoman, a policeman, and two National Guardsmen.

It was a stressful ride. We were bruised, tired, and hungry; some of the women were crying. Fortunately, the policewoman allowed them to sit next to me as I helped to calm them down and re-anchor to themselves, using our breath. The police knew it was a bad situation and they finally stopped at a police station maybe two hours from Bismarck to let two of the women off. We reached Fargo before midnight, exhausted. One of the women had actually been shopping in the mall with her boyfriend and got caught up unwittingly in the arrests. She was very stressed because they had two dogs in the car. We worked together, making calls to friends, using the phone cards the police gave us, as well as the legal office, and we finally learned that the dogs were okay.

Soon news came that we would all be bonded out and that a network of families in Fargo would pick us up. This is the magic of community-supported direct actions! A whole network had been activated to work on our behalf. We started to be released around 2 AM. We were taken to a family's home, where we found food, beds to sleep in, a shower, hugs, and love. It was hard to make sense of all that had happened, but I knew that though our arrest was brutal, our privilege had prevented even greater harm. We were battered but alive, and we had a community to embrace us on our return home.[13]

Stories to Build a Better World

The water protectors eventually settled upon a short phrase that came to encapsulate the story they wanted to tell—*Water Is Life*. Over my years as an organizer I have thought a lot about the importance of telling stories that build a counternarrative to the dominant culture. Concise messages like "Water Is Life" can spark fires in movements, piercing the hearts and minds of the larger society. These messages can help shift the narrative from the voices of oppression to the voices of liberation.

But at Standing Rock I was also reminded that stories are much more than just concise messaging. In today's world of social change nonprofits and labor unions, there is a whole communications industry being paid a lot of money to craft sanitized stories. They often start with focus groups, as if there's an exact science to it. These mainstream communicators avoid confrontational language, forgetting how important agitation and deeply emotional stories can be. But agitation is our fire. We have to tell stories that agitate around the problems, that tell the truth, that touch our emotions, that motivate around the solutions and raise up our humanity. Using a word like *empire* in our stories about the US government is confrontational, perhaps. It is also truthful, it exposes a problem, and it gives us an image of the monolith of "Power Over."

Stories are collectively formed and forged from realities of lived experience, not from focus groups. Stories emanate the power of the margins. Stories are as old as time and allow us to travel between worlds: past, present, and future. They inform who we are, what we believe in, what we consider important, and how we act. They allow us to reveal ourselves, if we are willing. To create a true crisis for the dominant culture, we need to continue to tell our stories, again and again, within and among our families, friends, communities, and institutions.

In her book *Emergent Strategy*, healer and social justice facilitator adrienne maree brown writes about how our stories create a shared social reality that can be very dangerous for some, and the power we carry within ourselves to change these stories:

> We are in an imagination battle. Trayvon Martin and Mike Brown and Renisha McBride and so many others are dead because, in some white imagination, they were dangerous. And that imagination is so respected that those who kill, based on an imagined, racialized fear of Black people, are rarely held accountable. Imagination has people thinking they can go from being poor to a millionaire as part of a shared American dream. Imagination turns

Brown bombers into terrorists and white bombers into mentally ill victims. Imagination gives us borders, gives us superiority, gives us race as an indicator of capability. I often feel I am trapped inside someone else's imagination, and I must engage my own imagination in order to break free.[14]

I love that movement gatherings, like Standing Rock, are called convergences, emphasizing that people come in person, allowing them to see, feel, and hear new stories. They are told in pictures, images, music, movement, art, and rituals. They are told with feelings: pain, grief, anger, rage, love, kindness, courage, and generosity. The convergence itself allows new stories to emerge; as each moment passes, stories are made and told as a new history is created. Our imagination is our most powerful tool. What we can imagine, we can create.

Stories create patterns. We tell them over and over again, laying down understanding and recognition for generations to come. At Standing Rock, we told many different kinds of stories, and some of the stories had not been known by many of us who were white. Stories about the Doctrine of Discovery. Stories about massacres, like the Dakota 38, Wounded Knee, or Sand Hill; about resistance and resistors like the Ghost Dances and the warrior Crazy Horse; and about victories, like the Battle of the Greasy Grass, also known as the Battle of Little Big Horn.

Standing Rock offered our nation and our movements lessons necessary for our survival and the survival of the planet. Indigenous peoples have always been the stewards of the land and the harbingers of our impending collapse. Their very existence and survival, always on the front line of settler colonialism, racism, and destruction, offers hope that perhaps Indigenous wisdom will prevail. This wisdom reframes who we are—not protestors but protectors, something I carry with me to this day.

Yet having seen the violence committed against the water protectors, it is difficult to be optimistic. Returning home from the camps, I was exhausted, vulnerable, and fragile. I still don't understand everything about what I experienced at Standing Rock. But I know deep in my heart that the love that was shared, the community that was built, and the courageous actions people took changed our world for the better, and we are not going back.

Life After Trump
and the Power of Healing

*And as we let our own light shine, we unconsciously give
other people permission to do the same. As we are liberated
from our own fear, our presence automatically liberates others.*

— MARIANNE WILLIAMSON

I n the wake of Trump's election and inauguration, I could feel collective trauma spread across the nation. I could see it in people's faces;
I felt it in my own body, too. The daily onslaughts continue today
as the mainstream cultural channels repeat Trump's words, even when
they know he is lying. This is taking its toll and doing its job of creating
feelings of powerlessness, confusion, despair, and instability, all of which
help this administration relentlessly drive the destructive agenda of the
1 percent. As time marches on, some have tuned out as a way of coping,
putting their heads in the proverbial sand. Some live quietly in fear. Some
have been reactive, thrashing out in anger at the president's hateful words
and his inhumane, deadly actions. Some have risen up.

As attention shifts to the 2020 election and the hope of a post-Trump
world, it's important to remind ourselves that the pursuit of social justice
is life's work. When Trump leaves office, he will not take our oppressive
culture and institutions with him. The divides that plague our country—
the divides that made Trump electable—will not disappear.

I'm old enough now to see the patterns around election cycles. When
an election approaches, money and people go into the campaigns, taking
needed resources from movement initiatives. If a Republican gets in, we
organize and protest. If a Democrat gets elected, our movements sit back
with a sense of relief and caution. But the problem with our focus on

elections is that politicians, be they Democrat or Republican, will not solve our problems. When the Democrats lead without accountability, we let them off the hook, like Clinton when he drove through welfare reform and NAFTA, or when Obama imprisoned immigrant children, refused to close the Guantanamo prison camp, and continued to bail out the banks.

Electoral organizing is just one part of the larger movement for change. I choose to take direct action outside *and* inside our legislative halls, knowing it is the power of the people-in-action that creates the mandate for change. Too many nonprofits, labor unions, political parties, and community-based groups utilize election campaigns, legislative fights, and public education as their primary strategies. History shows us this is not enough. Our lived experiences through our daily lives show us that we can't expect elected officials to do the right thing. This is a simple fact, yet people continue to entrust themselves, their schools, and their communities to the work of elected officials alone.

Democracy is not just an ideal, nor is it an annual event. It is not tied to any legislative session. It is a daily practice of working in community, engaging in decision making about things that affect our lives. The roots of the word *democracy* are in the ancient Greek language. *Demos* means "the people," and *kratia* means "power." People power is at the heart of democracy, and it is also the heart and soul of direct action. When people are empowered, they don't wait for permission. They do what needs to be done.

Democracy is not a political process separate from our personal lives. The personal is political. Every choice we make is an exercise of our power.

This is why healing ourselves is inseparable from healing the world around us. It has taken me a long time to understand that healing myself is the most important, and most difficult, part of my work. In order to heal, we must be willing to let go of what we think we know, and be willing to change into what we can be.

Looking Inward: Coming Home to Austin

When I returned to Austin from Standing Rock in December 2016, I was exhausted, traumatized, and cold to the bone. I welcomed the Austin sun and warm breezes, soaking it all in as I sat in my backyard. I lived in a lovely home in the Zilker Park area, a neighborhood undergoing rapid change as small homes were being torn down and replaced with new, larger, more modern ones. But ours was still there! The backyard was my sanctuary where I reconnected with my many friends—the birds, squirrels, and lizards. Gracie, my cat, was happy I was home, sitting next to me whenever she could, soaking in our connection and the warmth of the sun.

Aaliyah and Raven, my friends and next-door neighbors, came over to visit often. Raven, at age six, was still small enough to squeeze through the backyard fence. She is a tender soul, always caring for others. Her older sister Aaliyah is a born leader and fighter. From their births forward, we have been growing up together; Negar, their mom, was born in Iran and has a keen eye for oppression, and together we are raising the girls to see and take action against injustice. These girls, like all kids, are medicine for me, bringing joy and happiness. Together we would run, play, and explore our ponds and the plants in the garden. Getting my fingers in the soil tending a garden has always been one of my survival strategies.

I was glad to be home and taking some time to regroup after the intensity of Standing Rock and the outcome of the election. I started back with my tai chi class, making my way to the park off of Shoal Creek every Tuesday, Wednesday, and Thursday morning. It was a beautiful spot, a big open grassy area surrounded by huge live oak trees and a nearby creek. I would go early or stay late, sometimes just to sit by the water as it rushed by.

Healing has been a constant theme in my life. I am so grateful for my good body, my good health, and all the great healers who have supported me over the years. Much of my healing has been from injuries like fractures and sprains. My mom tells me I broke my collarbone when I was two. In the fourth grade I broke my wrist playing dodgeball, and in fifth grade I fractured my foot jumping off the deck. In sixth grade I fractured my other wrist playing touch football, and in seventh grade I fractured my right foot sliding into second base. In the eighth grade I got hit in the face with a baseball playing in the street—whew, did my eye and face swell! The doctors began to suggest that I stop playing sports, but that was not to be. In 2008 I fractured my wrist in March and then sprained my foot in April!

Then came the healing I've done from participating in protests where the police choose to harm with weapons, chemicals, and noise, or where counterprotestors have turned physical. In the mid-'80s, a Nicaraguan Contra grabbed a flag out of my hand, dislocating the upper tip of my ring finger. That finger is crooked to this day. I have been shot with a rubber bullet, tear-gassed, and pepper-sprayed, once taking a full shot directly in my face. I injured my hamstring during the Express Scripts labor campaign in Bensalem, Pennsylvania, in 2009. For several years after, my whole body got crooked. It was so bad that by 2012, I had to take a sabbatical to heal, only to injure myself again in 2017 when a fall in my garden resulted in a hematoma in my calf and knee.

It's pretty common knowledge by now that the body, mind, and spirit are all connected. As understanding of neurobiology has grown, we have learned that our bodies carry out a complex set of interactions through a neural network of dynamic connections, and when things are out of balance or stuck, sickness can occur. If care is not taken, injuries or sickness can linger, affecting other parts of your body, laying down patterns that can create future problems. Healing, like movement work, is life's work. It is an ever-evolving process, and the mind cannot be ignored in this process.

In addition to the physical injuries listed above, I have spent a lifetime healing from the difficulty my parents had when I was young and the feelings of neglect and loss after my father left home when I was four, and again more recently when he left the planet in 2015 after a traumatic year of trying to end his life. I have also been healing from the pain of knowing the history of what our government has done and continues to do, and have dealt with emotional assaults like hate mail, death threats, and being labeled a terrorist by media and Homeland Security. As I get older I realize some of the deepest healing needed is from white superiority and how it has affected all of us.

Healing work means accepting that we can't control all of our life's circumstances—but also recognizing that we have the ability to become whole again when something has fragmented us.

In the fall of 2017, my relationship of sixteen years came apart. I did not want it to end, but I wasn't in control of that. I plummeted into a period of pain, despair, and a sense of abandonment. I had to go through the pain, taking responsibility for saving my life as well as for my own patterns. I am learning and working to develop practices every day to keep myself regulated in a time of great dysregulation. It was during this time that my tai chi class kept me grounded.

One day as I walked to my spot on the creek, I felt called to two connected giant live oak trees nearby. I sat down to meditate with the sun on my face and my back to the tree. Waves of emotions came up as I found myself sobbing, releasing grief, old and new. I had lost my partner, my home, my cat, and my daily life with Aaliyah, Raven, the birds and the squirrels. I had a lot to grieve.

I found myself at home with these trees, a place of solace. I called them ONEE and ONEZ, based on the little metal tag placed on each, labeled 1988 and 1987. I sat there after class, and at times I hugged them close. They offered their strength, reminding me to ground myself deep in the earth, to stand tall, strong, and flexible, no matter what was happening around me. I'm not surprised that there's more information coming out these days about the healing power of trees, with a big study in 2015 showing the many health benefits of living near them.

For me, living a healthy life means being grounded in a state of wholeness, where there is room for both joy and pain. Wholeness is when all of our parts are in alignment with one another, with the universe, and in a loving relationship with our self and others. It means rejecting the denial, guilt, shame, and secrecy we have been socialized with. A woman named Buck at Standing Rock shared what her teacher taught her: "We are human beings. The human is physical, the being is spiritual." I liked that. Our bodies, brains, and minds are incredibly powerful, and they can be damaged in ways that are difficult to overcome. To my great relief, they can be healed. It's quite amazing, really.

When I was involved with Rise Up Texas in 2013, we offered our people a trauma workshop run by the International Center for Mental Health and Human Rights, which has worked with victims of violence around the world, particularly in Tibet. I learned more about neurology and physiology, and that trauma is not the triggering event itself, but the state of our nervous system during and after. They talked about our optimal window of arousal, or the *window of tolerance*, an idea first put forth by Dr. Daniel Siegal, a professor of psychology at UCLA.

The optimal window describes the mind-space where we're best able to notice our sensations, access our emotions, and choose how to respond instead of just reacting. In this space we are grounded, clear, and calm.

This optimal window contrasts with times when we are hyper-regulated (anxious, agitated) or hypo-regulated (depressed, apathetic). I've found that these three states correspond very well with the types of power discussed in chapter 6—Power Over, Power With/Within, and Power Under. Inspired by a framework that the international center offered, I now use these descriptions in some of my trainings:

Hyper-Aroused

ASSOCIATED WITH: Anger—Power Over—Superiority

WORD ASSOCIATIONS: Anxious, stress, agitated, manic, inflated, angry, talking fast, interrupting, no focus, no listening, no logic, buzzed, tense, seeing red, vengeful

Optimal Window of Arousal

ASSOCIATED WITH: Centered—Power With—Power Within

WORD ASSOCIATIONS: Sacred, open, grounded, fully alive, flexible, flow, non-attachment, light on feet, in the moment, needs met, clarity, hopeful, open to possibilities, clear, calm, rested, relaxed, generous, confident, capable, powerful, patient, kind, delighted, welcoming, breathing

Hypo-Aroused

ASSOCIATED WITH: Fear—Power Under—Inferiority

WORD ASSOCIATIONS: Tired, numb, depressed, apathetic, deflated, dissociated, lethargic, dull, worried, withdrawn, depressed, sleeping, paranoid, non-motivated, defeated, defensive

Trauma starts within our limbic system, the oldest part of the brain that enables us to respond to threats and processes our base instincts and emotions. Our limbic system commands our social feelings—our deep need to belong to community, which can in fact be the difference between life and death. When we're threatened, our limbic system is activated in a big way. When the threat passes, the system should return to baseline. But for many of us living with trauma, it does not.

Psychologist Peter Levine was one of the first to develop somatic healing methods by focusing on how the body manifests trauma at the physiological level. In the landmark book *Waking the Tiger: Healing*

Trauma, Levine describes how animals in the wild are able to shake out the residual energy from the limbic system's reaction to threat, discharging it, returning their bodies to a state of equilibrium. The problem with humans is we're not so good at that. The trauma gets embedded; our alert system gets stuck, leaving us constantly on alert, afraid, and unable to calm ourselves.

Post-traumatic stress disorder is what this triggered, reactive state is called. There are many techniques that are proving helpful for PTSD, like Eye Movement Desensitization and Reprocessing (EMDR) therapy, tapping, yoga, and shaking your body. The difficulty is, our modern environment too rarely offers the conditions we need to support our healing from trauma and to develop in healthy ways. Over the millennia, our survival was based on being part of a group—a herd, pack, clan, or tribe. The threats are not the same today, but our wiring is the same. From birth onward, we learn to be dependent, and then interdependent. The ability to develop what is known as secure attachment is at the core of all relationships and our navigation of the insider/outsider dynamic. We aren't usually conscious of it, but at some level we're always assessing/asking: *Do I belong? Is it safe? Will I be accepted? Am I loved?* Even in movement work, understanding this dynamic is key to how we organize our meetings and events. We want everyone to feel like they belong.

When people lack the social conditions or other resources to develop secure attachment or for moving themselves back to a state of equilibrium, they learn to feel better by reaching outside themselves for something to calm the pain. The common choices are alcohol, drugs (legal and illegal), nicotine, caffeine, but also shopping, overeating, television addiction, workaholism—any behavior that we overdo to escape the pain. Even behaviors like reading or exercise can become addictive and can keep us disconnected when we overdo them. These addictions become a vicious cycle. When we're caught up in avoiding pain, we're less able to act with clarity, maturity, and compassion, or from a place of security when dealing with other people, thus creating increased insecurity and pain.

One of the first steps to healing is simply being conscious of what is. In our culture many of the symptoms of Hyper-Arousal are rewarded and even celebrated, like overwork, while the symptoms of Hypo-Arousal (depression, lethargy) are shamed and thus people try to hide it. We all experience trauma at some level; it is impossible to escape in a country founded in colonization, white supremacy, patriarchy, and capitalism. For generations, people have lived with state violence and environmental destruction, passing their trauma on to the next generation. The dominant culture can make us sick on any given day, whether from environmental toxins, pharmaceuticals, or pollutants in the water, air, and land. This is particularly true for people of color, whose very survival is challenged daily.

In a culture where violence is glorified and all around, we are consciously and unconsciously afraid of what we might lose or have taken from us. Strategies for getting back to center include:

Asking for help
Eating well
Sleeping well
Developing self-awareness with breathing exercises, identifying
    emotions and sensations, and taking the time to scan and notice your
    body and what it's feeling
Learning to meditate
Taking long walks (this can reset your body)
Physical activity and exercise, especially yoga and dance
Connecting with someone safe and loving
Being easy on yourself and indulging in time-outs
Making eye contact with others, gazing into the other beings around
    you, recognizing their beauty and light
Doing things that make you happy—playing with babies, physical
    intimacy, and connecting with nature
With consent, we can offer others a hug, a gentle touch to the shoulder,
    or hold hands
Educating yourself about healing techniques
Being attentive to yourself and your personal hygiene
Connecting with friends, and community. Seek out teachers and
    healers—they are everywhere!

Another tool that I've found helpful for healing work is the practice of nonviolent communications (NVC) developed by Marshall Rosenberg. Oppression and trauma can lead to unhealthy communication, as it can cut us off from what we feel, need, or want. NVC offers us some literacy on emotions and needs. If you aren't feeling good about a dynamic with someone, you can follow this conversation process: (1) Say, "I noticed that . . ." (2) Ask, "How did it make you feel?" ("I felt . . .") (3) Ask, "What do you need?" ("What do I need . . .") (4) Make a request. "Would you . . ." This simple, elegant process can remove judgment and anger, and it can get to the heart of what you feel and what you need to heal the disconnection.

I recognize that there are many other ways to achieve health and fight disease, and we cannot underestimate the power of staying active, eating healthy foods, drinking clean water, breathing fresh air, and cleaning up the soil. I'm not trying to oversimplify the many health challenges that people face, but rather to offer suggestions that can help make life healthier and more rewarding. There is no one way to heal but many, so finding what works for you is what matters.

During the process of writing this book, I have been learning what it means to truly love and accept myself, knowing that I am enough just the way I am. Sometimes this just means knowing what I am feeling, needing, and wanting and being gentle with myself. From all of my learnings, I am hopeful. Here again, complexity science informs my understanding—we are amazing, complex beings made up of many systems that are always interacting and changing. That change can lead us to destruction and death, or to an ever-evolving process of wholeness and health. We are never done, because we are in relationship with an environment that is always changing. We in fact emerge new each day.

Act Locally, Think Locally: Working Against Trump in Austin

Organizing work is part of my healing, provided I do it in an intentional and conscious way. More and more, I am seeing the connections among self-healing, self-love, and the power of direct action. Taking direct action requires conscious choices as we exercise our power. It deepens our appreciation of what we have and what we can create.

Working within a beloved community is a powerful way to heal, and after the 2016 elections, many found both power and solace by connecting with others. Since Trump's election, there has been fear, but there has also been liberation. Millions of people have reclaimed their power, releasing tears of grief through action in a caring community. Many are taking risks they never imagined. While we have not won each battle, we are continuously gaining something greater—our belief in one another, that we can change things for the greater good.

After Standing Rock, I was hesitant to throw myself back in. But I knew I had to reconnect with my community and do what I could. I was planning to go to Washington, DC, for the J20 inauguration protests, but there was also a lot of work to be done in Austin.

In January I got a call from a friend who asked if I could do a de-escalation training for a group called Muslim Solidarity ATX, who were partnering with the Austin Sanctuary Network to support a big Texas Muslim Capitol Day rally at the capitol building. CAIR, the Council on American-Islamic Relations, was a main organizer. They were asking the community for support because white supremacists had disrupted their rally two years ago, and now with the rise in attacks against their community, they were especially concerned. Trump had just announced the Muslim ban, which targeted the predominantly Muslim countries of Iran, Iraq, Libya, Somalia, Sudan, Syria, and Yemen. The Muslim community in Austin has been active in resisting this and subsequent actions from the Trump administration.

I biked to the capitol early on Tuesday morning, January 30, feeling unsure about turnout since it was a workday. As the sun rose higher in the sky, I gathered people up in small groups for a quick briefing about our plan, role, and tactics. As more folks arrived, I headed up to the stage. From the capitol steps, I had a good view and was amazed at the sea of people showing up for their Muslim brothers and sisters.[1] Similar to many protective actions before, our intent was to make a giant circle of protection around the Muslim rally participants, who would fill the middle of the circle. We would stand together, shoulder to shoulder, arms linked, calm in our power to say, "No, you shall not pass" to the white supremacists.

Before the action began, I offered love and gratitude for the people's willingness to put their bodies on the line.

Over two thousand people showed up that Tuesday morning, standing in solidarity with hundreds of Muslims who had traveled, some from across the state, to be at the capitol. There was one crazy white supremacist heckler with signs near the back of the circle, but he had no real impact on the joyful rally. Our lines held, and our roving troubleshooting teams were able to keep that man at a distance from the line. Afterward, many folks stayed on as escorts, making sure that no one felt unsafe or had to walk home alone. We were there in community and in solidarity.

———

Most of this book has looked at the bigger campaigns I have been a part of internationally and across the US, but this doesn't imply that folks need to leave home to be a part of the movement. As I explored in chapter 1, our movements are most powerful when they comprise local networks linked together with other networks in a moderately dense, flexible, powerful web. Most of my work has been grounded in the communities where I have lived. This began with my work in high school and college in upstate New York, then in Boston, DC, Los Angeles, and most recently Austin, Texas.

Much of this work in Austin has come about organically as I follow the principles of direct action in my daily life. For example, in October 2013, Onion Creek in Austin rose at exponential rates, causing a deadly flash flood as the gauges failed. A raging river flowed across a dozen neighborhoods, killing six people, damaging over a thousand homes, and killing horses and thousands of chickens. I knew that a new friend, Ruth, from my tai chi class lived in one of those neighborhoods, so I entered the flood zone and got to her house.

Before long, Ruth's house and the cul-de-sac in front became an organizing center for Austin Common Ground Relief, which formed when activists started working together to support the flooded neighborhoods. We mobilized volunteers to gut homes, remove trash, provide hot meals, and distribute supplies to residents. We held holiday parties like a Thanksgiving Day dinner and Christmas party, giving away free bikes to all the kids. I also supported the residents in forming a neighborhood council and then a nonprofit, the Travis Austin Recovery Group, that was a legal structure allowing residents to raise desperately needed funds. Our work ensured that the residents were treated fairly in the city's buy-out of their homes.

Another Austin campaign that I'm proud of is Undoing Racism Austin. In 2013 my friend Bay Love showed me a slideshow that blew my mind. He was doing an internship with the Center for Elimination

Joy and Healing in Our Movements

I have greatly appreciated the book *Joyful Militancy* by Carla Bergman and Nick Montgomery, in which the writers analyze the types of toxicity in our movements and explore how we might embody joy and connection in our work. They explore the idea that the word *freedom* has the same Indo-European root as the word *friendship*: "I am free because I have ties!" We all have free will, and our connections help us feel our freedom. Perhaps this is why I love creative direct action. It requires action in the context of community, while it also requires conscious choice and self-responsibility. It provides us the support we need to willingly face what we fear most, with courage. If we are working in a good way, direct action will fill us with appreciation—appreciation we need to share, abundantly, as we enact a new world.

Today's movements are becoming more aware of healing work; making us less willing to accept toxicity. We must create places and spaces that value empathy. We can build authentic relations that allow us to trust one another. We can develop mindful awareness in our groups, embracing moments of silence or meditation to connect with ourselves and with one another. We can practice somatic healing techniques in our groups. We can act with compassionate curiosity toward what is painful, exploring why things are the way they are, and how we would like it to be different. With greater trust, we can be more honest, knowing that it fuels our integrity—and when we act with integrity, we feel good about ourselves and one another. When we do harm, which we will inevitably do, we can make amends and learn to change the behaviors that do not serve us or others.

of Disproportionality and Disparities, and under the leadership of Joyce James the center had hired the People's Institute for Survival and Beyond to offer Undoing Racism trainings to caseworkers in Child Protective

Services. Their pilot project in five counties showed that just attending an Undoing Racism training changed how the caseworkers saw their work, and the outcomes for Black kids—for all kids, in fact—improved in areas like kinship placement.[2]

Soon after, a group of us came together forming Undoing Racism Austin, with a vision of training the community and then the city leadership and staff in the PISAB Undoing Racism trainings.[3] We imagined the city of Austin as a leader in racial equity. We knew there was a lot of white liberal money, and we thought we could raise what we needed through house parties. At our first house party, one woman wrote a check for $8,000. Holy shit, we were on our way! In 2014 we rolled out five trainings, including one with two city council members and the mayor. We did a training with the Austin Independent School District. We did a training with Seton Family Health. We did a training with criminal justice groups.

Talking about racism had historically been taboo, but now it was becoming a regular feature of conversations, making its way into everyone's analysis of the city's problems. In one of our 2016 trainings, the police chief, the fire chief, two assistant police and fire chiefs, and two assistant city managers were in attendance. One of the assistant police chiefs later said, "Since the training, I'm seeing racism everywhere. I can't put it back in the box." *Yes!* We were chipping the armor, opening room for future work.

Parallel to Undoing Racism Austin, there were many new Black-led groups that formed, doing the heavy lifting of making the many problems caused by institutional racism a priority for the city. These groups include the Austin Justice Coalition, Black Lives Matter Austin, Black Sovereign Nation, Counter Balance, and a women-of-color-led coalition called Communities of Color United (CCU), which drove a landmark campaign that won an Equity Office and budget equity tool for the city. Over time, the White Caucus of Undoing Racism Austin renamed ourselves Undoing White Supremacy Austin and developed directly accountable relationships with several POC groups. In 2016 the Austin Justice Coalition, a Black-led group, began to organize more Undoing Racism trainings.

When Trump was inaugurated and communities in Austin were faced with an increase in hate crimes, raids, and deportations, we didn't need to create an anti-racist movement. It was already there. Austin was once part of Mexico, so there are many Latinx people in the city, along with many more recent immigrant communities. There is a strong history of organizing that has only gathered strength in the Trump era. In 2017 and 2018, for example, a Latinx-led coalition—the Eastern Crescent Right to Stay—fought back and defeated a major land redevelopment initiative called CodeNEXT that would have allowed a whole new wave of gentrification, displacing even more Black and Brown people in Austin.

When white supremacists started showing up at protests carrying guns and swords, we faced them with courage and in solidarity. There have been actions by the KKK, the Proud Boys, the March Against Sharia, the Patriot Front, and Identity Evropa. They marched in Austin the same weekend as they did in Charlottesville.

Meanwhile, in 2017 a coalition of POC groups in Austin worked together to establish demands for the new police contract that was being negotiated by the city that included a demand for true police oversight and accountability. In December 2017 over three hundred attended a nine-hour special hearing, and we won: The city council rejected that contract.[4] During the following year, Black leadership from the Austin Justice Coalition, among others, kept the pressure on, and in November 2018 a new police contract was approved, with all of the priority community demands included.

This was a major victory. Millions in funds were now available to support non-police services for public safety, and we won an independent Office of Police Oversight with some real teeth.[5] Under the leadership of Kellee Coleman and Brion Oaks in the Equity Office, the city started organizing Undoing Racism workshops, with hundreds of city staff going through. Even the Austin Police Department has starting paying for these trainings! In February 2019 the city council approved funds for eleven Undoing Racism trainings per year for the next five years. The visions we had, the demands we made, are now coming true. And we know we must stay vigilant and keep pushing!

As I write these words, important battles are being fought—ones that must continue until justice is achieved. In 2018 the fight against Trump's policy of family separation began on many fronts—in the courts, in the media, and in the streets. In June, with the leadership of the Women's March, over a thousand women marched to the Department of Justice and then filled the atrium of the Hart Senate Office Building with our bodies and our hearts. We rang bells to signal the banner drops from the floors above us and then raised our hands. On our right hands we had written WE, and on our left, CARE. We opened a huge black banner on the floor that said FAMILIES BELONG TOGETHER IN FREEDOM. As the police approached, we sat down and covered our bodies with space blankets similar to what the children in detention had been given. We became a shimmering sea of resistance. A sea of women connected through a powerful sisterhood, singing, "Women gonna rise like the water, gonna shut detentions down, I hear the voice of my great-granddaughter, saying free all families now!"[6]

Over 630 women were arrested that day in the largest act of civil disobedience in the history of the Hart Building.[7] This event fueled an even larger march the following Saturday, with over six hundred solidarity protests around the country.

Lisa training people in direct action at the US Capitol on the day of the Kavanaugh vote, November 2018. *Courtesy of Kisha Bari.*

OUT OF THE TOOLBOX
Manifestations of White Superiority

The manifestations of white superiority can be so subtle, but hugely impactful. Once seen, they can be changed. The ideas below originated with and are inspired by the lessons of the activist teachers Tema Okun and Kenneth Jones (a link to their workbook can be found in the resources). All of these are a result of our socialization into what I call our dominant culture of death, and thinking about these traits can offer insight into how white superiority has made us sick and harmed people who are not white. We live out these behaviors daily, believing that are natural.

OBJECTIVITY is praised over emotion, despite the fact that we are emotional beings, not linear machines. Our culture's chronic devaluing of our subjective, lived experiences invalidates ourselves and others.

PERFECTIONISM can lead to apathy and paralysis. It can prevent us from acting because of the fear that we're not good enough. It causes a lack of appreciation for others and low self-esteem as we believe that if we make a mistake, we are forever condemned.

SENSE OF URGENCY. This pervasive feeling makes us act without care as we override democracy and sacrifice the collective for individual actions. We take on more than we can do. We focus on *quantity*, not *quality*, valuing what we can measure or count as outcomes, rather than the process of creation and collaboration.

DEFENSIVENESS prevents us from being open to the perspective of others, leaving little room for growth and new ideas. We move toward *either/or thinking* and the dichotomies this creates—good/bad, right/wrong, us/them—centered on judgment instead of recognizing the and/both. We can be afraid to speak honestly. When we hide or lie, our shame and lack of integrity prevent our growth and the growth of others.

PATERNALISM fuels our entitlement to make decisions for other people, believing that we have the power, knowledge, and right to do so. We tend to think we know better, leading us to arrogance.

WORSHIP OF THE WRITTEN WORD leads us to believe there is only one right way as we value data and documentation over lived experience. We privilege those who can write or use the dominant language, limiting acknowledgment of the variety of perspectives that actually exist.

POWER HOARDING is based on a scarcity mentality and greed. It is a powerfully destructive trait of our culture that fuels competition, entitlement, criticism, and fear of open conflict. We constrict instead of expand, leading to disconnection and distancing.

RIGHT TO COMFORT. I believe it is our right to comfort that leads white people to call the police when a person of color (seen as a threat) is in their neighborhood. It also leads to a sense of fragility and helplessness and causes people to get angry if another person is rocking the boat. We don't like when people raise up issues or problems; after all, we hold the belief that we can, and must, do everything ourselves. This destroys our ability to work cooperatively and propels competition to prove we are better.

INDIVIDUALISM makes it difficult to work with others, instead desiring attention, recognition, and credit. We can become unaccountable and isolated from the very people who can help us and keep us honest. We are social beings and we need one another to fulfill our potential. Individualism keeps us stuck and disconnected from the sense of belonging, a basic human need.

PROGRESS IS BIGGER, MORE, AND BETTER. This mentality leads to the destruction of our planet through greed—our misguided desire to have more and more. It is what underlies consumerism and materialism and has created an insatiable desire for things we actually do not need, as we march forever forward unto death. The desire for more explains why storage space is the most valuable real estate today. Growth and evolution are part of life, but change does not mean "more." I like to remind myself that we already have everything we need!

Months later, in September, many of the same women hit the streets again to oppose the nomination and then the confirmation of Brett Kavanaugh to the Supreme Court. We filled the halls of the Senate for weeks. We marched in the hallways, occupied legislators' offices, blocked streets, and disrupted hearings. On the day of his confirmation, we outran the police to take the Capitol steps. Outside and inside the capitol building, we disrupted the vote from the Senate Galleries, yelling at the top of our lungs for justice. I was proud to be one of the women arrested in the gallery that day.

At the end of 2018, I participated in a strategic mobilization that focused on exposing something the government wanted hidden. In Tornillo, Texas, over twenty-five hundred children were still being imprisoned. A weeklong encampment called Christmas in Tornillo—The Occupation was planned to make sure the children being detained knew they were not alone, forgotten, or abandoned. The idea for an occupation grew out of a visit by Latinx women, including my friend Elizabeth Vega from Ferguson, who watched as white folks with a group called Witness Tornillo became buddies with the Homeland Security people, at times even thanking them. The women were outraged by this and knew that witnessing Tornillo was not enough.

Christmas in Tornillo became a camp dedicated to artistic resistance and focused on assisting the asylum seekers who were being dumped by Homeland Security at the bus station in El Paso on Christmas Eve.[8] Many of our siblings from the South had no coats, shoes, food, water, or money. Emergency shelters were set up, food was prepared, medical people donated their time, and thousands of dollars in community money were raised to house and transport people to sponsor families.

Back at the detention center, the resistance continued, with stilt walkers, giant puppets, and soccer balls with messages in Spanish being thrown over the wall to the children. On New Year's Eve a Christmas tree was made from slashed water jugs and mock tear gas canisters. The angel on top was a photo of Jakelin Maquin, the young Guatemalan girl who died from dehydration and septic shock in Homeland Security custody. The same water jugs were later used to shut down the entrance to the detention center, blocking five buses of workers from entering on New Year's Eve. These actions in Tornillo were built with Indigenous, Latinx,

Black, Muslim, and white organizers, including elders, children, and a sweet, beautiful baby.[9]

Soon after the Christmas action, the Trump administration announced that the Tornillo child camp was closing. This was a small victory, but the road ahead is long. Many children were sent to sponsor homes, but many more are being moved to a child detention camp in Florida. The reports from this new prison are not good, and the adult camp in Tornillo is still open. In January 2019 the administration revealed that thousands more immigrant children had been separated from their families than previously reported.

I don't know what the future holds, but I know that we must continue to fight this. Even as I write, people are using social media in an act of love to raise money to buy ladders to help our Latinx siblings get over. All the money raised will go to RAICES, the Refugee and Immigrant Center for Education and Legal Services, which provides free or low-cost legal services to immigrant families and children. Over Valentine's Day 2019 the Occupation group returned to Tornillo, while Indigenous leaders have established new camps along the Texas border to oppose Trump's monument to white supremacy—the wall.

Injustice existed long before Trump. He, like all of us, is a product of our sick culture. His sad life and toxicity remind us of the importance of building an alternative culture, one that rests upon the pillars of community and love. If you take one lesson from this book, I hope it is the understanding that resistance is not just about fighting *against* injustice, but *for* justice. It is a process of dismantling what no longer serves us, but also of building something better, which requires everyday intention.

No matter who is in power, or how difficult life may seem, we can choose to focus on the everyday beauty of the natural and human worlds. We can be open to learn. Nature is our greatest teacher, if we pay attention. Birds flocking, lion prides, herds of horses, and the schooling of fish teach us the power of moving together as a group. They teach us there is not one leader, but many. We might see a flower blooming and be reminded of how a simple seed takes root, or see a weed cracking through the concrete and be reminded that seemingly strong barriers can be broken through.

The roots of trees go down, weaving together, reminding us we are all interconnected, just like the running mycelia send information across the land. The laughter of children can fill us with joy, reminding us of the importance of playing in times of ease, and in challenging times as well.

We are so lucky to be alive. We are on this planet to evolve, to fulfill our potential, to love ourselves and one another, and to be of service to the greater good. What could possibly be better than that? I appreciate you taking the time to read this book. I am grateful to all who helped me birth it, and I hope you have found something here that will be useful as you create the life and the world you want for yourself and others. So mote it be!

Additional Out of the Toolbox Lessons

Included below are additional Out of the Toolbox lessons that I often use in my teachings and trainings. I believe there is no such thing as an original idea, and I'm working within a long lineage of people who have resisted the Power Over culture. We don't always know where the knowledge comes from, and we evolve what we have learned through our own lived experience.

I honor all who have come before, and hope that my offerings will be of value as we carry on and evolve the work even more.

Anti-Oppression Practices

These practices are modified/updated from a set of principles and practices I was involved with developing during my work with DAN-LA (Direct Action Network, Los Angeles) as well as my learnings from the People's Institute for Survival and Beyond. We have all been impacted by oppression, and we all have healing to do. Change looks different depending on who you are, but here are a few ideas to get you started. These lessons apply to racism, sexism, class, ageism, ableism, and more.

Educate yourself and others about the history, beliefs, and systems of oppression. Recognize that they manifest at a personal, an institutional, and a cultural level.

Recognize that power and privilege play out in group dynamics in destructive ways that marginalize, exclude, exploit, or dehumanize others. Power and privilege can be used for the good, but only after we have a clear analysis and conscious awareness.

Internalized racial oppression has two sides: superiority and inferiority.
   We can be conscious and committed to understanding how white
   supremacy, patriarchy, classism, heterosexism, and all other systems
   of oppression affect each one of us, granting unearned privileges to
   some while dehumanizing others.

We did not create these systems of oppression, but once we are aware
   of them, we must take responsibility to undo them internally and
   externally; otherwise, we are complicit and perpetuate harm.

Developing anti-oppression practices is lifelong work and requires a
   lifelong commitment. No single workshop is sufficient for learning to
   change our behaviors.

Challenge yourself to be honest, be open, and take risks to address
   racism, sexism, homophobia, and transphobia head-on.

Notice body language, like if you avert your eyes when encountering
   people different from yourself. Learn to make eye contact, offer a
   smile, and say hello so people feel seen and valued.

When you witness or experience an abuse of power or oppression,
   interrupt the behavior and address it on the spot or later in a
   compassionate way, either one-on-one or with a few allies; addressing oppressive behavior allows people to change.

Challenge the behavior, not the person. Be sensitive and promote open
   dialogue. Talk about how hateful, oppressive language makes you feel.

Don't generalize feelings, thoughts, or behaviors to a whole group.

Recognize that constructive criticism around oppressive behavior is a
   gift. Try not to get defensive, challenging the person or invalidating
   their experience. Give people the benefit of the doubt and don't
   make assumptions.

Be willing to lose a friend, but try not to "throw away" people who screw
   up. Having clear boundaries is important, but distancing perpetuates
   oppression. Help them see how what they did/said makes you feel
   and ask them to take responsibility for making amends/reparations
   for their behavior.

Challenge macho bravado, rugged individualism, saviorism, and paternalism in yourself, in your friends, and in activism.

Understand that you will feel discomfort and pain as you face your part
   in oppression, and realize that this is a necessary part of the process

of liberation and growth. We must support one another and be
gentle with one another in this process.

Feeling shame or guilt is paralyzing. Instead, feel responsible. Being part
of the problem doesn't mean you can't be an active part of the solution.

Respect different styles of leadership and communication. Remember
there is no one way or no right way. Create welcoming spaces and
prioritize time for those who have been most impacted by oppression.

Commit time to learn about one another, to share food and stories about
our lives, our history, our culture, and our experiences.

Learn more about trauma, as it is a cause and consequence of violence
and othering in our culture. Develop healing practices in all spaces
you participate in.

Relax, do the work, listen, learn, have fun, and love one another!

Complexity Science

Complexity science is the study of complex systems and how they evolve
and change organically through interactions and adaptations that allow
new self-organized systems to emerge. As understandings of complexity
science deepen and expand, many are translating it into social science and
organizing principles. I'm no expert on this, but this is how I think about
complexity science as it relates to organizing.

KNOW YOUR HISTORY. What came before impacts what will happen in
the future, how it happens, and when it happens.

KEEP ENVIRONMENTS OPEN. The natural world exists in an open
environment while humans tend to create closed environments. Open
environments allow for a free flow of information; closed environments limit what comes in, whether it be people, ideas, or culture.

RELATIONSHIPS MATTER. All individuals and groups are agents that are
part of something greater. Each agent is a form of self-organization
that is always growing and changing.

NETWORKS WORK. Agents are interdependent, and our impact is maxi-
mized when we are linked up in moderately dense decentralized networks.

FEEDBACK IS KEY. Our interactions in these networks are based on
feedback, both positive and negative.

BE OPEN, INCLUSIVE, AND WELCOMING. Positive feedback—collaboration, appreciation, gratitude—will lead to greater change, while negative feedback like competition, criticism, or judgment can lead to fragmentation or dissolution.

DIVERSITY IS OUR STRENGTH. It provides perspective, information, and ideas that can lead to the richest changes.

MULTIPLE STRATEGIES. Complexity science shows that the greater the variety of inputs, the greater the chances of change. There is not one way, but many. The more strategies we have, the greater our impact.

VIABLE PLANS. We can't wait for the perfect. We must choose and believe in ourselves that we can do what needs to be done. Imagination ignites our fire.

SMALL TO LARGE. Nature works in fractals or repeating patterns. When our tactics are replicable, we can scale up quickly, forming a tipping point where change can happen fast. Change is triggered by smaller, singular events that ripple out with increasing impact.

CHANGE IS NOT LINEAR. Change happens in cycles. We often have to begin again, adapting with new information and experience when we do not achieve what we want the first time around.

Table A.1. Complexity Science and the Dynamics of Power

QUALITIES OF SYSTEMS OF POWER OVER	QUALITIES OF SYSTEMS OF POWER WITH
Stable	Dynamic
Closed	Open
Hierarchical	Horizontal
Linear	Non-linear
Mechanical	Organic
Information controlled	Information Released
Predictable	Unpredictable
Ordered	On the edge of chaos
Exploitive	Exploratory
Decaying	Emerging self-organization

ESCALATION TO THE EDGE OF CHAOS. The edge of chaos is where
the greatest change happens. It is this sweet spot, the edge of
possibility, where what once was must change or transform. We are
not in control of the outcomes, but if we act with intention and the
full force of our conscious beings, we have tremendous power to shift
things in the direction we want.

EMERGENCE. In complexity science, emergence is when a system
self-organizes to replace what was with a new order. It is the process
of transformation. Change cannot be imposed. It comes from within,
just as it is our Power Within that makes all things possible.

Table A.1 shows how complexity science can be applied to the dynamics
of power.

Working in Groups

Working with people can be scary as well as fun and healing! We often
hesitate to extend ourselves because we're afraid of failing or being judged.
To be fully available, we need to settle our bodies and our minds. If we're
feeling anxious, insecure, or afraid, we can ask: Am I truly unsafe in this
moment? These feelings are often rooted in not feeling valued, respected,
or heard. We believe we are not good enough. But we are! We all carry
these feelings because we are all human. We are not better than or less
than; we are just different. Our differences are gifts of resources and
potential as we share ourselves, our power, and our dreams. Our creativity,
imagination, and interactions allow new things to emerge.

We gather together in groups because we need support and care in order to
fulfill our potential by healing oppression and injustice. Developing common
values or principles that guide your work will build cohesion and help
when there is conflict. Here are some of the basics for gathering in groups:

Find comfortable places to meet.
Share food and express gratitude for it.
Create time to check in—how are you doing?
Do some grounding work: Breathe, connect to Earth, stretch, sing, buzz,
hum, make eye contact, scan your body to feel what is going on inside.

Review your group contract or agreements.

Prioritize time to share cultural and personal histories as you learn about one another.

Be clear on why you are coming together and what you want to do. Allot most of your time for this purpose.

If decisions are being made, allow room to discuss your feelings and thoughts.

If requests are being made, allow time to reflect on what can be learned and the possible consequences, positive and negative, should you choose to move forward.

Discuss how the proposed actions are an opportunity for everyone to connect and grow.

Remind people of group values and principles.

Keep dynamics of power and privilege visible. Adjust practices to ensure power is shared and opportunities are accessible to all. This does not mean that everyone does everything, but that everyone is informed, has an opportunity for input, and feels welcome and connected.

Share appreciations of each other.

Angeles Arrien's Four-Fold Ways of the Warrior guides how I work in groups in a good way: Show up, pay attention, speak my truth, and stay unattached to outcomes.

Facilitation

Facilitation can make or break a meeting. Facilitators must be confident, be authentic, and work with integrity. They need to be aware of the energy of the group, group needs, and watch for body language cues. They need to work with intention in creating the physical space as well as the space for discussion. They must be strategic in how they use time. Facilitators need to understand the dynamics of power and oppression to release blockages. They must be flexible at all times, willing to change or put the agenda aside if needed.

The Role of the Facilitator

Build a container, a space that allows diverse participation.

Attend to basics, include sitting in a circle or other seating arrangements and thinking about lighting, food, drink, and breaks.

Skillfully and gracefully utilize the power to interrupt.

Visibly demonstrate or model the use and dynamics of Power With.

Take responsibility for the group journey and process: You don't make
decisions, but make sure decisions are made.

Be intentional about the kind of culture they are building/want.

Work with energy: pacing, energizing, punctuating, silence,
stretching, music.

Produce powerful documentation: notes, charts, and so on.

Good Practices

Cultural opening: song, poem, music

Getting permission from the group to fill the facilitator role

Staying neutral or transparent on power and views; staying unattached
to outcomes

Agenda prep: prioritizing group needs, decisions to be made, and space

Presenter prep, to ensure participants have all the information they need

Roles: Assign a notetaker, timekeeper, scribe, vibes watcher, door greeter,
sign-in person, and so on

Guidelines or agreements for how we will work together and what we
need from one another (for example, turn off phones)

Introductions, icebreakers, grounding, somatic tools, to help everyone
feel welcome and present

Group process tools: small groups, brainstorms, go-arounds, dyads, active
listening, straw polls, pro/con, progressive stack lists, and so on

Working with flip charts: People learn in different ways; visual tools can
help, as well as using different-colored markers

Make the gathering cooperative and participatory

Set a tone with goodwill, spirit, creativity, and fun

Consensus

Decision making is how we exercise our power through the choices we
make. Decision-making processes set the patterns that will either liberate
or oppress. Consensus, if done well, is a process that supports liberation
because it allows for all voices to be heard, and for everyone to decide. It is
not about unanimity but consent. It is not a process of winners and losers

like voting, but a process of building maximum support, knowing that not everyone will go along with everything all the time.

For consensus to truly work, the group needs to explicitly develop a set of shared values, common principles, and group agreements that can align/guide/inform our interactions. Without this, we are vulnerable to internal discord and external forces that want to undermine or stop us. Make sure everyone understands the consensus decision-making process, and work with an experienced facilitator. Deal with only one item or proposal at a time. Straw polls, or asking for a show of hands on the proposal or different options on the table, are often used in consensus because you can get an immediate sense of where the group is at. Each amendment made must be affirmed by the group as you go along, then the proposal as a whole.

All decisions start with identifying the problem or need, visioning a
   solution, and then developing a proposal for action.
The proposal is created by or brought to the group and presented.
The group is first asked if there are clarifying questions. Do you understand what is being presented? After all clarifications are made, you
   move to the next step.
Ask if there are any concerns. List concerns, then open discussion on
   how to address them. Modify the proposal accordingly. Once the
   concerns have been addressed, the proposal is restated in its new
   form to make sure everyone is clear on it.

Then the actual decision making begins in this order, which creates the space for each party to really be sure before saying yes:

ARE THERE ANY OUTSTANDING CONCERNS OR RESERVATIONS?
   At this point, nothing major should come up, but if it does, an
   additional amendment can be made.
ARE THERE ANY STAND ASIDES? This is where people may choose
   to opt out. They don't have major concerns and don't oppose the
   proposal, they're just not called to it and may choose not to be a part
   of it. If there are a lot of stand asides, it is worth assessing if this is
   really what the group needs to move forward with.

ARE THERE ANY BLOCKS? This is when a group or an individual feels that the proposal is counter to the beliefs and principles of the group and that it could do harm to the integrity of the group and work. By blocking, they are choosing to stop the whole group from moving forward. It is my belief that if the process has been done well during the concerns discussion, all potential blocks would be addressed. If a person or group blocks without first raising their concerns, I do not consider it a legitimate block, but an abuse of power of someone trying to derail the work.

DO WE HAVE A CONSENSUS? If there are no blocks, then consensus has been reached. It is typically signified by people twinkling their fingers (this is the silent clap in American Sign Language), putting their thumbs up, clapping, or saying yes.

ONCE A DECISION IS MADE, you move to discuss implementation. Who will do what and by when.

Strategic Campaigns

Campaigns can be understood as the larger containers for our actions. Campaigns allow for escalation over a period of time. The more strategies you use, the greater and sooner the change will come. Campaign have phases and steps and can be changed based on external conditions and political opportunities. Broadly, there are four phases:

Phase 1: Prep

INVESTIGATE AND RESEARCH your opponents and allies. Learn all you can about who they are, where they are, and what they care about. Where do they make their money? Who influences them? Develop demands, maps, calendars, and plans.

NEGOTIATE. Give your opponent the opportunity to make a change to resolve the problem and implement your solution. Communicate your message through letters, delegations, meetings, and phone calls.

Phase 2: Launch

EDUCATE your allies and the public to garner support and pressure your opponent with teach-ins, flyers, social media, public events, and more.

MOBILIZE increasing numbers.

NEGOTIATE, AGAIN. Are they ready to make a change? If not, move to
phase 3.

Phase 3: Battle

DEMONSTRATE. Organize protests, delegations, marches, rallies, street
theater, and more.

DIRECT ACTION. Use delegations, pickets, strikes, and civil disobedience to take space and disrupt business as usual.

PROTRACTED STRUGGLE. The action continues and must be antici-
pated, with many rounds of strategic campaigning and escalating
actions, bringing the situation to the edge of chaos.

Phase 4: Winning Win-Wins

COMPRESSION. Your opponent must feel that they have no place to go
other than settling, going out of business, or losing their job.

SETTLE. Which outside or neutral party can bring both sides together
to negotiate the change? Are the people most affected at the table?

PARALLEL ORGANIZATION. Make plans for replacing the bad actor
with a community alternative.

CELEBRATE AND FOLLOW UP to ensure that all solutions are
implemented.

Action Planning

At core, actions are all about having an impact. No matter where you are,
who you're with, what your goal is, or what materials are at your disposal,
here are questions I ask myself when thinking about an action:

Is the action symbolic or direct?
Will the action be public or secret?
Does the action have a beginning, a middle, and an end?
Does the action make sense in the context of what came before and
what will happen after?
How can we make the action colorful, life affirming, fun, and dramatic?
What visuals can we use that will tell our story?

How will all of the basic needs of the participants be met—water, food,
    bathroom, transportation?
How will the action engage participants and observers emotionally,
    physically, mentally, and spiritually?
Always remember that vision counts and details matter!

I have also found it useful to think about goals, the target, the message,
the mobilization, and the scenario or framework for the action.

GOALS. The goal must be concrete, tangible, and winnable. What does
    victory/change look like?
TARGET. Who are we trying to impact? Who has the power to decide?
MESSAGE/DEMANDS. What is the problem, and what is the solution?
    Are there audiences besides our target, and what do we want them to
    know and do?
MOBILIZATION. How many people do we need and want to participate?
    How will we get them / keep them informed, committed, and
    involved? What are the logistical factors needed to support their
    participation?
SCENARIO/ACTION FRAMEWORK. What will happen? Where will it
    happen? When will it happen? Have we scouted the location? What
    does it look like? How will people join in? Is it creative, impactful,
    and visual? Will it attract people?

Most actions, especially during mass mobilizations, will also include
some form of the following elements that require planning and strategy:

PUBLICITY. Social media campaigns, flyers, ads, PSAs, emails, mailings,
    calendars, et cetera.
PROGRAM. Are those impacted speaking for themselves? Have we
    included cultural elements—song, spoken word, music?
SCHEDULE. What happens when, by whom, from pack-up to cleanup.
LOGISTICS. Everything that is needed, from transportation to water
    bottles.
PROPS. All the materials we need to tell the story, engage participants,
    and offer images that inspire.

SECURITY/TRAFFIC PLAN. What is needed? Who will coordinate, train, and recruit?

COORDINATION/PREP. Training and prep meetings, communication, art, and a final pre-action meeting to make sure everyone understands the plan and their role.

Civil Disobedience

Making a decision to risk going to jail requires additional infrastructure and support beyond typical actions. This infrastructure gives us the confidence needed to take additional risks. A few things to put in place if you're planning for civil disobedience include:

SCOUT AND MAP. Make sure you scout and map the site.

TRAININGS. Organize trainings, including nonviolent direct action trainings, legal trainings, and street medic trainings.

MODEL OF ORGANIZATION. Choose your model of organization and put it in place, whether you're using affinity groups, action teams, buddies, or swarms.

SPOKES COUNCILS OR TACTICAL LEADERSHIP. Have a system in place for how decisions will be made in advance and during the action, like a street spokes council.

TACTICAL COMMUNICATIONS. This might include bikes, radios, text loops, flags, and runners, or a specified time, movement, or sound to trigger the action.

CIVIL DISOBEDIENCE PROPS. Signs, banners, or full-page stickers with message for arrestees to wear.

LEGAL PLAN AND STRATEGIES. Do you have lawyers and legal observers? What is the legal hotline number? What are the laws and consequences? What are the politics of the DA?

POLICE STRATEGIES AND SETUP. Will you inform the police about the action, get permits, or rely on the element of surprise? Will you ask for rules of engagement that would protect people and communities?

JAIL STRATEGIES. Is outside support organized—rides, food, love? And is inside support planned for, including jail solidarity? Will people be cooperating or not?

MEDIA. Make plans for the action to be documented with video, photos, and social media.

STREET MEDICS. Do you have street medics? Do participants have basic first aid information as well as information on police tactics and weapons for crowd control? Do you know where hospitals are?

TRAUMA AND HEALING. If people are hurt, what is your plan for dealing with trauma?

POST-ACTION LEGAL FOLLOW-UP. Have you set up an arrestee meeting and secure ways to stay in touch? Track the court dates and possible legal options—diversions, community service, or lawsuits.

CELEBRATE AND APPRECIATE those who have gone to jail and those who have supported them.

Anatomy of an Intersection

Intersections are not just physical spaces, but symbolic ones that in many mythologies represent a place of deep power and energy where choices are made. In the more literal sense, there are many kinds of intersections where roads, cars, trains, buses, people, stores, parks, homes, or fields meet, come together, or move apart. Some intersections have more energy or juice than others, so it's important to scout them beforehand. Look around, pause, and observe, especially around the same time of day you're planning your action. Questions to ask include:

How many lanes are there? Single, double, or multilane?
How many cars are going through? What is the flow of traffic like?
What surrounds the street? Is it open and wide with fields or parking lots? Or constricted with stores, buildings, or fences?
Are there construction sites? Bus stops, trains, or subway entrances? Stop signs and traffic lights?
What are the escape routes?

All of these things matter when you want to take that space. Single lanes can be closed with a handful of people, while multiple lanes obviously take more. When taking an intersection, here are key things to think about:

What is your goal? Are you stopping traffic to get your message out, holding
it temporarily, or trying to shut it down? Are you willing to take arrests?
If you are not prepared to take arrest, standing makes it faster to get out.
If you are prepared to take arrests, sitting sends a determined message.

Make sure your line of people extends from curb to curb. If drivers sense
even a little space or opening, they may try to drive through.

Long banners or signs not only help take the space, but make your
message clear.

Have a few people designated to talk to the drivers. Prepare leaflets
about the cause with actions to take: "If this makes you angry, please
call this representative about this issue."

In big intersections, assign people to every lane to stand right in front of
the car, maybe wearing a safety vest. This can deter cars from advanc-
ing to your line, especially if you're sitting.

In big intersections, it can be helpful to have teams of people on every
corner who initially move in on the side of the street just before the
light turns green, with other teams poised to move in soon after.

It is key to stop the incoming traffic first, allowing all the cars in the
middle to get out before shutting the whole thing down.

You need to be prepared for moments of chaos when you first deploy—
Whoa, everything goes in slow motion—but this quickly settles
down once you have secured the space.

Once you have shut the intersection down, be prepared for the crazy driver
who decides to drive through. I have learned that sometimes it's better
to just open your lines, let them through, then shut it down again.

I tend to like doing these kinds of actions earlier in the day when people are
headed to work or at lunch as opposed to when they're headed home.

As scary or complicated as this all sounds, it's really quite easy. The
safety of everyone involved is the highest priority, and having a clear plan
makes all the difference.

Solidarity in Practice: Sample Agreements

We are very different groups. We are not necessarily immediate allies nor
are we each other's greatest enemy. There are many things on which we do

not agree. But we will be in the streets together during the protests. We know that the police and media are trying to divide us in order to crush our movements. Solidarity is the way in which our diversity becomes our strength; we build our movements, and we protect each other's bodies, rights, and lives.

We believe we have some things in common. We believe in basic human rights and the need to live with respect and dignity. We believe we must protect this planet—our air, water, earth, and food—or we will all die. We believe these global corporate and political institutions are only serving the interests of the rich. We all agree it's time for fundamental change.

As we take to the streets together, let us work to be in solidarity with one another. The following suggestions offer ways in which we can make our solidarity real.

Personal

Challenge and critique other groups and individuals in constructive
    ways and in a spirit of respect.
Listen without getting defensive. Be open in thinking, not rigid
    in positions.
Don't make assumptions based on what a person looks like or what
    groups they belong to.
Don't assume tactics are the only way to measure militancy or radicalness.
Refrain from personal attacks, even with people with whom you strongly
    disagree. (Focus on how you feel, not what they did.)
Understand that even though we may disagree, we have come to our
    politics, strategies, and choice of tactics through thoughtful and
    intelligent consideration of issues, circumstances, and experiences.

Street

Do not intentionally put people at risk who have not chosen it.
Do not turn people over to the police.
Do not let people within our own groups interfere with other groups.
Respect the work of all medics, legal observers, and independent
    media people.
Share food, water, medical, and other supplies.
Support everyone who is hurt, gassed, shot, or beaten.

Respect other groups' rights to do a certain type of protest at certain times and places. If you choose to participate, do so within the tone and tactics they set. If you do not agree, do not participate in that protest or bring another protest into that time and space.

Understand that our actions and tactics have repercussions that go beyond ourselves and our immediate groups. And that some tactics overrun the space of others.

If you choose to negotiate with the police, never do so for other groups of which you are not a part.

Media

Do not denounce other demonstrators.

Talk about your strategy, not those of others.

Acknowledge other groups' existence and the roles they play in creating change.

Acknowledge that we sometimes disagree about strategy and tactics.

Avoid using the word *violence*.

Condemn police repression and brutality.

Share media contacts and do not monopolize the media's attention.

Jail

No one is free until everybody is free.

ONLINE RESOURCES

Organizing for Power and Shut It Down Now

These are the author's websites. In the Organizing for Power site, you'll find
    links taking you to the *Organizing for Resistance* manual, Common Ground
    organizing materials, a list of Common Ground's accomplishments in their
    first year, the *Direct Action Handbook*, and more.

www.organizingforpower.org

www.shutitdownnow.org

Documenting Ferguson Archive

http://digital.wustl.edu/ferguson/

Ferguson Action

http://fergusonaction.com/

Justice for Janitors Oral History Project

http://georgetownlaborhistory.org/

National Pledge of Resistance Manual

www.reclaimingquarterly.org/web/handbook/DA-Handbk-Pledge86-lo.pdf

The New Bottom Line

www.buildingmovement.org/reports/entry/the_new_bottom_line

No DAPL Archive

www.nodaplarchive.com/

On May 12th

http://www.onmay12.org/

People's Global Action

www.nadir.org/nadir/initiativ/agp/en/

People's Institute for Survival and Beyond

http://pisab.org/our-principles

Starhawk's Writings Archive
With information on the Gaza Freedom March and more.
https://starhawk.org/writing/activism/israelgaza/

Swarmwise
https://falkvinge.net/files/2013/04/Swarmwise-2013-by-Rick-Falkvinge-v1.1
-2013Sep01.pdf

Unsettling America
https://unsettlingamerica.wordpress.com/

White Supremacy Culture
http://www.cwsworkshop.org/PARC_site_B/dr-culture.html

WTO History Project
http://depts.washington.edu/wtohist/index.htm

NOTES

Chapter 1: Election Night 2016 and the Power of Decentralized Networks

1. On January 24, 2017, Trump took executive action and approved the Dakota Access Pipeline. In June 2017 a federal judge ruled that Trump did not follow proper environmental procedures, but the ruling did not stop the oil from flowing.
2. Becky Bond and Zack Exley, *Rules for Revolutionaries: How Big Organizing Can Change Everything* (White River Junction, VT: Chelsea Green, 2016), 44.
3. L. A. Kauffman, *Direct Action: Protest and the Reinvention of American Radicalism* (New York: Verso, 2017), xi.
4. adrienne maree brown, *Emergent Strategy: Shaping Change, Changing Worlds* (Chico, CA: AK Press, 2017), 3.
5. Margaret Wheatley and Deborah Frieze, "Using Emergence to Take Social Innovations to Scale," Margaret J. Wheatley website, https://www.margaret wheatley.com/articles/emergence.html.
6. Marty Jezer, *Abbie Hoffman: American Rebel* (New York: Rutgers University Press, 1993), 296.
7. Texas Women's Healthcare Coalition, "Texas Women's Healthcare in Crisis," https://texaswhc.org/wp-content/uploads/2017/04/Texas-Womens -Healthcare-in-Crisis.pdf.
8. Jordan Smith, "HB 2 Protestors Return to Court," *Austin Chronicle*, April 22, 2014.
9. Rocio Villalobos, "The People's History: The Birth of the New Feminist Army in Texas," *Rewire News*, June 25, 2014, https://rewire.news/article/2014/06 /25/peoples-history-birth-new-feminist-army-texas.
10. Ben Ramalingam et al., "Exploring the Science of Complexity: Ideas and Implications for Development and Humanitarian Efforts" (working paper, Overseas Development Institute, February 2008), https://www.odi.org/sites /odi.org.uk/files/odi-assets/publications-opinion-files/833.pdf, 4.
11. Ramalingam et al., "Exploring the Science of Complexity," 6.
12. Ramalingam et al., "Exploring the Science of Complexity," 8.
13. Victor Hugo, "History of a Crime," 1877.
14. Martin Luther King Jr., "Letter from a Birmingham Jail" (April 16, 1963), Martin Luther King, Jr. Research and Education Institute, https://king institute.stanford.edu/king-papers/documents/letter-birmingham-jail.
15. "Edge of Chaos," Systems Academy, http://complexitylabs.io/edge-of-chaos.

Chapter 2: Shutting Down the CIA and the Power of Bottom-Up Organizing

1. Kate Aronoff, "Peace Activists Pledge Resistance Against U.S. Military
   Intervention in Central America, 1984–1990," Global Nonviolent Action
   Database of Swarthmore College, February 10, 2011, https://nvdatabase
   .swarthmore.edu/content/peace-activists-pledge-resistance-against-us
   -military-intervention-central-america-1984-1990.

2. The Chicago 8 were put on trial for conspiracy to cross state lines to commit a
   riot at the Democratic National Convention. At the convention the Yippies
   ran a pig for president and were brutally attacked by the police.

3. At this time Abbie was on the run from authorities and living under a pseud-
   onym, Barry Freed, with only a few select friends knowing his real identity.
   After the Save the River victory, he turned himself in, which he did in a
   dramatic way, with Barbara Walters coming to the river for an exclusive. She
   was put on a boat and taken out into the middle of the river, where another
   boat brought Abbie to meet her. He ended up serving four months in prison.

4. This was a huge victory that continues to protect the river to this day. I was
   given a key to the Thousand Islands for my work. Yes, it was made of tinfoil,
   but I was honored.

5. Adam Taylor, "The CIA's Mysterious Role in the Arrest of Nelson Mandela,"
   Washington Post, May 16, 2016, WorldViews section.

6. Gary LaFree, Laura Dugan, and Erin Miller, Putting Terrorism in Context: Lessons
   from the Global Terrorism Database (Abingdon, UK: Routledge, 2003), 56.

7. Lucinda Glenn, "Inventory of the Pledge of Resistance Collection," Graduate
   Theological Union Archives, collected 2011, https://oac.cdlib.org/findaid
   /ark:/13030/kt7c60424f/entire_text.

8. In addition, Paul Shannon, a local leader with the American Friends Service
   Committee (AFSC), and Tony Palumbo at the Mobilization for Survival
   office were instrumental in launching the Pledge in Boston. Other key
   organizers included Dakota Butterfield, Ann Shumway, Frank Dorman,
   John Hoffman, Athena Lee Bradley, and Paul Miller. Noam Chomsky was
   also a huge backer of this work.

9. Athena Lee Bradley and Paul Miller were two of my good buds and partners
   in protest. I became roommates with Diane Adler from CPPAX and Ted
   German, living in their pantry closet. Ted and I remain good friends to
   this day!

10. Christian Smith, Resisting Reagan: The U.S. Central America Peace Movement
    (Chicago: University of Chicago Press, 1996), 303.

11. This action was conceived by Athena Lee Bradley, Paul Miller, Karen
    Dobak, and C. T. Butler.

12. We negotiated to do community service in exchange for dismissing our trespassing charges. I spent days cleaning up trash on the Boston Common for this action.

13. In 1991 riots broke out in Mount Pleasant after a Latinx man was shot by a Black policewoman.

14. Folks working on the DC Pledge included Brian Adams, Paul Ruther, Pete Caplan, Sara Mahy, Amy Markowitz, Laura Worby, Jane Zara, Paul Rhemer, Doug Fishman, and Nadine Bloch.

15. This included Margie Swedish and Lee Miller at the InterReligious Task Force on Central America, the Nicaragua Network, CISPES, NISGUA, the Fellowship of Reconciliation, Mobilization for Survival, and the Coalition for a New Foreign and Military Policy, who convened the Central America Working Group, an essential strategy table of all the key players. I also started working with Stephen Slade and then Ken Butigan and Judy Rohrer, the national Pledge coordinators in the National Resource Center, which along with the Pledge shuttered its doors in March 1993.

16. The city mobilization group was staffed by Clarence Lusane. The mobilization and outreach group was staffed by Josh Bornstein. The fund-raising group was led by Greg More; the media group, by Ned Greenberg; the logistics and programming group, by Leslie Cagan, who served as the national coordinator.

17. Personally I was wowed by the members of the steering committee itself, which included big names in my mind like Joseph Lowery from the Southern Christian Leadership Conference, Kathy Engle from MADRE, Alice Cohan from NOW, Randall Robinson from TransAfrica, Damu Smith and Imani Countess from the Washington Office on Africa, and David Cortright from SANE/FREEZE.

18. A congressional lobby day was also scheduled for Monday, which disappointed some of us because it would split our ranks. But recently I have reevaluated this. Complexity science has helped me appreciate that multiple options allow for greater participation. Many who attended the lobby day would not have joined us at the CIA anyway.

19. Lee Hockstader, "560 Arrested at CIA Headquarters," *Washington Post*, April 28, 1987.

Chapter 3: Justice for Janitors and the Power of Escalation

1. Maryann Haggerty, "Protest of Carr Companies Blocks Bridge; 38 Arrested," *Washington Post*, December 9, 1994, http://georgetownlaborhistory.org/news -article/protest-carr-companies-blocks-bridge-38-arrested.

2. Frank Swoboda and Maryann Haggerty, "Janitors Approve Contract," *Washington Post*, June 21, 1998.

3. Stephen Lerner and Jono Shaffer, "25 Years Later: Lessons from the Organizers of the Justice for Janitors Campaign," *The Nation*, June 16, 2015.

4. She also taught me what it was like to be part of a big, loving family. She is the oldest of eight kids, born and raised by politically conscious parents in Philadelphia.

5. Stephen had a long history organizing low-wage workers, including farm-workers and garment workers. He has always believed that disruption has to be part of the mix!

6. Along with a group of courageous union leaders, including Jay Hesse, Valarie Long, and organizers like Bill Ragen in DC and Jono Shaffer in Los Angeles. Other key organizers included Lenore Friedlander, Mary Anne Hohenstein, Maria Naranjo, Mauricio Vasquez, Jaime Contreras, and Lynn Turner. Some key researchers include David Chu, Manny Pastreich, and Carol Tyson.

7. Alyssa Russell, "Cleaning Up the Service Sector: The Justice for Janitors Campaigns in Washington, D.C. and Atlanta, Georgia" (honors thesis, Georgetown University, May 2017).

8. Ross Eisenbrey, "Employers Can Stall First Union Contract for Years," *Economic Policy Institute*, May 20, 2009.

9. Mark Jenkins and Charles Paul Freund, "The Man Who Tore Things Down," *Washington City Paper*, May 12, 2000.

10. Chin-chinas are noisemakers made out of empty soda cans that have been washed, dried, and then filled with popcorn kernels, BBs, or dried beans, which are then sealed with a little piece of paper covered with duct tape. Drying the can's contents and the little piece of paper are important so that the contents don't get sticky. These make a great sound when you shake them!

11. Russell, "Cleaning Up the Service Sector."

12. Ken Cummins, "Brazil's Surprise Victory," *Washington City Paper*, February 17, 1995.

13. Wendy Melillo, "D.C. Police Dispute Clarke's Description of Protest," *Washington Post*, March 9, 1995.

14. We thought we were being clever with "DC Has Carr Trouble" since we knew we would be impacting the streets, but nobody really understood what we were talking about. Our second round of messaging made much more sense to everyone.

15. I developed a long-term relationship with Bob King and his team and supported the UAW on a number of campaigns. When Governor Rick Snyder was driving Michigan to be a Right to Work State in 2012, Bob's chief of staff, Wendy Fields, called me and said, "Lisa, we broke the emergency glass, and your name came out!" I traveled to Michigan to coordinate a week of actions at the capitol. We did not win, but we gave them a hell of a fight!

16. Mary Ann French, "Taking It to the Streets," *Washington Post*, April 14, 1995.

17. "Penalty for Bridge Blockers," *Washington Post*, August 5, 1997, http://georgetownlaborhistory.org/news-article/penalty-bridge-blockers.

18. The agreement included wages raised from $3.35 an hour to $6.50, then $8.50 within a five-year period. The contract also included health care, retirement funds, and a fund to help mostly immigrant workers learn other skills that would allow them to move to higher-paying jobs.

19. John Howley, "Justice for Janitors: The Challenge of Organizing in Contract Services," *Labor Research Review* 1, no. 15 (1990), https://digitalcommons.ilr.cornell.edu/lrr/vol1/iss15/4.

Chapter 4: The Battle of Seattle and the Power of Going to Jail for Justice

1. Miguel passed away from a heart attack on May 6, 2005.

2. "Highest to Lowest—Prison Populations Rate," World Prison Brief, Institute for Criminal Policy Research, Birkbeck University of London, updated November 2018, http://www.prisonstudies.org/highest-to-lowest/prison-population-total.

3. In 1987 Katya broke into the Vandenberg Air Force Base and destroyed a computer mainframe that she believed was part of a first-strike nuclear launch system. She served a five-year sentence for this action, during which time she studied for the LSAT and was accepted into Harvard Law School.

4. "Contras Set to Free 8 Germans," *New York Times*, June 6, 1986, https://www.nytimes.com/1986/06/06/world/contras-set-to-free-8-germans.html.

5. Black bloc is a tactic used around the world by people who dress typically in black clothes and masks to hide their identity. A black bloc is more inclined to engage in property destruction and fighting back against the police.

6. Seattle Police Department, *After Action Report*, compiled after the World Trade Organization Ministerial Conference in Seattle, Washington, November 29–December 3, 1999, April 4, 2000.

7. Katya Komisaruk, "Solidarity Tactics in Seattle, Washington, D.C., and Los Angeles," https://organizingforpower.org/wp-content/uploads/2009/06/solidarity-tactics-seattle-on.pdf.

8. Elizabeth Betita Martinez, "Where Was the Color in Seattle? Looking for Reasons Why the Great Battle Was So White," *Colorlines*, March 10, 2000.

Chapter 5: The Global Justice Movement and the Power of Creative Nonviolence

1. We had been collaborating with the folks in Philly organizing against the RNC in July. Unlike the RNC efforts, we put a central focus on anti-racist organizing. They, too, faced infiltration and a terrifying crackdown down by

the police, under the leadership of Chief Timoney. Timoney was later hired as chief of the Miami police and orchestrated a brutal crackdown during the FTAA protests in 2003.

2. We won an injunction to prevent them from raiding our space. We won the right to assemble close to the convention when they tried to force us into Pershing Park, and we embraced non-cooperation in our jail strategies and ultimately won reduced charges for all.

3. One of our actions involved fifty people engaging in civil disobedience shutting down all the doors of the Rampart Police Station.

4. These action guidelines are the same ones I was raised up on during the Central America movement. I believe they may have originated within the Clamshell Alliance that was organizing mass direct action to stop the Seabrook Nuclear Power Plant in New Hampshire. They have since been passed on to generation after generation, to those who are committed to disciplined nonviolent direct action. At times, "We will not destroy property" has been modified to say "We will not destroy property, unless it is obstacles put in our way."

5. Years later I learned that at least three European direct-action trainers groups emerged from that mobilization.

6. During this march my friend David Rovics, an anarchist troubador whose music fills my soul, sang "We Will Shut Them Down."

7. Kate Connolly, "Prague Protestors Say They Were Beaten in Jail by Police," *The Guardian*, October 3, 2000.

8. This formation grew out of a response to the moralistic and controlling nonviolent position held by the Montreal-based organizing group Operation SalAMI.

9. Nicolas Phebus, "Radicalize This! Building the Resistance to the FTAA and Summit of the Americas," *Northeastern Anarchist*, January 19, 2001.

10. Paul D'Amato, "Diversity of Tactics or Unity in Action?" SocialistWorker .org, March 26, 2012, https://socialistworker.org/2012/03/26/diversity-of -tactics; the concept of a diversity of tactics has a much longer history going back to the 1960s, at least, but this was the first that I became aware of it being codified as an action agreement.

11. Oscar Olivera, a Bolivian labor leader, was a key leader in this fight.

12. Andrew Boyd and Dave Oswald Mitchell, *Beautiful Trouble: A Toolbox for Revolution* (New York: OR Books, 2012).

13. Once again, the air was our ally, and in this moment I learned the importance of moving into the wind as it blows the tear gas away.

14. James Vassilopoulos, "We Live to Tread on Kings: The Significance of Genoa," *Links International Journal of Socialist Renewal*, http://links.org.au/node/96.

15. Paddy Agnew, "Italy Found Guilty of Using Torture During G8 Protest," *Irish Times*, April 8, 2015.
16. Bob Arndorfer, "People Stream Out as Security Move in Around G8 Summit," *Gainesville Sun*, June 9, 2004.
17. A year later they practiced domestic internment at the 2004 Republican National Convention when they arrested 1,800 people and put us in cages at a bus depot at Pier 57. We called it Guantanamo-on-Hudson. Most of the charges were dismissed. You can read about it here: https://www.thevillager.com/2004/09/pier-57-pens-are-called-guantanamo-on-hudson/.
18. The infiltrator, Brandon Darby, was someone I had worked with and never trusted, the same misogynist who created problems at Common Ground after Hurricane Katrina.
19. In 2004, during the Republican National Convention, *Nightline* showed pictures of the twenty most dangerous anarchists in the country, and I was one of them.
20. At this meeting I met Mike McGuire, an organizer from Baltimore with long-standing connections in the Global South, and it was lucky I did because he spoke fluent Spanish and became my translator both before and during the mobilization. Our collaboration was a real gift, and I consider him my brother to this day.
21. There were concerns about Plan Puebla Panama (PPP), a regional development initiative that would create a protected biological corridor that would make privatization of biodiversity profitable and legally possible.
22. At the initial gathering Walden Bello, a well-known and respected movement leader from the Philippines, reminded us that the weak link in WTO is consensus—all countries must agree for a rule to be adopted. He also said that the WTO with its policies of trade liberalization was like a bike—it must keep moving forward or it collapses.
23. At another international meeting, it was agreed that there would be a People's Forum on Alternatives to the WTO and a call for a Global Week of Action from September 7 through 14. The 9th would be an International Day of Action, the 10th would have a forum on Agriculture, the 11th would be an International Day of Mourning against war and economic violence, the 12th would focus on privatization of services, and the 13th would be a big anti-WTO march.
24. Merging permaculture with political action was something we did a lot with the Pagan Cluster. One of my favorites was the compost toilet at the anti-FTAA mobilization in Miami that said GIVE A SHIT FOR THE REVOLUTION.
25. When I moved to Austin, I befriended Skotty Kellogg and his partner, Stacy Pettigrew, the initiators of the Rhizome space in Austin, an amazing permaculture, political, and art space that was a model for how things could be. I

was in love with its beautiful flowers, fruit trees, and vegetable gardens, which extended outside and up the street. There was a bike shop, a welding shop, and a laundry area that channeled the water out through a series of bathtubs with gravel and plants, cleaning it before watering the gardens. There was also a child-care room, a stage, an art space, and a pirate radio station.

26. The Group of 22 was a recent formation of developing nations that were working together to stop the destructive policies of the WTO.

27. The 2003 FTAA protests in Miami were a pivotal moment for our movement. We brought forward a set of Solidarity Principles and Practices that were designed to bridge the divide on tactics in our movements. We wanted to avoid getting stuck on the questions of nonviolence or diversity of tactics, instead focusing on a set of beliefs and behaviors that would allow all to be in relationship, even with those with whom we did not agree. It was at a spokes council meeting in Miami, attended by direct actionists, NGOs, and representative from the AFL-CIO, that these were agreed to. A new era of solidarity was beginning, and while it was not perfect, it opened up new relationships and understanding. The police were brutal in Miami, and when they turned their guns on labor activists, many finally understood that we were not the cause of the violence, and that the media criminalization campaigns were lies.

Chapter 6: Hurricane Katrina and the Power of Solidarity

1. A. C. Thompson, "Post-Katrina, White Vigilantes Shot African-Americans with Impunity," ProPublica, December 19, 2008.

2. Matt Taibbi, "Apocalypse in New Orleans: Five Days After Hurricane Katrina, a Journey into the Nightmare," *Rolling Stone*, October 6, 2005.

3. And even within the Hurricane Harvey relief efforts, it was the Black and Brown communities in the area that received the least help.

4. Brentin Mock, "Why Louisiana Fought Low-Income Housing in New Orleans After Katrina" *CityLab*, August 27, 2015.

5. Each RV carried Iraq veterans, military families, and those we called Gold Star families, who had lost a loved one. The Veterans for Peace bus that had joined the southern route diverted in NOLA and set up a hurricane relief center in Covington, north of Lake Pontchartrain. From them, we got daily reports on what was happening on the ground. Veterans for Peace was one of the earliest supporters of Common Ground, providing money and material aid.

6. Common Ground was one of three locally led radical relief efforts that emerged in the month or so after Katrina. One of the others, the People's Hurricane Relief Fund, was founded by Curtis Muhammad, a longtime organizer in NOLA who worked with his sons and other key nationalist-oriented

Black organizers to build both material and political relief. And then there was Mama D, a Black leader who stayed through the storm in the Seventh Ward. With the help of the Soul Patrol, she organized a relief effort to support her neighborhood. More than once she clashed with both Common Ground and the People's Hurricane Relief Fund, saying they were taking credit for her work, enabling them to raise money that they did not share. Mama D showed up for her community again and again, on her own terms.

7. I worked with scott at the Exxon Mobil Shareholder meeting in 2002 in Dallas and on several training camps. My friendship with scott was challenged by patriarchy in scott's relationship with and support for Brandon Darby. When it became clear that Darby was an FBI informant, our relationship broke down, but we have since healed, knowing we all were harmed.

8. There were many people, especially women, that were the engines behind our work early on. Bork was instrumental in home and eviction defense. Soliel led the legal team that fought for prisoner rights and supported the residents with legal clinics. Emily drove the effort to restore community gardens and bring fresh food to the people. Jenka ensured that essential information was available through the radio station and setting up centers where people could access computers. Carolina brought heart and soul to residents in the Ninth Wards, gathering needed resources and organizing immigrant workers. Genevieve coordinated the gutting of thousands of homes. Kerul also helped to secure resources and disseminate information using corporate and social media. Mo, Aislyn, Catherine, Jennifer, and Carrie anchored a lot of the healing work at the clinic. Alex and Lou Lou did whatever needed to be done. Sue, Kimber, and Sam coordinated volunteers. Jen and Isabelle helped with distro. Kim, Jessie, and Anna worked the Ninth Wards. Marina managed the finances and Liz organized the bikes! Scott, Suncere, Sean, Jeremy, Brian, Tyler, Topher, Justin, Matt, Kobe, Francisco, Mikkel, Pauly, Randeep, Grumble, Nick, Peter, Kone, Benji, Alain, Jimmy, Jon, Glen, and more brought their skills, labor, and kindness to the work. Eric, Scott W., Scott M., Iggy, Greg, Noah, Bay, and Roger were key players in the clinic. There were many more key people as time went on including Olivia, Claire, Luke, Drew, Casey, Gabe, Sylvia, Sonia, Matthew, Shada, Alan, Jake, Renee, Rebecca, Molly, Annie, Jeremiah, Bronwyn, Ethan, Maddie, and Shakoor. And oh so many more!

9. A. C. Thompson, "If It Moved, You Shot It," *Texas Observer*, January 5, 2009.

10. Thompson, "If It Moved."

11. Thompson, "If It Moved."

12. Campbell Robertson, "New Orleans Police Officers Plead Guilty in Shooting of Civilians," *New York Times*, April 20, 2016.

13. Rebecca Solnit, "Reconstructing the Story of the Storm: Hurricane Katrina at Five," *The Nation*, August 26, 2010.

14. "10 Years Later: Remembering Hurricane Katrina," National Guard, https://www.nationalguard.mil/Features/2015/Katrina.

15. While scott, Malik, and Sharon were putting together ideas for Common Ground, there was a rescue effort under way for Robert King, a former Black Panther and member of the Angola Three, the group who were framed for a crime while in prison and locked in solitary confinement for decades. This was in Angola State Prison in Louisiana—the former site of the Angola Plantation. King was stranded with his dog, Kenya, in the Seventh Ward because he had refused to evacuate without her. As the story goes, it was King who suggested the name Common Ground when they got to Malik's house.

16. One of our members, Elizabeth West, had grown up in Louisiana, and her aunt's home off Grand Isle was badly damaged. The Pagan Cluster mobilized to support her and the whole relief effort.

17. Gary Rivlin, "Why the Lower Ninth Ward Looks Like the Hurricane Just Hit," *The Nation*, August 13, 2015.

18. Rivlin, "Lower Ninth Ward."

19. Deborah Sontag, "Months After Katrina, Bittersweet Homecoming in the 9th Ward," *New York Times*, December 2, 2005.

20. Campbell Robertson and John Schwartz, "Decade After Katrina, Pointer Finger More Firmly at Army Corps," *New York Times*, May 23, 2015.

21. Some street medics had arrived four days after the storm and with the help of Malik were able to establish the first civilian medical clinic in the Majid Bilal Mosque.

22. Tim Shorrock, "Common Ground: Post-Katrina Volunteer Medics on Bicycles Sparked a New Model of Community Health Care in New Orleans," *Mother Jones*, March 2006.

23. In retrospect I feel deep awe at the fact that after Katrina, radical organizers from the Global Justice movement—folks who had spent the past several years developing skills at setting up alternative social structures to support mass mobilizations—were now applying what we knew to disaster recovery.

24. Grumble has served many movements both before and after Common Ground, and is a true unsung hero.

25. Rivlin, "Lower Ninth Ward."

26. Rivlin, "Lower Ninth Ward."

27. Roberta Brandes Gratz, "Who Killed Public Housing in New Orleans?" *The Nation*, June 2, 2015.

28. Rivlin, "Lower Ninth Ward."

29. Laura Bliss, "10 Years Later, There's Still So Much We Don't Know about Where Katrina Survivors Ended Up," *CityLab*, August 25, 2015.

30. Bliss, "10 Years Later."

31. Sarah Carr, "New Research Sheds Light on Fates of Thousands of New Orleans Teachers Fired After Hurricane Katrina," *New Orleans Public Radio*, June 18, 2015.

32. Our work was informed by our practice of direct action. Opening the Little Blue House was against their rules. No one was supposed to stay in the area, but we slept there, defying the police. We organized protests to disrupt media events organized by public officials and created a rapid response to stop bulldozers that came to demolish what was left. I remember one day we got a call that the bulldozers had been seen in the area. We all dropped what we were doing and sped over. We stood in the road, letting them know we were there and watching. There was no question that at some point, the debris and destroyed homes would need to be cleared, but we were determined to make sure that didn't happen until the residents had a chance to come home and see what, if anything, could be saved.

33. Rivlin, "Lower Ninth Ward."

34. In February we were looking for a place to house the influx of volunteers for spring break. Driving through the Upper Ninth Ward, I spotted a church and school called St. Mary's of the Angels and happened to see a man standing in the parking lot. This turned out to be Pastor Bart Pax. When Katrina hit, he stayed behind and opened the school to shelter residents who hadn't gotten out in time. Two hundred people were evacuated off the roof by helicopter. I talked to the pastor about using the school as a new volunteer center for Common Ground. He was hesitant, unsure if the archdiocese would support it. In the end he opened the space to us despite uncertainty about the rules—a man after my own heart! After the hard work of cleaning St. Mary's, including feces left behind by two hundred people, it became a full-on hub that housed hundreds of volunteers.

35. One of the great tragedies is that the US government has covertly co-opted this work, training and funding uprisings like the "color" revolutions of the '00s and right-wing coups like we are witnessing in Venezuela today.

36. Taibbi, "Apocalypse in New Orleans."

37. Brian Thevenot and Gordon Russell, "Rape. Murder. Gunfights," *Times-Picayune*, September 26, 2005.

38. Jarvis DeBerry, "Danny Brumfield's Death at the Hands of New Orleans Police Shouldn't Be an Aside," *Times-Picayune*, December 11, 2011.

39. We also supported the immigrant "guest workers" who were brought in by the private sector on H-2B visas to do the hard cleanup and rebuilding work, pitting them against local Black workers who needed the jobs. The guest workers were living in horrible conditions in City Park and in the back of trailer trucks around the Gulf Coast starting in the fall of 2005. Carolina took this situation on. The workers sued for and eventually won a multimillion-dollar settlement. Black and Brown workers organized a massive May Day march in 2006, and Carolina secured a $20,000 grant that led to the creation of the New Orleans Workers' Center for Racial Justice, which is still organizing strong today!

40. In March 2006 the Archdiocese of New Orleans announced plans to close St. Augustine Church in the Tremé, the first free Black neighborhood in the city, and merge it into a predominantly white church, much to the shock and outrage of the parishioners. When Father Jerome, beloved in the community, was replaced during Mass, many of the parishioners walked out. Suncere from Common Ground took action. Suncere arrived early on after the storm and was one of the anchors of our work, running a distribution center in Houma and then one called Hope just east of the Lower Ninth Ward. Suncere, along with residents and other Common Ground volunteers, occupied the church offices. As the media exposed the story, the clear unwavering commitment of the occupiers forced the archbishop to back down. The church was reopened in April 2006 and continues to serve the community today.

41. Others went on to organize with Indigenous and local leaders to oppose the expansion of the nuclear complex in Los Alamos; Oak Ridge, Tennessee; and Kansas City, Missouri. We worked together for a year organizing Disarmament Summer. This included a week-long training for about forty youth leaders, a convergence in NY for a UN Summit, a two-week encampment in Chimayo, and a civil disobedience at Los Alamos Nuclear Lab. It was a heavy lift and we won some of what we fought for. There was no expansion of the Chemistry and Metallurgy Research Facility at Los Alamos!

42. In Puerto Rico we are continuing to see the importance and power of self-organized local groups who rise up to help themselves when nobody else can or will. A network of Centros de Apoyo Mutuo—community-based centers for food and goods—has emerged. In many cases these are helped by grassroots groups in the US, including UPROSE in New York, the Climate Justice Network, the Grassroots Global Justice Alliance, and Mutual Aid Disaster Relief.

Chapter 7: The Gaza Freedom March and the Power of Taking Space

1. Mark was the main driver of this work, as my focus was on the wars in Central America, but together we hosted some significant events, including a Mass Teach-In with Hanan Ashrawi, who was and continues to be an important leader in the Palestinian struggle. She worked to humanize the struggle to help people in the US understand what life under occupation was like, including how stones, the primary weapon of the youth, were no match for tanks, fighter jets, and IDF assault rifles.

2. Sheila MacVicar, "Rights Group on Jenin: Massacre, No; Human Shields, Yes," CNN, May 4, 2002, World.

3. My friend Charles was arrested and thrown in jail in one of these settlements.

4. Recent resistance began on March 30, 2018, when the Palestinians started weekly marches to the border fence called the March of the Great Return. Since then 210 people have been killed, and up to 18,000 have been wounded by Israeli snipers, including paramedics and journalists.

5. "Egypt Blocks Travel of Gaza Freedom March Activists," *Electric Intifada*, December 28, 2009.

6. Sharat G. Lin, "Gaza Freedom March Marches in Cairo against Blockade," *Dissident Voice*, January 4, 2010, https://dissidentvoice.org/2010/01/gaza-freedom-march-marches-in-cairo-against-blockade.

7. Mona El-Naggar, "Protestors Gather in Cairo for March to Gaza," *New York Times*, December 29, 2009.

8. Joshua Brollier, "Lessons Learned from the Gaza Freedom March," Wisconsin Network for Peace, Justice, and Sustainability, published December 21, 2009, http://www.wnpj.org/node/3154.

9. "Gaza Freedom Marchers Issue the 'Cairo Declaration' to End Israeli Apartheid," *Electric Intifada*, January 4, 2010.

10. Ali Abunimah, "Gaza Freedom March Protests Continue in Cairo, Organizers Say Egypt Offer to Allow 100 into Gaza Not Sufficient," interview by Amy Goodman, *Democracy Now!*, December 30, 2009, https://www.democracynow.org/2009/12/30/cairo_protests.

11. Mark Landler, "Germany Conducts Raids Ahead of G-8 summit," *New York Times*, May 10, 2007.

12. There were multiple actions leading up to the summit in Heiligendamm. For example, on June 1 about seven hundred of us went to a military site in Bombodrom where hundreds had established an additional encampment. One of my favorite memories was when a standoff between military police and a group of peaceful people praying was broken when a group from the

Clandestine Insurgent Rebel Clown Army (CIRCA) came in with feather dusters and started to dust the police's boots.

13. This affinity group included Erik Forman, Causten E. Rodriguez-Wollerman, Logan Price, and Nick Simmons. Logan and Nick were Common Ground volunteers!

Chapter 8: On May 12th, Occupy Wall Street, and the Power of Multiplying Our Strategies and Tactics

1. Michael Mulgrew, "Letter from the President: September 2011," *The United Federation of Teachers*, September 1, 2011.

2. Adam Gabbatt, "Michael Bloomberg's 12 Years at the Helm of New York City Come to an End," *The Guardian*, December 31, 2013.

3. Sean Thomas-Breitfeld and Marnie Brady, *The New Bottom Line: Building Alignment and Scale to Confront the Economic Crisis*, Building Movement Project, http://www.buildingmovement.org/reports/entry/the_new_bottom_line.

4. Jon Kest passed away from cancer in November 2012 at the age of fifty-seven. This was just weeks after his daughter was killed by a falling tree during Hurricane Sandy. He was a longtime fighter for poor and working people and will be long remembered. Jon was a leader from ACORN who became the director of New York Communities for Change, a group advocating for poor communities of color. They worked closely with another new consortium, Strong Economy for All, comprising labor unions, community-based organizations, and nonprofits. Strong Economy for All was headed by Michael Kink, an organizer with a range of connections and a willingness to take action.

5. "Who's Doing It," On May 12, http://www.onmay12.org/about/who-is-doing-it.

6. The May 12 Coalition, *Payback Time: $1.5 Billion Ways to Save Our City's Budget and Make the Big Banks and Millionaires Pay Their Fair Share*, http://www.onmay12.org/sites/default/files/MAY%2012%20COALITION%20FULL%20REPORT%20PAY%20BACK%20TIME.pdf.

7. To this day we are family. I work with Johanna on the Abbie Hoffman Activist Foundation. Johanna and Abbie's "kids" include myself, Joanna Balcum, Eliot Katz, Ola Manana, Al Giordano, Adrian Mann, Monica Behan, and dear Velvet Wells, who passed away in late 2018 from cancer.

8. In the early 2000s, law enforcement tactics were changing to using barricades, fences, nets, and pens to contain marches, rallies, or protests. Today we've become accustomed to this, but prior to the new millennium, it was not my experience that police would force peaceful protestors into demarcated areas.

9. The beauty of effective organizing is that last-minute changes—like changing the schedule to disrupt this meeting—are possible when each delegation has capable leaders in place and props ready to go.

10. Tactical communications are essential during big actions. Over the years we have used walkie-talkies, UHF radios, Nextel radios, and bikers. With all the cell phones around these days, we can just use signal groups, texts loops, or a secure conference call line as a way to all be on together.

11. "Teacher's Choice a Casualty of Budget Cuts this Year," United Federation of Teachers, August 4, 2011.

12. The Movement of Squares was emerging as people around the world rose up against austerity measures imposed by the EU and the big banks.

13. Matt Sledge, "Reawakening the Radical Imagination: The Origins of Occupy Wall Street," *HuffPost*, November 10, 2011.

14. I developed a manual for creating large, citywide mobilizations and called it *Kicking Corporate Booty*. The material was the initial basis for this book.

15. I first met Marisa in Detroit in July 2007 when I was facilitating the second national gathering of the new Students for a Democratic Society. There were hundreds of young people there from all around the country who were deeply inspired and passionate about ending the US Global War on Terror and rebuilding a radical student movement. My friendships with the young people I met there have continued through today, with me often supporting them through movement questions, struggles, and collaborations, while they keep me connected and informed about a wide range of movement work.

16. It was Marisa Holmes who asked the question.

17. Kari Huus, "Homeowner Taps Occupy Protest to Avoid Foreclosure," *NBC News*, October 17, 2011.

18. Marie Diamond, "Hundreds of Wall Street Protestors Shame Bank into Letting One Woman Keep Her Home," *ThinkProgress*, October 18, 2011.

19. Peter Dreier, "Occupying Wall Street, Building a Movement," *The Nation*, October 5, 2011.

20. The fact that it was the teachers who were fighting to save their jobs inspired many. Soon after On May 12th, the Chicago teachers went on strike and won. More recently we have seen amazing teacher uprisings, from West Virginia to Ohio and Los Angeles, going on the offensive in strategic campaigns to win wage increases and improved conditions. As Stephen Lerner once said, good actions set the stage for better ones!

21. Occupy was also reminiscent of Common Ground for me. We gathered enormous amounts of material and financial resources that we redistributed, free of charge, to those who needed things most. Many homeless people

joined our ranks at OWS, and they were fed, clothed, and offered medical treatment. Our library provided free educational material, and artists contributed time and resources to help others create as well, with cardboard signs being our favorite medium.

22. The Occupiers had less fear, making direct action and the taking of space easier and fun. One such action during Occupy was when a group occupied a bank by setting up a living room inside a bank lobby.

23. In fact, $15 an hour in New York City was enacted on January 1, 2019.

Chapter 9: Ferguson and the Power of Liberation

1. MSNBC Staff, "Timeline: How the Ferguson Crisis Unfolded," *MSNBC News*, August 7, 2015, http://www.msnbc.com/msnbc/crisis-ferguson -michael-brown-unfolded-photographs.

2. Amanda Taub, "What Was That? A Guide to the Military Gear Being Used against Civilians in Ferguson," *Vox*, August 18, 2014.

3. Montague Simmons and Jamala Rogers were two of the elders at OBS who provided important counsel to the youth. Jelani Brown coordinated lots of the amazing art and props.

4. Tef Poe and Taureen "Tory" Russell were the strong local leaders for Hands Up United.

5. Laurie brought a thousand shirts that said UNARMED CIVILIAN with her. She had been in touch with the leaders in Millennial Activists United, Ashley Yates, Brittany Ferrell, and Alexis Templeton.

6. At MORE, Jeff Ordower was the director who understood the importance of putting MORE into the fight. Julia Ho organized with the youth and supported the actions. Molly Gott, a fantastic researcher, coordinated the legal team. Arielle Klagsbrun helped to coordinate direct actions, and Derrick Laney and Tia Bird became the co-coordinators of MORE in 2015.

7. Matt Apuzzo and John Eligon, "Ferguson Police Tainted by Bias, Justice Department Says," *New York Times*, March 4, 2015.

8. Kim Bell, "Protestors Stage Sit-In at St. Louis University," *St. Louis Post-Dispatch*, October 13, 2014.

9. James Anderson, "St. Louis University Occupation Ends, but Movement for Justice in Ferguson Continues," *In These Times*, October 25, 2014.

10. Olga Khazan, "In One Year, 57,375 Years of Life Were Lost to Police Violence," *The Atlantic*, May 8, 2018.

11. Sophia Kirby, "The Top 10 Most Startling Facts about People of Color and Criminal Justice in the United States," *Center for American Progress*, March

13, 2012, https://www.americanprogress.org/issues/race/news/2012/03/13 /11351/the-top-10-most-startling-facts-about-people-of-color-and -criminal-justice-in-the-united-states.

12. Evie Blad and Alex Harwin, "Analysis Reveals Racial Disparities in School Arrests," *PBS News Hour* and *Education Week*, February 27, 2017. Previously published by *Education Week*, January 24, 2017.

13. I reached out to Michael at the urging of Sarah Coffey, who had been on the ground in Ferguson supporting the legal operations. She had been part of the Midnight Special Law Collective for years, and when we talked she strongly urged me to come back, saying that many of the young folks were excellent and could use some mentorship in putting together mass actions.

14. The Don't Shoot Coalition was the primary overall space that supported this effort, but within that larger group I was working with the staff of MORE, Julia and Arielle in particular; Montague and Kayla from OBS; Michael and Taylor from the Don't Shoot Coalition; Bree, Diamond, and H.J., E.J., Doruba, and Talal from Freedom Fighters and Tribe X; and Sekou, with his team Gretchen and Lizzy, and Damon from Whose Streets.

15. These new affinity groups helped to shift the political calculus in the city, but the preexisting structural barriers of racism still made it difficult for newly politicized Black folks to get involved. Many of the new affinity groups were predominantly white people from South City, and some Black people could not travel across the city to attend the meetings there. And knowing the long history of infiltration in our movements and the vengeance of the local police, participating in the council could increase their risks of exposure.

16. Action tip: The flowers were scavenged from the dumpster at the flower wholesale market, and the coffins were made from the flower boxes we got there, spray-painted black!

17. The people with the Deep Abiding Love Project included Lizzey Padget, Gretchen Honnald, and Reverend Sekou.

18. Lizzy Jean, *Coming to Ferguson: Building a Nonviolent Movement* (Boston: Creative Commons, 2015), http://nonviolence.rutgers.edu/s/digital /document/IIP0302F07.

19. Resmaa Menaken, *My Grandmother's Hands: Racialized Trauma and the Pathway to Mending Our Hearts and Bodies* (Las Vegas: Central Recovery Press, 2017).

20. Bayard Rustin, *I Must Resist: Bayard Rustin's Life in Letters*, ed. Michael G. Long (San Francisco: City Lights, 2012), 366.

21. Along with Brittany Packnett and Samuel Sinyangwe, Deray Mckesson and Netta Elzie launched Campaign Zero, a policy platform to reform the police.

DeRay and Netta got a lot of attention as leaders of the movement because of their social media work. DeRay was born in Baltimore and had worked with Teach for America. He was living in Minneapolis when the uprising broke out. Netta was from North St. Louis and became active after Michael Brown was killed. As with many movements, the media likes to make stars, creating discontent within the movement, as it did especially with DeRay.

22. A sadder outcome of the movement work is the arrest of nineteen-year-old Joshua Williams, a brilliant street warrior whom I had the honor to work with. He was arrested for property destruction at the QuikTrip and was sentenced to eight years in prison. The police needed to make an example out of someone, and he is still incarcerated as I write.

23. During the uprising the Artivists created beautiful defensive shields and large banners to mitigate police assaults. They later sent shields of beauty to Standing Rock during their struggle. Today the Artivists continue to engage in creative direct actions, organizing out of a house they secured in St. Louis.

Chapter 10: Standing Rock and the Power of Stories and Spirit

1. The ancient prophecies tell of a separation of the people into two worlds— North and South. The North, represented by the Eagle, holds our mental, technical, and masculine energies. The South is the land of the Condor, and it holds the energies of intuition, love, and an alignment with nature. When these worlds reunite, a new era will be born.

2. Saul Elbein, "The Youth Group That Launched a Movement at Standing Rock," *New York Times*, January 31, 2017.

3. Alleen Brown, Will Parrish, and Alice Speri, "Leaked Documents Reveal Counterterrorism Tactics Used at Standing Rock to 'Defeat Pipeline Insurgencies,'" *The Intercept*, May 27, 2017.

4. Some of the elders and important leaders at Standing Rock included Leonard Crow Dog, Sicangu Lakota; Chief Arvol Looking Horse, the Lakota, Dakota, and Nakota Nations; Regina Brave, Oglala; Nathan Phillips, Omaha Nation; Raymond Kingfisher, Cheyenne Nation; Cheryl Angel, Sicangu Lakota; Theresa Black Owl, Sicangu Rosebud; Sonny Wonase, Standing Rock Sioux; Phyllis Young, Standing Rock Sioux; and Linda Black Elk, the Catawba Nation. There was also essential youth leadership from the International Indigenous Youth Council.

5. While the original website for the Standing Rock Solidarity Network has been taken down, you can still find their resources packet here: https:// theantioppressionnetwork.com/2016/11/01/standing-rock-solidarity -network-resources-packet/.

6. Desiree Kane also lived in the yurt. She helped to document and coordinate media for a lot of the actions.

7. The team grew to include Carolina Reyes, L.J. Amsterdam, Griffen Jeffries, Dylan Cooke, and Micah Hobbes Frazier.

8. It was during this meeting that I met Thomas Joseph II from the Hoopa Nation in Northern California. His family were the primary hosts of the California Camp, and they nourished us deeply with food before and after our actions! Thomas was one of the key organizers and leaders I had the honor of working with in the actions to come. My friend Kerul Dyer, whom I worked closely with at Common Ground, was also a key anchor for the California Camp.

9. This was due in part to security concerns over infiltrators, plus many of those who showed up at camp were transient, only intending to stay for a few days.

10. People came in and out, but the Action Gaggle had a solid crew that included myself, Carolina Reyes, Remy, Thomas Joseph II, Chris, Desiree Kane, Lola, Little Feather, Badger, Griffen, Dylan, Christina, Felicia, Noah Dillard, Kayla, Ethan, Anders, Ashley, Maria, Brandon, and Eric. Sorry for the names I may have missed. Ray Kingfisher offered prayers and leadership for many of our actions.

11. During the actions at the capitol, I was targeted and arrested by the police. I was so bummed until I was put in jail with Red Fawn. Her wisdom, her power, and the beauty of her spirit were a great gift to me. When I said we can't wait for you to be free, she said, "I am free!" I was able to offer her a gift in return: the gift of stories from actions and camp. Forces greater than ourselves work in mysterious ways. I have never been so happy to be arrested.

12. Reuters Media, "Anti-Pipeline Protestors Arrested at North Dakota Shopping Mall," *Duluth News Tribune*, November 25, 2016.

13. When the folks with the dogs returned to their car, they found that all their tires had been slashed.

14. adrienne maree brown, *Emergent Strategy: Shaping Change, Changing Worlds* (Chico, CA: AK Press, 2017), 18.

Epilogue: Life After Trump and the Power of Healing

1. Alexa Ura and Alex Samuels, "At Texas Muslim Capitol Day, Supporters Form Human Shield around Demonstrators," *Texas Tribune*, January 31, 2017.

2. Joyce James and Bay Love, *Overview of the Texas Model for Eliminating Disproportionality and Disparities*, Texas Health and Human Services Commission, August 29, 2013, http://www.undoingracismaustin.org/wp-content/uploads/2013/10/CEDDslideshow.pdf.

3. Undoing Racism Austin came together during a meeting at the Cherrywood Café with Kellee Coleman, Eve Hernandez, Marisa Perles, Carmen Llanes, her father and longtime community organizer, Daniel Llanes, Juniper Lauren Ross, Tane Ward, and me. Kellee Coleman, born and raised in Austin, was a founder of Mamas of Color Rising, Communities of Color United for Racial Justice and has now become a fierce leader at Austin's new Equity Office. I was able to support her family, who tragically lost their home in the Halloween Flood.

4. Alicia Inns, "No Contract: Austin City Council Votes for More Negotiations with APD," *KXAN News*, December 13, 2017.

5. Michael Barajas, "New Contract Could Give Austin One of the Most Transparent Police Departments in the Country," *Texas Observer*, November 16, 2018.

6. This was a revised version of the song we sang during the Flood Wall Street Action in August 2014 when over three thousand of us sat down in the streets around Wall Street, shutting the whole area down.

7. Jen Kirby, "Nearly 600 Women Arrested at Immigration Protests in Senate Building," *Vox*, June 28, 2018.

8. Elizabeth Vega, founder of the Artivists in Ferguson along with local Indigenous organizers in El Paso and Dallas, put out a call to action. Mama Cat from Ferguson came and cooked a delicious holiday dinner while Vega was wrangling the white folks who were afraid, asking them to understand that raising giant puppets above the barbed-wire-covered chain-link fences was not violent.

9. At some points, white fears got in the way of the tremendous care and heart the people of color organizers were bringing. Leaders from Witness Tornillo, a white group that was there just to witness, led tours around the facility, taking newcomers away from the assemblies the Occupiers were holding. They developed close relationships with the security, much to the dismay of the Occupiers. When the Occupiers threw soccer balls with messages of solidarity, the youth inside wrote their names on the balls and threw them back over the fence. But the Witness Tornillo folks would not give the soccer balls to the Occupiers, who wanted the names to help identify the kids inside. This is *not* what solidarity looks like.

INDEX

Note: Numbers followed by "t" refer to tables, and numbers followed by "f" refer to figures. Numbers with "n" or "nn" refer to endnotes.

ABOUT THE AUTHOR

Leon Alesi

L isa Fithian is an anti-racist organizer working for justice since the 1970s. Using creative, strategic nonviolent direct action and civil disobedience, she has won many battles and trained tens of thousands of people while participating in a range of movements and mobilizations, including Occupy Wall Street, anti-WTO and corporate globalization protests all over the world, the climate justice movement, and more. Lisa enjoys walking, playing with children, gardening, cooking great food, being in the wild, and raising up new generations to be agents of change. She is grateful to play her part in manifesting a world rooted in respect, justice, and liberation.

the politics and practice of sustainable living

CHELSEA GREEN PUBLISHING

Chelsea Green Publishing sees books as tools for effecting cultural change and seeks to empower citizens to participate in reclaiming our global commons and become its impassioned stewards. If you enjoyed reading *Shut It Down*, please consider these other great books related to social justice and social change.

A PRECAUTIONARY TALE
*How One Small Town Banned Pesticides,
Preserved Its Food Heritage, and Inspired a Movement*
PHILIP ACKERMAN-LEIST
9781603587051
Paperback • $19.95

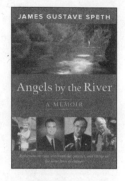

ANGELS BY THE RIVER
A Memoir
JAMES GUSTAVE SPETH
9781603586320
Paperback • $17.95

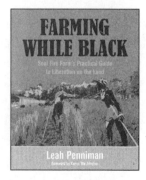

FARMING WHILE BLACK
*Soul Fire Farm's Practical Guide
to Liberation on the Land*
LEAH PENNIMAN
9781603587617
Paperback • $34.95

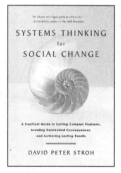

SYSTEMS THINKING FOR SOCIAL CHANGE
*A Practical Guide to Solving Complex Problems,
Avoiding Unintended Consequences,
and Achieving Lasting Results*
DAVID PETER STROH
9781603585804
Paperback • $24.95

the politics and practice of sustainable living

For more information or to request a catalog,
visit **www.chelseagreen.com** or
call toll-free **(800) 639-4099**.